Join In

English

for Child Care and Education

von
Ruth Fiand
Heidi Kreber
Bernd Müller-Knospe
Anke Schweer

5., durchgesehene Auflage

Handwerk und Technik – Hamburg

Vorwort

JOIN IN
ist ein Lehrwerk für das Fach Englisch, das sich an Schülerinnen und Schüler der Berufsfachschulen für Sozialassistenz und Kinderpflege richtet. Das Buch ist für zwei Schuljahre konzipiert und bietet neben dem Grundkurs (Units 1 – 6) die Möglichkeit, über Basiskenntnisse des Englischen hinaus den mittleren Bildungsabschluss im Erweiterungskurs (Units 7 – 16) zu erwerben.

Die wichtigsten Grundlagen der englischen Grammatik werden kapitelbegleitend und in den Kontext eingebunden wiederholt. Dabei werden zunächst Basiskenntnisse (A2) aufgefrischt und im Erweiterungskurs werden die Lernenden auf das Sprachniveau des mittleren Bildungsabschlusses (B1) geführt.

In diesem Lehrwerk werden grundsätzlich die britische Schreibweise und britische Fachausdrücke verwendet. Ergänzend wird der Unterschied zwischen amerikanischem und britischem Sprachgebrauch herausgearbeitet.

Die Themenbereiche wurden so zusammengestellt, dass sie berufliche Schwerpunkte der Kinderpflege, Sozialassistenz sowie des Sozialwesens aufgreifen und hier insbesondere die Arbeit mit Kindern und Säuglingen in den Mittelpunkt stellen. Ausgangspunkt für den Grundkurs ist die Arbeit im Kindergarten sowie in der Krippe und in der Tagespflege. Es werden Themen bearbeitet, die den Alltag widerspiegeln. Daneben werden allgemeine Themen und Problembereiche behandelt, die sich z. B. mit Erziehung zur Gesundheitspflege, einem Auslandsaufenthalt oder der Inklusion von Kindern mit Behinderung befassen. Der kreative Umgang mit englischer Kinderliteratur und englischen Reimen und Liedern kann Ansätze bieten, die englische Sprache im deutschen Kindergarten einzuführen.

JOIN IN
legt einen besonderen Schwerpunkt auf handlungsorientierte Aufgabenstellungen, die berufliche Handlungssituationen aufgreifen und ein fächerübergreifendes Arbeiten anstreben. Sie sind gekennzeichnet durch die Überschrift **"Hands-on task"**. Ziel dieser Aufgaben ist es ebenso, Methoden- und Sozialkompetenzen zu fördern.
Die Kompetenzen nach dem Europäischen Referenzrahmen werden bei Aufgaben ausgewiesen, in denen

`Reception`

`Interaction`

`Production`

`Mediation`

besonders geübt werden.

Im Anhang des Buches finden die Lernenden verschiedene **Methodenseiten,** die ihnen die für diese Aufgaben benötigten Informationen und Anleitungen zur Verfügung stellen. Zum besseren Lernen befinden sich die Vokabeln am Ende jedes Kapitels (mit Lautschrift) und zusammengefasst in einem alphabetischen Verzeichnis im Anhang.

SO JOIN IN AND ENJOY THE BOOK!

Autoren und Verlag

 Als Audiotrack auf Audio-CD erhältlich

Inhaltsverzeichnis

	Skills	Grammar
Unit 1 Me and my job .... **1** This is me .... 1 Talking about hobbies .... 3 At the job centre .... 6 Training on the job 8	Working with a text Talking about hobbies Working with a text Writing a letter, creating a brochure	Personal and possessive Pronouns I The verb "to be" Simple Present
Unit 2 In the nursery school .... **11** A day in the nursery school .... 12 Janet's first day .... 14 Meeting and greeting people at work ... 18 Inside the classroom 19	Working with a text Speaking about daily routines Meeting and greeting people Describing a nursery classroom	Present Continuous Present Continuous and Simple Present Prepositions of place
Unit 3 Outside the nursery school ..... **23** Outdoor play areas .... 23 Outdoor activities .... 24 Safety first .... 26 Going on an outing .... 28 Giving directions 31	Describing a play area Writing a letter to parents Giving directions	Can and can't Need, needn't – must, mustn't Prepositions describing directions
Unit 4 Families .... **35** What makes up a family? .... 35 Who is who in Sandra Miller's family? .. 36 What is a typical family? Four family portraits .. 39 Childminders .... 42 Work report 46	Describing family trees Describing family types	Genitive Possessive Pronouns II Simple Past
Unit 5 Toys and games .... **49** Choosing toys for children .... 50 Buying toys .... 52 Children, children, children .... 56 Play with me 56	Giving advice on toys Making suggestions, filling in forms Playing games	Adjectives and Comparison Quantifiers
Unit 6 Holidays around the year .... **59** Celebrating Halloween .... 60 Preparing for Halloween in the classroom ... 61 Thanksgiving – the story 66	Working with a text Performing, decorating in class Working with a text	Future
Unit 7 Children from birth to three .... **69** Caring for infants and toddlers .... 70 The care environment for children under three .... 73 Training and learning in crèches 75	Analysing body language Planning a baby-friendly environment Planning activities for children under three	Reported Speech
Unit 8 Nursery school and kindergarten abroad .... **79** At an American kindergarten in Wamego, Kansas .... 79 At a British nursery school .... 80 The terms kindergarten and nursery school ... 82 A daily report 85	Analysing different approaches to childcare Keeping track of a child's development	Present Perfect
Unit 9 Being ill .... **87** Signs that children are not feeling well .. 88 A phone call to Nora's mother .... 89 Poorly children, worried parents .... 90 Hygiene in a nursery school .... 91 The first-aid box .... 94 Small accidents and injuries 95	Working with a text Making a phone call Working with a text Setting rules for hygiene Recording accidents	Plural Present Perfect

Inhaltsverzeichnis

	Skills	Grammar
Unit 10 Food and drink for children .... 97 Give them a good start: breakfast .... 98 A balanced diet. .... 100 Breast or bottle? The importance of milk ..... 103 Planning meals for children .... 104 Making meals fun .... 106 Baking muffins 108	Talking about breakfast Analysing cereal boxes Finding arguments, writing an essay Analysing a menu Understanding and writing a recipe Explaining a recipe	Conditional sentences type I and II Some and any
Unit 11 Family problems .... 111 Searching for help – letters to the agony aunt 112 Aggression in the family .... 114 A child suffers .... 118 Why didn't we react? 119	Answering letters, giving advice Working with a text	The Passive
Unit 12 Children with special needs .... 123 Andrew McArthur – a child with special needs 124 Windham Integrated Nursery School .... 126 Choosing toys for children with special needs 130	Talking about special needs Working with a text Giving advice on the integration of children	Who – which – that
Unit 13 Story time, rhyme time .... 133 Books and stories for children................ 134 Organizing a reading-aloud activity .... 135 When are you coming back? .... 136 Nursery rhyme time – traditionals............ 140 Activities with nursery rhymes .... 141 Creative writing .... 142 Let's sing a song 142	Working with a text Working with a children's story Working with nursery rhymes Writing creatively Singing songs with children	Conjunctions
Unit 14 Children and TV .... 145 Sesame Street – one of the most famous children's programmes .... 146 Walt Disney and Donald Duck. .... 150 Children's TV heroes – what should they look like?................................... 151	Working with a text Giving point of views Discussing point of views	Adverbs Use of Adjective and Adverb
Unit 15 Nursery school as movie topic..... 155 Let's talk about the movies................... 155 The movie "Kindergarten Cop " 156	Interpreting pictures Analysing a movie	British and American English
Unit 16 Working abroad.................. 163 European countries......................... 163 Changing places – Frederic's diary .... 164 Applying for a job abroad.................... 168 The job interview........................... 169 Thoughts about my work experience in Britain 170	Talking about people's origin Working with text and language Writing letter of application and CV Working with a text, role playing	Conditional sentences type III

Anhang

Methodenseiten 173
Wortschatz erweitern und Vokabeln lernen 173
Textfragen schriftlich beantworten 174
Wörter und Ausdrücke auf Englisch erklären..... 175
Konnektoren und Einleitungen 176
Häufige Fehlerquellen im Englischen 178
Einen zusammenhängenden Text schreiben 180
Eine Erörterung („Essay") schreiben 181
Die Mindmap................................ 182
Der Geschäftsbrief 183

Mediation 184
Feedback geben 185
Informationen im Internet suchen 186
Die Präsentation................................ 188
Folie oder Plakat gestalten 189
Das Rollenspiel 190

Unregelmäßige Verben 191
Alphabetische Vokabelliste 193

Unit 1 — Me and my job

Hi!
My name is Janet Smith. I'm 16 and I'm from Liverpool, England. My hobbies? My hobbies are swimming, reading and playing the guitar. I like meeting friends and going out in the evenings. I like dancing – and music, of course! My favourite music is pop music. I also like watching TV. My favourite programmes are films and soap operas.
I live with my mother and father. I have a little sister and a little brother. Sometimes I look after my sister and my brother when my parents work or when they go out.
I don't go to school anymore, I have passed my GCSEs! Now I am looking for an interesting job or a good training course.

This is me

Working with the text

A The following statements are wrong. Give the correct answer.
1. The girl's name is Carol. *Example: The girl's name is Janet.*
2. She is 17 years old.
3. She comes from London.
4. She likes playing the piano.
5. She has her own flat.
6. She is an only child.
7. She is a student.

B Your own introduction
1. **Write a short text about yourself. You can look at Janet's text for help:**
   Example: My name is… I'm… years old….

2. **Work with another student and introduce yourselves to each other.
   First read out your texts to each other. Then ask questions, for example:**
   1. What are your hobbies?
   2. Do you go out in the evenings? Where do you go?
   3. What is your favourite pop group?
   4. Why do you want to become a nursery nurse?

Unit 1 Me and my job

C Introduce your partner to the class. Look at the grammar boxes for help. *Example:*

This is Linda, she comes …

Für Übungen und weitere Pronomen vgl. Unit 4.

Grammar box:
Personal and possessive pronouns I
– Pronomen / Fürworter

Singular / Einzahl

I	ich	my	mein
you	du / Sie	your	dein / Ihr
he	er	his	sein
she	sie	her	ihr
it	es	its	sein

Plural / Mehrzahl

we	wir	our	unser
you	ihr	your	euer
they	sie	their	ihr

Grammar box: The verb to be

Aussagen		Verneinungen	Fragen
Singular / Einzahl			
I am	I'm	I am not / I'm not	am I?
you are	you're	you are not / you aren't	are you?
he is	he's	he is not / he isn't	is he?
she is	she's	she is not / she isn't	is she?
it is	it's	it is not / it isn't	is it?
Plural / Mehrzahl			
we are	we're	we are not / we aren't	are we?
you are	you're	you are not / you aren't	are you?
they are	they're	they are not / they aren't	are they?

Practising grammar

A Answer the questions.
1. Are you tired?
   Example: Yes, I am.
2. Are you hungry? No, …
3. Is Janet from England?
4. Are you a teacher?
5. Is your father old?
6. Are shoes expensive in Germany?
7. Are the children happy?
8. Are you married?
9. Are we too late?
10. Is Janet's sister younger than Janet?

B Make up questions with these words. Use am / are / is.
1. you interested in books?
   Example:
   Are you interested in books?
2. your mother at work?
3. the cinema expensive?
4. the shops open on Sundays?
5. I in your group?
6. Peter 18 years old?
7. this answer wrong?
8. we in the same class?

C Make up questions with Who / What / How / Where / Why. Use am / are / is.
1. What / your favourite music band? *Example: What is your favourite music band?*
2. What / you doing?
3. How old / Janet's little brother?
4. Where / my keys?
5. Why / the banks closed after 5 o'clock?
6. Where / you from?
7. Why / your answers always correct?
8. What colour your eyes?

Me and my job Unit 1

Talking about hobbies

Janet likes swimming, reading and playing the guitar. She likes meeting friends and going out in the evenings. Look at the pictures. What do you like? What do you not like?

A Write sentences. Use as many different expressions from the box as you can.
Example:
I like swimming. / I don't like swimming.
I am good at playing the guitar. / I am not …

There are many expressions you can use to say what you like or don't like:
- to hate something – etwas hassen
- to love something – etwas lieben
- to adore something – etwas anbeten, für etwas schwärmen
- to fancy something – Lust haben, etwas zu tun
- to be a fan of something – ein Fan von etwas sein
- to be good at something – gut sein in etwas
- to be fond of something – etwas gern haben, etwas mögen

B Work together with your partner. Read your sentences from exercise A to your partner. `Interaction`

C Present the hobbies of your partner to the class. `Interaction`
You must change your partner's sentences into the 3. person singular. Look at the grammar box for help.
Example:
She likes swimming. She doesn't like …
She is not …

handwerk-technik.de

3

Unit 1 Me and my job

Grammar box:
Simple Present – Einfache Gegenwart

Aussagen

I	like	reading.
You	like	books.
He	likes	dogs.
She	likes	children.
It	likes	sleeping.
We	like	pop music.
You	like	playing tennis.
They	like	comics.

- Das Simple Present wird gebildet mit der Infinitiv-Form (ohne to).
- Aber: Bei den Formen der 3. Person Singular wird ein zusätzliches ‚s' angehängt: **He / she / it – ‚s' muss mit!**

- Das Simple Present wird verwendet,
  – wenn eine Handlung regelmäßig geschieht,
  – wenn eine Gewohnheit ausgedrückt wird,
  – wenn Tatsachen beschrieben werden (vgl. auch Unit 2).
- Signalwörter: *always, never, usually, sometimes, often, every week, on Mondays*

Ausnahmen
- Bei Verben, die auf –o, -sh, -ch, -ss oder -x enden, wird in der 3. Person Singular –es angehängt:
  go – he goes
  rush – he rushes
  touch – he touches
  kiss – he kisses
  mix – he mixes
- Bei Verben die auf –y enden, gilt in der 3. Person Singular folgende Regel:
  Konsonant + y → ies: try – he tries
  Vokal + y → ys: play – he plays
- *have – he has*

Practising grammar

A Put the verbs in brackets into the correct form.
1. Peter usually (to walk) to school.
   Example: Peter usually walks to school.
2. Mr Carter (to work) for a computer company.
3. Steve (to smoke) ten cigarettes every day.
4. On Tuesdays, Sheila (to play) the piano.
5. You often (to drink) a glass of milk.
6. Every week, my sister (to go) to the cinema. She (to watch) comedy films.
7. I never (to get up) before 6 in the morning.
8. Paul (to catch) the train to London every morning. His daughter Linda always (to cry) when he (to leave).
9. The child always (to finish) his / her dinner.
10. We (to clean) the rooms twice a week.

B Janet's weekly timetable
Make up sentences to describe Janet's typical week.
Example: On Monday morning, she goes shopping. From 2 to 3 p.m. she has …

Monday	Tuesday	Wednesday	Thursday	Friday
		9:00 breakfast		
9:30 shopping			10:00	help mother to clean the house
			library	
		12:00 lunch		
2:00 – 3:00 guitar lesson	4:00 meeting with Cathy	4:00 – 6:00 swimming pool	3:00 appointment at the job centre	
		6:30 dinner		
	8:00 babysitting		9:00 good film on TV	7:00 cinema

Um die Uhrzeiten auszudrücken, nutzt man im Englischen

- *a.m.*   für vormittags
- *p.m.*   für nachmittags und abends
- *midnight* für 0:00 Uhr.

Me and my job Unit 1

Grammar box: Simple Present – Einfache Gegenwart (Fortsetzung)

Verneinungen

I	do not	like reading.
You	don't	go for a walk.
He	does not	have a job.
She	doesn't	meet a friend.
It		rain.
We	do not	read a book.
You	don't	know the grammar.
They		work very hard.

Fragen

Do	I	like reading?
Don't	you	go for a walk?
Does	he	have a job?
Doesn't	she	meet a friend?
	it	happen often?
Do	we	read a book?
Don't	you	know the grammar?
	they	work very hard?

C Make up negative sentences and put the verbs in brackets into the correct form.

1. I (not / to smoke) cigarettes.
   Example: I don't smoke cigarettes.
2. I am rich. I (not / to work).
3. Sally (not / to go) to school any more.
4. We (not / to learn) enough grammar at school.
5. The children (not / to like) to watch horror films.
6. Jim (not / to play) football very often.
7. Sue (not / to live) in London.
8. I (not / to know) the answer.
9. The cat (not / to catch) a lot of mice.
10. We (not / to have) problems learning vocabulary.

D Make up questions.

1. you / to smoke?
   Example: Do you smoke?
2. he / to like going to the cinema?
3. Susan / to hate playing tennis?
4. we / to get up early on Sundays?
5. they / to speak English?
6. I / to work at weekends?
7. your parents / to live in Liverpool?
8. you / to wash your hair every day?
9. the cat / to play with the mouse?
10. a lot of people / to adore lying on the beach in the summer?

E Make up questions with Who / What / How / Where / Why / When.

1. How many cigarettes / you / to smoke?
   Example: How many cigarettes do you smoke?
2. When / she / to do the shopping?
3. Where / they / to buy clothes?
4. Why / you / not know the answer?
5. What / this word / to mean?
6. Who / to speak Japanese?
7. When / you / to go to bed in the evenings?
8. How much / the apples / to cost?
9. Where / your father / to work?
10. When / you / to have lunch?

- Fragewörter wie
  What / How / Where / Why / When
  stehen am Anfang des Fragesatzes.

- Nur *Who* hat kein *to do,* wenn nach dem Subjekt des Satzes gefragt wird.
  Beispiel:
  Who likes hamburgers?

- Vgl. auch Unit 4, Grammar box: Questions

Unit 1 Me and my job

At the job centre

Janet wants to find a good job. It is Thursday afternoon and she goes to the job centre. There she talks to Mrs Grand, a job advisor.

Janet:	Hello, my name is Janet Smith. I want to find a good job. Can you help me?
Mrs G:	Hello, Janet. I'm Mrs Grand. Well, I hope I can help you. How old are you?
Janet:	I am 16 years old.
Mrs G:	Do you still go to school or have you done your GCSEs?
Janet:	I have already done them.
Mrs G:	That's good. Now, let's find out about your qualifications. Can I see your certificate?
Janet:	Yes, of course. Here you are. *(She pulls the certificate out of her bag and hands it to Mrs Grand.)*
Mrs G:	Thank you. Let's have a look … Oh, your grades in sport and biology are very good, and English of course … What are your hobbies?
Janet:	My hobbies are swimming, reading and playing the guitar.
Mrs G:	So you are a very sporty person with musical talent. What about social skills or meeting other people?
Janet:	I like being with people. I often meet friends and sometimes I go out in the evenings. I like music and dancing! I also like watching TV.
Mrs G:	Do you like children?
Janet:	Yes, very much. I have a little sister and a little brother. Sometimes I look after them.
Mrs G:	Really? And would you like to work with children?
Janet:	Yes, why not? I think that it is fun to play with them. But playing with children is not a job, is it? What job can I do?
Mrs G:	You can work in a nursery school as a nursery nurse.
Janet:	That's a good idea. When can I start?
Mrs G:	You have to do a training course first. It takes two years to train. You go to a college of further education and learn all the things you need to work in a nursery school.
Janet:	College? But I want to work!
Mrs G:	Okay, but good training is important. You can't work with children without being trained. And vocational training at college is work! At college you often work in projects and you learn both theory and practice. You also do a lot of work experience in nursery schools.
Janet:	Okay, okay, that's alright. What about exams?
Mrs G:	After two years there is a written exam and a practical test.
Janet:	Do you have any more information?
Mrs G:	Here, this is a brochure about the training course. It gives you a lot of information. *(Mrs Grand hands a paper to Janet.)*
Janet:	Thank you. It looks very interesting.
Mrs G:	Yes, read the brochure and think about it. You can come back and ask more questions if you want.
Janet:	Thank you very much. Goodbye.
Mrs G:	Goodbye.

Me and my job Unit 1

Working with the text

A The following statements are wrong. Give the correct answer.
1. Janet goes to the job centre on Wednesday morning.
2. The lady's name is Mrs Great.
3. Janet has no certificate.
4. Janet has artistic talent.
5. The training takes three years.

B Answer the following questions.
1. What does Mrs Grand want to know?
2. Where can Janet learn to become a nursery nurse?
3. What will she learn there?
4. How does the training end?
5. Does Janet decide to become a nursery nurse?

C Find words in the text that mean …
1. a person who works at the job centre
2. a piece of paper that shows your school grades
3. a characteristic to say that you like being together with people
4. a school in which you can learn a profession
5. a piece of paper that gives you information about something

D Match each sentence beginning with a suitable ending.

Janet goes to the job centre …	… to find out about Janet's qualifications.
Mrs Grand wants to see her certificate …	… but she does not know that playing with children can be a profession.
Mrs Grand describes Janet as a sporty person …	… you do a work experience.
Janet likes looking after her brother and sister in her free time …	… because she likes swimming.
When you put into practice what you have learned in school …	… to become a qualified nursery nurse.
Janet has to pass written exams and a practical test …	… because she wants to find a good job.

Hands-on task

Play the role of people below. Choose one of the following scenes: **Interaction**
1. Act out the conversation between Mrs Grand and Janet.
2. Act out a conversation between a job advisor and yourself.
3. Imagine Janet meets some friends who also went to the job centre. They all speak about their visit and their future jobs.

For more information on role plays see page 190.

Unit 1 Me and my job

x = General Certificate of Secondary Education

Training on the job

Janet reads the brochure about the job training:

Have you passed your GCSEs? ⓧ
Do you like working with children?
Are you a sociable person who likes music?
Then this is the perfect profession for you:

A nursery nurse

A nursery nurse usually works in a nursery school. She or he works in a team and looks after groups of children who are 0 to 6 years old.
Your tasks are, for example:
- to play with children, to sing with them, to read stories to children, to paint with children or be creative etc.
- to plan activities and outings
- to look after the children and their needs, e.g. help them to eat, help them to use the toilet and give first aid etc.
- to choose healthy food for children
- to create a pleasant and safe environment
- to choose suitable toys
- to work in a team
- to do administrative paperwork
- to work with parents

The training course
Training takes two years. It is a fulltime course at a college of further education. You learn both theory and practice. After two years, there is a written exam and a practical test.

You learn about:
- the social, emotional, physical and intellectual development of children
- the importance of playing and organising play activities
- children's needs and problems
- communication
- the health and nutrition of children
- arts and crafts
- sports
- family life, social institutions and services
- employment

Practical work experience
You spend some of your time at college in 'placements' working with children. Most work placements are in nursery schools, in private families, in crèches or with a childminder.

Working on projects
You often work on projects. For example, you work on one topic for a week and plan an activity for children. Then you invite a group of children to put your plan into practice.

Are you interested? We are looking forward to your application!
[Details of application: see back of paper]

Me and my job Unit 1

Janet thinks that this is a wonderful training course and decides that she wants to become a nursery nurse. She completes the application form and sends it to the college of further education. Janet also writes a letter to her German penfriend. She wants to inform her friend about her plans.

Working with the text

Copy the following letter and fill in the gaps with words from the brochure.

Dear Melanie,
How are you? I'm fine. I am so happy because now I know what I want to do. Last week I went to the (1)… and I spoke to a lady. She gave me
5 a (2)… which has all the information I need. As you know, I have passed my GCSEs and I like working with children. Now I am starting a (3)… as a nursery nurse. A nursery nurse usually works in a (4)…. There she looks after (5)… who are 3 to 6 years old. Of course, a nursery nurse plays with children but she also (6)… with them. This is what I like because I can play the guitar. I also like reading and at work you have to read (7)… to the children. A lot of work
10 is creative but a nursery nurse also plans (8)… and (9)…. Another part of the job is actually caring for children: You help them to eat, to use the (10)…, to get dressed and undressed or you help them when they are ill. When an accident happens you must give (11)…
As a nursery nurse you must be a responsible person. It is part of the job to choose healthy (12)…, to choose suitable (13)… and to create a pleasant and (14)… environment.
15 But the good thing is that you don't work alone. You work in a (15)…. Training takes place at a (16)…
It takes two years. After the two years there is a (17)… exam and a (18)… test. You learn theory and practice. But there will also be practical work, for example in a nursery school or (19)…. The course also includes working on (20)…
20 Doesn't that all sound very interesting? I'm really looking forward to it.

Lots of love
Janet

Hands-on tasks

A Write a reply to Janet. Write something about yourself, your age, your family, your hobbies and your training course. `Production`

B Get a brochure about your school and explain the main aspects (in a letter) to Janet. `Mediation`

For mediation: see page 184.

Unit 1 Me and my job

This is me
favourite ['feɪvərɪt]	Lieblings-…
soap opera [səʊp 'ɒpərə]	"Seifenoper", Fernsehserie
GCSE (General Certificate of Secondary Education) [dʒiː siː es iː]	Mittlerer Bildungsabschluss an britischen Schulen, vergleichbar mit dt. Realschulabschluss
training course ['treɪnɪŋ kɔːs]	Lehre, Ausbildung
own [əʊn]	eigene/r/s
flat [flæt]	Wohnung
only child ['əʊnlɪ tʃaɪld]	Einzelkind

Talking about hobbies
(to) adore [ə'dɔː]	anbeten, über alles lieben, für etwas schwärmen
(to) fancy s. th. ['fænsɪ]	Lust haben, etwas zu tun
usually ['juːʒʊəlɪ]	gewöhnlich, üblicherweise
twice [twaɪs]	zweimal
typical ['tɪpɪkl]	typisch
weekly ['wiːklɪ]	wöchentlich
timetable [taɪm'teɪbl]	Stundenplan, Zeitplan
appointment [ə'pɔɪntmənt]	Termin, Treffen
job centre [dʒɒb 'sentə]	Arbeitsamt, Arbeitsagentur
mouse (sg.), mice (pl.) [maʊs, maɪs]	Maus, Mäuse

At the job centre
job advisor [dʒɒb əd'vaɪzə]	Arbeitsberater/in, Mitarbeiter/in des Arbeitsamtes
qualifications [ˌkwɒlɪfɪ'keɪʃns]	Qualifikationen
certificate [sə'tɪfɪkət]	Zeugnis, Zertifikat
social skills ['səʊʃl skɪls]	soziale Fähigkeiten
nursery school (British English) (auch: nursery)	Kindergarten
nursery nurse (British English) ['nɜːsrɪ]	Kinderpfleger/in, Mitarbeiter/in im Kindergarten
college of further education	Berufsbildende Schule, Berufskolleg
vocational training [vəʊ'keɪʃnl]	Berufsausbildung
work experience [wɜːk ɪk'spɪərɪəns]	Praktikum

Training on the job
profession [prə'feʃn]	Beruf
(to) look after [lʊk 'ɑːftə]	sich kümmern um
task [tɑːsk]	Aufgabe
outing ['aʊtɪŋ]	Ausflug
need [niːd]	Bedürfnis
healthy [helθɪ]	gesund
pleasant ['pleznt]	angenehm
environment [ɪn'vaɪərənmənt]	Umgebung
suitable [suːtəbl]	passend, angemessen
administrative [əd,mɪnɪ'strətɪv]	Verwaltung-…
development [dɪ'veləpmənt]	Entwicklung
nutrition ['njuː'trɪʃn]	Ernährung
arts [ɑːts] and crafts [krɑːfts]	Kunst und Basteln
social services ['səʊʃl 'sɜːvɪsəs]	Sozialdienste
employment [ɪm'plɔɪmənt]	Beschäftigung, Berufstätigkeit
placement ['pleɪsmənt]	hier: Praktikumsstelle
crèche [kreʃ]	Krippe
childminder [tʃaɪldmaɪndər]	Tagespflege
topic ['tɒpɪk]	Thema, Themenstellung
(to) look forward to [lʊk 'fɔːwəd tuː]	sich freuen auf
application [æplɪ'keɪʃn]	Bewerbung

Unit 2 In the nursery school

What can you see in the pictures?

Describe the nursery school in the pictures. Would you like to work there?
Does your nursery school look like this one?

handwerk-technik.de

Unit 2 In the nursery school

A day in the nursery school

After some weeks at college Janet is finally starting to do her practical training at nursery school. Her work placement is with "Tiny Tots" nursery school. Their website is full of information for parents. Here is their page about the daily routine:

---

www.tiny-tots.uk **Welcome to Tiny Tots**

| Where to find us | Our concept | Daily routines | Staff | Q&A |

7:30 a.m.	Our nursery opens. The first hour in the morning is free play. The children choose their own activities. At 8:30 a.m. the children split into two groups and go to their own playrooms. Between 8:45 and 9:30 a.m. the children can have breakfast if they are hungry or if they have not had breakfast at home. They clear away their own dishes, wash them and put them back into the cupboard.
10:00 a.m.	Morning circle time. All children take their chairs and form a circle in the middle of the room. First they join hands and sing a song together. They can share news, sing songs or nursery rhymes. After that, theme time begins. The children listen to a story from a book. Then they carry out activities that are linked with the theme. These can be painting or drawing, handicrafts or small experiments.
11:15 a.m.	Clean-up time. It starts with a clean-up song and the staff help the children to put away toys and clear away other activities.
11:30 a.m.	The children get ready to go outside. In the playground they can choose from many activities: there are swings, slides, climbing frames and a large sand-pit. They can ride tricycles and bikes. We try to go outside every day even if the weather is not so good.
12:00 a.m.	All children come back inside. They go to the bathroom and wash their hands before lunch. Some children only stay during the mornings. Now their parents come and pick them up.
12:30 p.m.	The children have lunch, sitting together in small groups. The children serve themselves (with help) and afterwards wash and put away their dishes. Then all children go back to the bathroom to brush their teeth. After lunch they normally enjoy quiet activities: some of them take a nap, some relax or listen to music CDs. They listen to stories that our nursery nurses read out to them.
3:00 p.m.	Outdoor play again. Now the first parents come and pick their children up to take them home. *The nursery closes at 4:00 p.m.*

Working with the text

A Right or wrong? Correct the false statements.
1. The nursery opens at half past seven and is open for eight and a half hours. 8:30 ✓
2. When the children arrive they cannot play the games they want.
3. All children have breakfast together. Between 8:45/9:30
4. At circle time the children sit down on chairs.
5. After circle time it is clean-up time. home time
6. The children go to play outside even if it is raining a little bit. ✓
7. After lunch only some children brush their teeth. all
8. The nursery nurse washes the dishes and puts away the toys. children
9. After lunch all children go to sleep. some of them
10. The children go home on their own. Parents pick up

B The Q&A page lists questions that parents ask frequently. Answer their questions in your own words.

www.tiny-tots.uk	*Welcome to Tiny Tots*			
Where to find us	Our concept	Daily routines	Staff	Q&A

Q: What meals do you offer?
A: We offer breakfast and lunch. Your child can eat her breakfast when he / she feels hungry. We eat our lunch all together in the groups.

1. Q: What activities are there in your nursery school?
2. Q: I only work in the morning. Does my child have to stay all day?
3. Q: What can my child learn at nursery school?
4. Q: My child enjoys exercise outside. What do you offer and when?
5. Q: How do you help children to get independent?

Hands-on task

Interaction

And your nursery school?

Work alone: What is the daily routine of the nursery school where you work? Make notes.

8:00 a.m.   nursery opens

Work with a partner: Tell each other about the routines (use the Simple Present).
Presentation: Now be ready to present it in class.

Unit 2 In the nursery school

Janet's first day

Today is Janet's first day at the Tiny Tots nursery so she is feeling a bit nervous. When she arrives at the nursery school, her new colleagues are already expecting her. They
5 are Mary, the nursery school teacher, and Tom, the nursery assistant.
Mary is greeting Janet at the entrance: "Good morning, Janet," she says, "welcome to your first day at Tiny Tots. Let me show you
10 around. Look, here's the toddler room. The children here are between 6 months and 2 years old."
Janet takes a look inside and sees a nursery nurse singing a song to a baby. She is mov-
15 ing her hands to the words of the song. Two toddlers are sitting on an activity quilt.
"Now let's go to your classroom, Janet." Janet already knows that the children in her group are between 3 and 6 years old.
20 When Janet and Mary enter the room, two girls are playing with play dough. Some others are building a big tower. One boy is drawing a picture, the others are helping Tom, the nursery assistant. He is laying the table for
25 breakfast. "Hello, Janet, welcome. Would you like to join in with breakfast?" asks Tom.
After breakfast it is circle time and Janet is beginning to feel more relaxed.
At 11 o'clock it is time for outdoor play. But
30 everybody is staying inside today because it is raining heavily. After lunch, while the children are relaxing, Janet and her colleagues have their own lunch breaks. In the afternoon the sun is shining again, so everybody
35 is getting ready for outdoor play.
Soon Janet's first day is over and Mary asks Janet: "So how did you like your first day with us?"
Janet says: "I really enjoyed it. Now I'm look-
40 ing forward to my work with Tiny Tots."
All of a sudden she is feeling very tired; it was a long day.

Working with the text

Match up the two halves of the sentences.

While Mary is showing Janet around,	is for children from 6 months to school age.
The toddler room	but today it is raining too heavily.
After circle time the children usually go outdoors,	but they also help the nursery assistant.
In the morning Janet is nervous	Tom is preparing breakfast.
The nursery school	but at the end of her first day she is feeling happy.
In Janet's group the children play a lot of games	is for children under 2 years.

Grammar box: **Present Continuous** – Verlaufsform der Gegenwart

Aussagen und Verneinungen

I	**am**		
He			doing a puzzle.
She	**is**	**(not)**	
It			
We			
You	**are**		playing with children.
They			

Fragen Kurzantworten

Am	I		Yes, I am. / No, I'm not.
Is	she		Yes, he / she / it is.
	he	singing a song?	No, he / she / it isn't.
	(it)		
Are	we		Yes, we / you / they are.
	you	playing with children?	No, we / you / they aren't.
	they		

- Das Present Continuous wird mit einer Form von *to be* und der *ing*-Form des Verbs gebildet.
- Bei den meisten Verben hängt man nur die Endung *–ing* an.
- Wenn jedoch die Grundform des Verbs auf *–e* endet, fällt das *–e* weg: *make → making*;
Bei einigen Verben wird der Endkonsonant verdoppelt: *run → running; stop → stopping; swim → swimming;*
-ie wird zu → *ying: lie → lying*

- Das Present Continuous drückt aus, dass eine Handlung jetzt, d. h. zum Zeitpunkt des Sprechens oder Schreibens geschieht.
- Signalwörter: Es wird oft benutzt mit Zeitbestimmungen wie *at the moment, now, right now*.
- Man benutzt das Present Continuous auch, um zu beschreiben, was man auf einem Bild sieht: *In the photo the children are playing with play dough.*

Grammar box: **Present Continuous and Simple Present**

Im Englischen wird zwischen zwei Formen der Gegenwart unterschieden:

- Das **Simple Present** wird verwendet, wenn eine Handlung regelmäßig geschieht.
- Signalwörter: Es wird mit *always, often, sometimes, rarely, never* und mit Ausdrücken wie *every day, twice a week, usually* etc. benutzt: *I always start work at 8 o'clock.*

- Das **Present Continuous** drückt aus, dass eine Handlung jetzt oder vorübergehend geschieht: *This week my colleague is on holiday, so I'm starting work at 7 o'clock.*
- Signalwörter: *at the moment, now …*

Practising grammar

A Make up sentences in the Present Continuous.
They may be positive or negative.
1. I (do) my homework.
   Example: I am doing my homework.
2. He (not/go) home.
   Example: He is not going home.
3. Tom (help) to tidy up right now.
4. The nursery nurses (plan) a project.
5. At the moment Janet and Lisa (inform) some parents about the outing.
6. The students (study) hard before their exam next week.
7. I (not/feel) good at the moment.
8. We (not/go) to the cinema.
9. When Janet arrives, the staff (prepare) breakfast.
10. The children (not/brush) their teeth.
11. Me and my family (stay) at home.
12. She (not/read) a book.

B Make up questions in the Present Continuous.
They may be with or without question words.
1. What/the little girl/ask/Janet?
   Example: What is the little girl asking Janet?
2. Tom/help/with breakfast?
3. When/Janet/begin to enjoy her work?
4. Who/prepare/lunch?
5. Why/they/sit/there?
6. The boy/draw/a picture?
7. What/the children/build?
8. Where/Mary and Tom/go?
9. What/she/play with?
10. How/you/lay/the table?
11. You/enjoy/your meal?

C Describe what the children are doing in these photos.
Write at least one sentence to each picture.

a)

b)

c)

D What happens usually and what is happening now?
Write out sentences as in the example.

1. Sarah / go to college – this week / work in a family.
   Example: Sarah usually goes to college, but this week she is working in a family.
2. The children / play outside – today / stay inside because it is raining.
3. Janet / start work / at 8:00 a.m. – this week / start at 7:15 a.m.
4. The children / play in the nursery – today / go to the zoo.
5. Mary / stay / with her group all day – at the moment / take a lunch break.
6. I / read a story to the children – today / sing a song and play the guitar / with the children.
7. Normally / the children in our group / go home at 4:00 p.m. – today / stay longer / because of a party.

Unit 2 In the nursery school

E Simple Present or Present Continuous?
Complete the text with the correct form of the verb.

This is Sue. Look! There you can see her in the nursery. She … (1 play) the guitar and … (2 sing) a song. The children … (3 sing) along with her. They … (4 join) hands. Tom and Mary are also there. Tom … (5 tidy up) together with some children and Mary … (6 get) an activity ready for theme time. The rest of the children … (7 play) with blocks.
Sue … (8 come) to the nursery once a week. Four days a week Sue … (9 go) to college. She … (10 work) hard because she … (11 want) to pass her written exam in two months. "Qualifications are important," she says, "I … (12 need) a good job, that's why I … (13 study) hard at the moment. I … (14 not want) to be jobless after my training."

Meeting and greeting people at work

Read the information in the box, then decide what is correct to say in the situations below. Act out the scenes.

Some things are really different in Britain. People only shake hands when they meet for the first time. It is quite amazing for foreigners that the answer to *"How do you do?"* is the same question. If you meet that person the next time or you want to know how somebody is, you ask *"How are you?"*

Senior staff use the first name when they speak with somebody who works under them. Junior staff or trainees use Mr, Mrs, or Ms and the surname unless first names are offered.
Good morning, good afternoon, goodbye are formal, with friends *hello, hi, bye, see you* are alright.

1. Janet meets Mary Parson for the first time.
    Mary Parson: Take a seat, Miss Smith. Janet Smith, isn't it?
    Janet: …

2. One hour later.
    Mary Parson: Well, Janet, you can do your practical training here with us.
    Janet: …
    Mary Parson: Please call me Mary.

3. Janet meets Tom on her first day in the nursery.
    They know each other because they went to the same school some years ago.
    Tom: … Great to see you here with us.
    Janet: … I'm so glad to be here …
    Tom: …

4. Janet says goodbye after her first day. What does she say to Tom and to Mary Parson?

Inside the classroom

The nursery school classroom is a large room with windows and a door to the playground. The room offers areas for different activities: the block area, the home
5 corner, the quiet area, the puzzle table. There is a child-size sink and a cupboard for the dishes. Bookcases and shelves help to store books, games and toys.
The block area is located along the side with
10 the windows. This area is carpeted and the children use it to play with building blocks. Besides blocks there are also toy trains and tracks, toy trucks and buses, figures and plastic toy animals. The toys are kept in the
15 bookcases that divide the block area from the home corner.
The home corner is on the other side of the room along the window. A large wooden structure serves as a playhouse with a child-
20 size kitchen, tables and chairs, a mirror and clothes for dressing up.
Opposite the home corner is the quiet area. There are often times in the day when children like to be quiet and to rest. Some chil-
25 dren just relax while others want to look at a book or play quietly with a toy. The quiet corner is furnished with mattresses, pillows and a curtain which the children can close for a cosy feeling.
30 There are different tables for different play activities. Near the quiet area there is a large round table that the children often use for puzzles and other games.
There are two other tables in the classroom:
35 they are used for play and artwork during free play and for breakfast and lunch. Playing with play dough, painting and drawing are typical activities at these tables.
Near the door is the sink. It is a child-size
40 sink where the children wash their own dishes after breakfast and lunch. They really enjoy this work because it makes them feel "grown-up".
The atmosphere of the room is pleasant
45 and welcoming. It is decorated with the children's own artwork.

Working with the text

A Match the parts of the room to the children's activities.

1. block area
2. home corner
3. quiet area
4. sink
5. puzzle table
6. shelves
7. bathroom
8. tables

a) wash their hands
b) dress up
c) play with blocks, toy trains and figures
d) brush their teeth
e) take a nap
f) relax
g) wash their dishes
h) store toys
i) listen to music CDs
j) play with child-size kitchen equipment
k) do puzzles
l) play with play dough

Unit 2 In the nursery school

B Where do you find these parts of the room and its equipment?
Match the words from the box to the numbers in the picture.

child-size sink 2
breakfast table 6
dishes 3
curtain 4
quiet corner 7
block area 5
shelves 9

mattresses 8
pillows 11
carpet 10
potted plants 1
dustbin 13
artwork 12

C Make up sentences about the children's activities. Write one sentence for each part of the room or each piece of equipment. You can add activities that are not in the list.
Example: In the block area the children play with blocks, toy trains and figures.

In the nursery school Unit 2

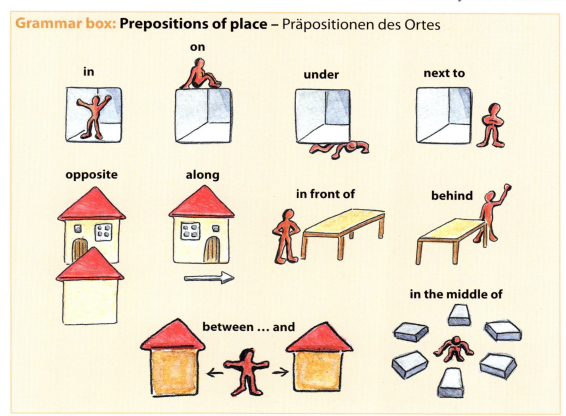

Practising grammar

Put in the correct preposition according to the plan on page 20.
1. The door is … the window. next to
2. The bookcase is …block area … home corner. between and
3. The tables are … the group room. in the middle of
4. The sink is … the entrance door. next to
5. The door to the playground is … the entrance door. opposite
6. The puzzle is … the table. on
7. The artworks are hanging … the walls. along
8. The children are … the room. in
9. The block area is …, window. opposite along the

Hands-on task

Production

Write a letter to Janet. Tell her what a typical classroom in your nursery school looks like and what the children can do there. The expressions in the box below may help you.

- **There is** a puzzle table.
  There are two lunch tables.
- The home corner **is / is located** in one corner of the room.
- The room **is divided into** different areas.

handwerk-technik.de

Unit 2 In the nursery school

A day in the nursery school

tot (von: toddler) [tɒt]	Knirps, Kleinkind
free play [friː pleɪ]	Freispiel
(to) split [splɪt]	sich aufteilen
(to) clear away [klɪə əˈweɪ]	wegräumen
dishes [dɪʃəz]	Geschirr
cupboard [ˈkʌbəd]	Schrank
circle [ˈsɜːkl]	(Stuhl-)Kreis
(to) join hands [dʒɔɪn hænds]	sich die Hände geben
(to) share [ʃeə]	teilen, hier: sich mitteilen
(to) carry out [ˈkærɪ aʊt]	etwas ausführen
theme time [θiːm taɪm]	Arbeit an einem Thema
(to) be linked with [bɪ lɪŋkt wɪð]	verbunden mit
staff [stɑːf]	Personal
playground [pleɪgraʊnd]	Spielplatz / Außengelände
swing [swɪŋ]	Schaukel
slide [slaɪd]	Rutsche
climbing frame [ˈklaɪmɪŋ freɪm]	Klettergerüst
tricycle [ˈtraɪsɪkl]	Dreirad
(to) pick s.o. up [pɪk ʌp]	jemanden abholen
(to) brush teeth [brʌʃ tiːθ]	Zähne putzen
(to) take a nap [teɪk ə næp]	ein Schläfchen machen
daily routine [ˈdeɪlɪ ruːˈtiːn]	Tagesablauf

Janet's first day

colleague [ˈkɒliːg]	Kollege / Kollegin
(to) expect s.o. [ɪkˈspekt]	jemanden erwarten
(to) accept [əkˈsept]	akzeptieren
activity quilt [ækˈtɪvɪti kwɪlt]	Spieldecke
play dough [pleɪ dəʊ]	Knete
blocks (auch: building blocks) [blɒks]	Bauklötze
(to) lay the table [leɪ ðə ˈteɪbl]	den Tisch decken
(to) take turns [teɪk tɜːns]	sich abwechseln
break [breɪk]	Pause

Inside the classroom

block area [blɒk ˈeərɪə]	Bauecke
home corner [həʊm ˈkɔːnə]	Puppenecke
quiet area [ˈkwaɪət ˈeərɪə]	Kuschelecke
child-size [tʃaɪld-saɪz]	in Kindergröße
sink [sɪŋk]	Spüle
bookcase [bʊkkeɪs]	Bücherregal
shelf (sg.), shelves (pl.) [ʃelf, ʃelvz]	Regal(e)
carpeted [ˈkɑːpɪtɪd]	mit Teppich ausgelegt
besides [bɪˈsaɪdz]	außer, außerdem
track [træk]	Schiene
(to) divide [dɪˈvaɪd]	unterteilen
wooden [ˈwʊdn]	aus Holz
mirror [ˈmɪrə]	Spiegel
(to) dress up [dres ʌp]	sich verkleiden
(to) rest [rest]	sich ausruhen
furnished with [ˈfɜːnɪʃd wɪð]	möbliert mit
mattress [ˈmætrɪs]	Matratze
pillow [ˈpɪləʊ]	Kissen
curtain [ˈkɜːtn]	Vorhang
cosy [ˈkəʊzɪ]	gemütlich, kuschelig
grown-up [grəʊn-ʌp]	erwachsen
welcoming [ˈwelˈkʌmɪŋ]	einladend

Unit 3 — Outside the nursery school

Outdoor play areas

swing – seesaw – climbing frame – car tyre swing – slide – sand pit

Look at pictures 1 to 5.
What can you see in the pictures?
What do you have in the outdoor play area of your nursery school?

Unit 3 Outside the nursery school

Outdoor activities

A Look at the circles and talk about what you can do in the outside play area of your nursery school.
Example:
At my nursery school the children **can** make mud pies in the sand pit but they **can't** slide down a slide because there isn't one.

B Now ask your classmate about her or his nursery school.
Example:
Can the children make mud pies in a sand pit at your nursery school?
Yes, they **can**. There is a sand pit.
No, they can't. There isn't a sand pit but there is a slide and the children **can** slide down it.

outdoor activities

make mud pies — sandpit
swing to and fro — swing (car tyre)
bob up and down — seesaw
jump over
run around — grass
play chasing games — grass
seesaw — seesaw
play ball games — playingfield

bounce up and down — trampoline
play hide and seek — grass (pit grass)
play with the sand — sandpit
slide down — slide
skip — rope (ladder)
pile up sand
climb up and down — climbing pole
ride a bicycle — tricycles & bicycles

outdoor equipment

seesaw
swing
climbing pole
tricycles and bicycles
trampoline
car tyre swing
slide
grass pitch
climbing frame
skipping rope
benches
playingfield
rope ladder
sand pit

Outside the nursery school Unit 3

Grammar box: Can und can't

Aussagen	Verneinungen	Fragen
It is nice weather.	It is bad weather.	Can the children play outside?
The children **can** play outside.	The children **can't**	
I	cannot play	Can I
you	outside.	you
he / she / it		he / she / it
we		we
you		you
they **can** ride a bike.		they ride a bike?

Can und can't können ausdrücken

1. eine Fähigkeit bzw. Unfähigkeit	He can speak English but he can't speak Chinese.
2. eine Erlaubnis bzw. ein Verbot	You can have my car this afternoon. I am sorry but you can't have my car this evening.
3. eine Möglichkeit bzw. Unmöglichkeit	Perhaps it's nice tomorrow and we can go out. If it rains we can't. You cannot go out. You haven't done your homework.
4. eine Annahme	Can this be John's football?

Practising grammar

Fill in can or can't with a verb from the box below.

~~keep~~   swing   ~~ride~~   pile up   ~~come~~   ~~find~~   be   go   sit

1. It is raining. The children … (not) outside today. They … only … out when the sun is shining. *can't go*
2. … these … Mike's yellow rubber boots? I think he has got yellow boots. *can you see*
3. John is six now and he … a bike, but his little brother Samuel who is only three … (not) his balance on a bike. *can ride / can not*
4. It's raining this morning. All the sand is wet, so you … (not) in the sand pit without getting wet and dirty. *cannot sit*
5. John likes to play with his toy spade. He … the sand with it. *can pile up*
6. All parents … to the nursery school and have a look around. *can come*
7. Don't let Samuel go on the swing. He is too little and … (not) alone. *can't swing*
8. Wait for me! I want to go out playing football with you but I … (not) my football boots. *can't find*

handwerk-technik.de

Unit 3 Outside the nursery school

Safety first

It is a sunny day and Janet thinks she has a good idea. But Mary Parson who is in charge of the Tiny Tots nursery school wants her to think her plans over.

*The sun is shining. Let the children go out and do what they want to in our outdoor play area. There is a swing, a sand pit and a climbing frame. So there are lots of things they can do and play with. And I **need** some more time to plan my outing so I **needn't** look after them all the time.*

*Oh, it's not that easy. You can't let the children go out and let them do what they want. You **must** watch them closely. You **mustn't** let them just run around. Think of what you want them to do outside and perhaps prepare a game. And don't forget, you **must** always think of their safety first and take good care of them. There is a handbook in my office which gives you some information on outdoor safety. Have a look at it!*

Working with the text

A Answer the questions on the text.
1. What does Janet want to do with the children on this sunny day?
2. Why does she want the children to go outside?
3. What does Mary think about Janet's plan to send the children outside?
4. What does she tell Janet to do?

B Why does Janet use the words *need* and *needn't* but Mary uses *must* and *mustn't*? Look at the grammar box and try to find out.

Outside the nursery school Unit 3

Grammar box: Need, needn't – must, mustn't

Children (I/you/we/they)	need	to be outside in the fresh air.
Janet (he/she)	needs	some more time to plan her outing.
The children (I/you/we/they)	needn't / don't need to	put on warm clothes, it's sunny.
Janet (he/she)	needn't / doesn't need to	hurry. There is enough time.

→ *need to* = brauchen
→ *needn't* in Verbindung mit Verb = nicht brauchen

You	must	always supervise the children outside.
Children	must	never be left alone.
I/he/she/we/they	must	keep a close eye on the children.
I/you/he/she/we/they	mustn't	leave the children alone.
Children	mustn't	be left alone.

→ *must* = "müssen" (Gebot)
→ *mustn't* **in Verbindung mit Verb** = nicht dürfen (Verbot)

Practising grammar

This is what the handbook tells Janet about safety in the outdoor play area of a nursery school. Fill in *need to, must* or *mustn't*.

Outdoor safety

Children (1)… be outside in the fresh air and they (2)… be active. But when children play outside the play area (3)… be safe. For this reason you (4)… always think about what you plan to do outside with the children before you go out.
First you (5)… check the area for safety. The outdoor equipment (6)… be intact and of course it (7)… be clean before you go out and use it. You (8)… always be sure that the children are safe when they play outside. For example: children (9)… have enough space for outdoor chasing games. Sometimes there are more than twenty children in a group and perhaps you (10)… ask a second or third person to help you to supervise the children. You (11)… always take special care that you can see all the children. For this reason you (12)… stay in one place but always walk around. Look out for children who (13)… receive some help with the equipment. Sometimes they are too little to swing or to seesaw alone. Children who are getting too tired (14)… take a rest, so look out for them and tell them to rest.
Children feel more at home when their play area is nice and attractive. When you leave the play area you (15)… check that the play equipment is safe and clean.

Unit 3 Outside the nursery school

Going on an outing

Janet is planning an outing with the group she works with. Mary Parson asks her about her plans.

Mary: Hi, Janet. Theresa says you are planning to go out with your group next month.
Janet: Yes, I'm planning to go to the pet zoo in Green Park. Do you know it?
Mary: Yes, it's a nice place to go to.
Janet: I think it fits in exactly with what we are doing with the children at the moment. We are talking about pets and we are planning some activities like making an animal mobile. Today we are going to sing different songs about animals and we're planning to do a mime game. I think it will be nice for the children to see some of the animals and how they live in real life.
Mary: Yes, I think it's a good idea. It's always special for the children to go out.
Janet: I hope we are going to enjoy it and have a lot of fun!
Mary: Oh, but it's not always a lot of fun for us, you know. There are many things you must think of first and take care of. The parents must be informed, for example.
Janet: Yes, they will be informed. And I know we must keep an eye on the children on our way to the pet zoo and of course watch them at the zoo as well.
Mary: Well, what about the walk?
Janet: It's not a long walk, just 10 or 15 minutes and it's not very complicated. I know the route very well. I often walk along it with my little nephew.
Mary: It's different with a group. A group takes more time and is not that easy to look after.
Janet: That's true. It can take more time.
Mary: Yes, and it needs preparation. Perhaps you should walk along it once more today and do a risk assessment. Is there a dangerous crossing? And what about the traffic? Does the road you walk along have much traffic?
Janet: Well, the traffic is just normal but we have to cross Baker Street at one point. But I don't think it will be a problem because there is a pedestrian crossing a bit further down. We can also take the zebra crossing not far from our nursery school. So we should be safe.
Mary: That's good. Always use pedestrian crossings! Never take a risk! You must always be careful and you mustn't leave the pavement if you don't need to.
Janet: I'm not going alone, Theresa, Sandra and three mothers are coming with me.
Mary: It's always good to have someone else with you to supervise. It is important to have enough supervision of a group. At least one person at the front and one at the back, with plenty in between. How many children are in the group?
Janet: There are 19 children but one is ill with chicken pox.
Mary: 18 children, that's a good number. Tell the children to join hands. That is a simple way to keep the group together and no one can get lost.
Janet: I am becoming a bit nervous now. There are so many things I must think of.
Mary: Don't worry. You will cope if you are well prepared and Theresa and Sandra will give you a helping hand.

Outside the nursery school Unit 3

Working with the text

A Here are all the different things you have to think about or do before you go on an outing. Match the verbs with the correct nouns and phrases.

1. choose — b
2. hand out — h
3. inform — f
4. talk — e
5. present — i
6. do — j
7. walk along — c
8. find — d
9. do — g
10. introduce — a

a) the children to the most important traffic rules
b) a good place for an outing like the pet zoo
c) all the streets and dangerous traffic spots which you will pass on your outing
d) at least two more colleagues or parents who accompany you on the outing and help you to supervise the children
e) about the outing with the children
f) the parents about the outing at least three weeks in advance with a letter and a flyer
g) some preparatory activities with the children like reading out a book, singing songs, doing a mime play
h) a list with all the things the children will need on the outing like something to drink, a healthy snack, weatherproof clothes and shoes
i) your plans for an outing at the staff meeting and ask for help or further ideas
j) a risk assessment before you set off with the children

B Janet writes a letter to the parents to inform them about the outing. Fill in the missing words taken from the text.

Dear parents,

I would like to inform you that I'm planning an (1)… with the children in my group on Monday, May 17th 20…
We are going to start at about 9:30 a.m. from our nursery school and we are going to visit the (2)… in Green Park. You might be interested in coming with us and helping to (3)… the children. In order to make sure that they are (4)…, I will do a (5)… and walk along the streets and crossings which we will pass on Monday. For the children's safety we will always stay on the (6)… and use the (7)…
For our outing your child needs weatherproof clothes and shoes, a drink and maybe a small, healthy snack. (8)… and … are coming with me but you are also welcome to join in and give us a (9)…

Thanks for your interest and help.
Yours sincerely,
Janet

Hands-on task

Production

Choose a typical outing you could do with your nursery school class and think of how to organise your outing. What are the first things you have to do, what the last? Use the words and phrases from exercise A and take down your organisation plan.

Unit 3 Outside the nursery school

Grammar box: Prepositions describing directions

from	to	It takes 20 minutes to walk **from** the nursery school to the pet zoo.
into	out of	In the morning the children come **into** the nursery school at 8 o'clock. When does Anna come **out of** the nursery school?
on	off	The children like to climb **on** top of the climbing frame. Be careful! Don't fall **off** the swing!
up	down	Look at that boy over there. It takes him a minute to climb **up** the ladder of the slide and only a few seconds to go **down**!
over	under / underneath	Go **over** the bridge. Lots of traffic goes **underneath** it.
through	round / around	It's a sunny day. Let's go for a walk **through** the park. You have to walk **around** that big house to get there.
along	across	Don't walk **along** the river with the children. It's too dangerous. The ferry will take him **across** the river.
past		Are you angry with me? Why do you walk **past** me without saying a word? Go past the building.

Practising grammar

Fill in the correct prepositions.

1. Children love to play with the cardboard boxes. They can jump … them or hide … them.
2. On their first day we take children … and show them everything.
3. This is the wrong way. Don't go … Church Street, walk … it and then turn … Green Park Street.
4. How long does it take us to walk … the nursery school … the playing ground in Green Park?
5. Don't walk … Baker Street here. Use the pedestrian crossing down there.
6. A lot of traffic goes … Station Road.
7. Sometimes children jump … the climbing frame and don't watch out for other children.
8. Let's walk … the park, it's nicer than walking … the street.
9. The children like to bob … and … on the seesaw.

Giving directions

**Look at this map of the city.
Can you find the Tiny Tots nursery school?
Where is Green Park and the pet zoo that Janet wants to visit with her group?**

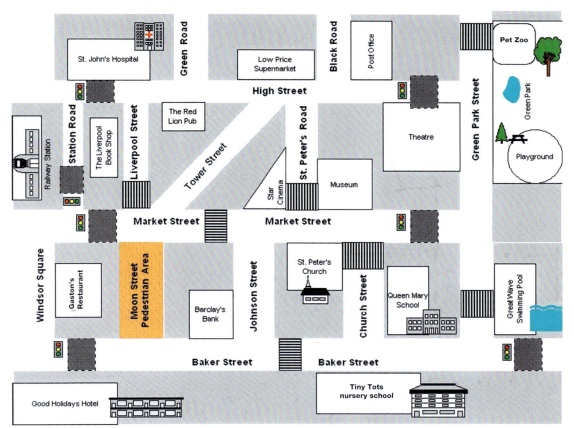

Unit 3 Outside the nursery school

Some time later Theresa asks Janet about her outing.

Theresa: Is everything all right for your outing?
Janet: Yes, I think so. After talking it over with Mary I'm now sure which way I want to go. It's not difficult to get to the pet zoo with the whole group.
Theresa: Which way do you want to go?
Janet: I think we stay on the pavement in front of our nursery school, turn right and walk along Baker Street till we reach the pedestrian crossing by the traffic lights. We could cross Baker Street at the zebra crossing nearby. But then we would have to go along Church Street and there is no zebra crossing or anything else – and I think this can be dangerous with a group!
I would prefer to walk along Baker Street on the pavement till we come to the pedestrian crossing by the traffic lights. Then we cross Baker Street and only walk down that road till we reach Green Park Street and turn right there. We can stay on the pavement again and just go straight on. After a five-minute-walk we can see Green Park on our right hand side. From there it's just a short and easy walk through the park.
Theresa: That's a good plan. With a group it's always better to use a longer but safer way!

Working with language

A Here are some words Janet uses to describe her way to the pet zoo.
Look at the vocabulary and work on the exercises on the next page.

Giving directions

Go straight on / up / down / along …. Street	Gehe / Gehen Sie die … Straße entlang / runter / hoch
Turn left into … Street	Biege / Biegen Sie links in die … Straße ein
Turn right into … Street	Biege / Biegen Sie rechts in die … Straße ein
Turn left at the traffic lights / at the corner	Biege / Biegen Sie links an der Ampel ein / an der Ecke
Walk along … Street	Gehe / Gehen Sie die … Straße entlang
Go / Walk down … Street	Gehe / Gehen Sie die … Straße hinunter
Cross … Street	Überquere / Überqueren Sie … Straße
Take the third road on the right …	Biege / Biegen Sie in die dritte Straße auf der rechten Seite ein
Walk past the church on your left …	Gehe / Gehen Sie an der Kirche auf deiner / Ihrer linken Seite vorbei
Go past the … building	Gehe / Gehen Sie an dem … Gebäude vorbei
The building is on your right / left hand side	Das Gebäude ist auf deiner / Ihrer rechten / linken Seite
The school is opposite the church.	Die Schule ist gegenüber der Kirche
The school is on the corner of … Street and … Street	Die Schule ist an der Ecke … Straße und … Straße

Outside the nursery school Unit 3

B Look at the map of the city on page 31 and fill in the missing words.
Sometimes the gap can be filled with more than one word.

Sandra: Hi, Janet. Can you help me? I want to go to the Great Wave Swimming Pool with my group. But I am not quite sure which way to take. Perhaps you can think of a good and safe route?
Janet: Well, you can (1)… Baker Street on the (2)… nearby. And then (3)… right and (4)… down Baker Street. But there is one problem. After a few minutes you must (5)… Church Street and there is no (6)… So it's better to stay on the (7)… in front of our nursery school and turn right and walk (8)… Baker Street till you come to the traffic (9)… (10)… Baker Street and turn left. Carry on for a bit and then (11)… (12)… into Green Park Street. Here you can see the swimming pool on your (13)…
Sandra: That's a good route. Thanks a lot.
Janet: Not at all.

Hands-on tasks

A Now Theresa asks Janet the way.
Look at the beginning of this dialogue and then try to complete it.

Theresa: Hi, Janet. Did you know that they are showing the new Walt Disney film at the Star Cinema?
Janet: No, I didn't. Do you want to go?
Theresa: Yes, it's a nice idea to take the children. But I'm not sure about the route. Can you tell me the best way to go?
Janet: Well, let me think … Oh, of course, there is a safe way to walk to the cinema. First of all stay on the pavement in front of our nursery school, turn left and walk down Baker Street till you come to the …
…

B Can you tell me the way to …? **Interaction**
Take the Tiny Tots nursery school as starting point on the map on page 31.
Ask someone in your class how to get to the museum, to the theatre, to St. John's Hospital or to any direction you choose.

C Imagine you are planning an outing with your nursery group.
Draw a map and tell the class where you want to go on your outing and which route you want to take.
Don't forget to look for a safe way!

Unit 3 Outside the nursery school

outdoor, outside [aʊtdɔː, aʊtsaɪd]	außen, außerhalb, im Freien	**Going on an outing**	
play area [pleɪ ˈeəriə]	Spielbereich	(to) go on an outing [gəʊ ɒn æn ˈaʊtɪŋ]	einen Ausflug machen
Outdoor equipment		pet zoo [pet zuː]	Streichelzoo
swing, car tyre swing [ˈswɪŋ, kɑː ˈtaɪr]	Schaukel / Autoreifenschaukel	mobile [ˈməʊbaɪl]	Mobilé, Windspiel
seesaw [ˈsiːsɔː]	Wippe	mime game [maɪm]	Pantomime-Spiel
climbing pole [ˈklaɪmɪŋ pəʊl]	Kletterstange	(to) cope with [kəʊp wɪð]	bewältigen, meistern
		prepared [prɪpeəd]	vorbereitet
slide [slaɪd]	Rutsche	adult [ˈædʌlt]	Erwachsener
sand pit [sænd pɪt]	Sandkasten	(to) be informed [bɪ ɪnˈfɔːmd]	informiert sein
toy spade [tɔɪ speɪd]	Kinder- / Spielspaten	preparation [ˌprepəˈreɪʃn]	Vorbereitung
trampoline [ˈtræmpəlɪn]	Trampolin	risk assessment [rɪsk əˈsesmənt]	Risikoabschätzung
skipping rope [ˈskɪpɪŋ rəʊp]	Hüpfseil	pedestrian, walker [pɪˈdestrɪən, ˈwɔːkə]	Fußgänger
bench [bentʃ]	Bank	crossing [ˈkrɒsɪŋ]	Kreuzung
rope ladder [rəʊp ˈlædə]	Seilleiter, Strickleiter	pedestrian crossing [pɪˈdestrɪən ˈkrɒsɪŋ]	Fußgängerüberweg
playing field [pleɪɪŋ fiːld]	Spielfeld		
grass pitch [grɑːs pɪtʃ]	Rasenfeld, Rasenfläche	zebra crossing [ˈziːbrə ˈkrɒsɪŋ]	Zebrastreifen
rubber boots [ˈrʌbə buːts]	Gummistiefel, "Wellies"	pavement [peɪvmənt]	Bürgersteig
Outdoor activities		pedestrian subway [pɪˈdestrɪən sbweɪ]	Fußgängerunterführung
(to) swing to and fro [swɪŋ tu ænd frəʊ]	vor und zurück schaukeln	preparatory [prɪˈpærətəri]	vorbereitend
(to) seesaw [ˈsiːsɔː]	wippen	weatherproof [ˈweðəpruːf]	wetterfest
(to) bob up and down [bɒb ʌp ænd daʊn]	auf und ab wippen, sich auf und ab bewegen	cardboard boxes [kɑːdbɔːd bɒksɪz]	Pappkartons
(to) climb up and down [klaɪm ʌp ænd daʊn]	herauf- und herabklettern	**Safety first**	
(to) slide down [slaɪd daʊn]	herunter rutschen	(to) be in charge of [bɪ ɪn tʃɑːdʒ ɒv]	verantwortlich sein
(to) make mud pies [meɪk mʌd paɪs]	Kuchen aus Sand bauen	safety [ˈseɪftɪ]	Sicherheit
(to) pile up (sand) [paɪl ʌp (sænd)]	auftürmen / aufhäufen	handbook [hændbʊk]	Handbuch
(to) bounce up and down [baʊns ʌp ænd daʊn]	auf und ab springen	(to) check sth. for safety [tʃek fɔː ˈseɪftɪ]	etw. auf Sicherheit
(to) skip [skɪp]	Seil springen	intact [ɪnˈtækt]	intakt, nicht beschädigt
(to) jump over [dʒʌmp ˈəʊvə]	springen über	space [speɪs]	Raum, Platz
(to) play chasing games [pleɪ tʃeɪzɪŋ geɪms]	Nachlaufspiele spielen	(to) stay in one place [steɪ ɪn wʌn pleɪs]	an einer Stelle stehen bleiben
(to) play hide and seek [pleɪ haɪd ænd siːk]	Verstecken spielen	(to) walk around [wɔːk əˈraʊnd]	herumgehen
(to) hide [haɪd]	verstecken	(to) look out for [lʊk aʊt fɔː]	Ausschau halten nach
(to) ride a tricycle [raɪd ə ˈtraɪsɪkl]	Dreirad fahren	(to) take a rest, to rest [teɪk ə rest, tuː rest]	eine Pause einlegen
		Sich um jemanden kümmern	
		(to) take care of / care for [teɪk keə ɒv]	sich kümmern um
		(to) supervise [ˈsuːpəvaɪz]	beaufsichtigen
		(to) keep an eye on [kiːp æn aɪ ɒn]	ein Auge haben auf
		(to) pay attention to s.o. [peɪ əˈtenʃn tuː]	jmd. beachten, jmd. Aufmerksamkeit schenken
		(to) watch s.o. [wɒtʃ]	jmd. beobachten, hier: beaufsichtigen

Unit 4 — Families

What makes up a family?

- family
  - family members
  - immediate family circle
  - family parties
  - family circumstances
  - family life

A What keywords come to your mind when you think of a "family"? Work in groups and draw your own "family mind map" on a poster.

B Pin up your posters in the classroom. Walk around and look at the different results. You can also try to sum up all your results in one mind map.

If you don't know how to create a mind map, look at page 182 for help.

Unit 4 Families

Who is who in Sandra's family?

This is a typical family tree. Look at the tree and answer the following questions.
1. What are the names of Sandra's grandparents?
2. What are her mother's and father's names?
3. How many aunts has Sandra got and what are their names?
4. Has Sandra got a sister or a brother?
5. How many uncles has Sandra got and what are their names?
6. Have all of her uncles and aunts got children?
7. How many cousins has Sandra got? What are their names?
8. Has Sandra got a niece or nephew?
9. Is your own family smaller or larger than Sandra's family?

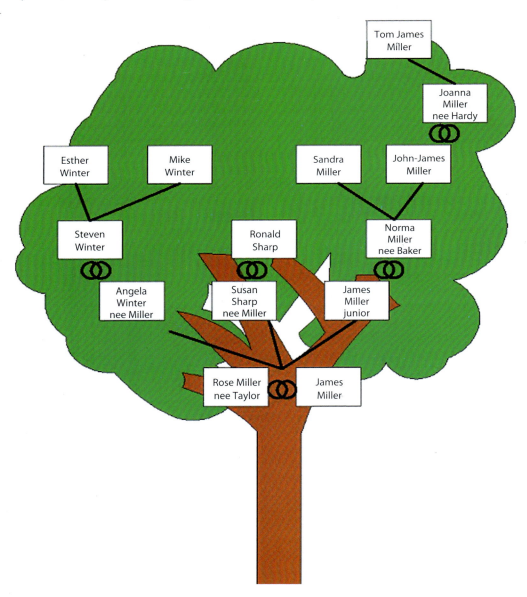

Families Unit 4

Working with language

The following words describe family relationships. Read them and make sure you know what they mean. Then try to fill in the gaps in the text.

great-grandparents 1
granddaughters 8
grandsons 9
married 5
father 4
son 3
daughter 2
brother 12
sister 19
sons-in-law 6
daughter-in-law 7
great-grandchild 10
aunt 15
uncle 16
brother-in-law 21
sister-in-law 13
cousin 18
nephew 14
nieces 17
husband 20
wife 11

1920

Sandra likes to look through her grandparents' family album. The first photo shows her grandmother's parents, Sandra's (1)… on their wedding day. Then there is a wedding photo showing James and Rose Miller, Sandra's grandparents. Two years after their wedding their eldest (2)… Angela was born. Angela was followed by Susan and James junior, Rose's and James's only (3)… and Sandra's (4)…. It's a tradition in the Miller family that the first born son always carries the name James. All three children are (5)…. Now there are two (6)…, Steven and Ronald and one (7)… Norma, two (8)…, Sandra and Esther and two (9)…, Mike and John-James called JJ. Last year Rose and James were very proud to have a (10)…, baby Tom. His parents are their grandson JJ and his (11)… Joanna. Sandra likes to visit her (12)… JJ and her (13)… Joanna because she is very fond of her little (14)… Tom. The whole family sticks together. Although Sandra's (15)… Susan and her (16)… Ronald haven't got any children, they have a very close relationship with their (17)… and nephews, Esther, Mike, Sandra and John-James (JJ). Sandra likes to get together with her (18)… Esther because she hasn't got a (19)… only her brother JJ. Angela's (20)… Steven likes to spend his time with his … Ronald because they have the same hobby. The whole family likes to come together for family parties. The next one will be Tom's christening and Rose and James are looking forward to it.

Grammar box: Genitive – Das Genitiv-S

Mary's parents are teachers.	Singularform des Vornamens → + 's
Thomas's parents are doctors.	Singularform des Vornamens endet auf s → + 's
Mrs Evans' daughter is five years old.	Singularform des Familiennamens endet auf s → + '
Some parents can't understand their children's problems.	Pluralnomen ohne Plural-s → + 's
My grandparents' house is very old.	Pluralform des Nomens endet auf s → + '
The colour of the car is black.	**of** + Artikel / Pronomen + Nomen im Singular
The colour of the car**s is** red.	**of** + Artikel / Pronomen + Nomen im Plural

Hands-on task

Production

Draw your own family tree and give a short talk about your family in class.

Unit 4 Families

Grammar box: Possessive Pronouns II – Possessivpronomen / Fürwörter

Possessivpronomen drücken ein Besitz- oder Zugehörigkeitsverhältnis aus.

Sie können

- attributiv = vor dem Nomen

This is Sandra's photo album.
→ *This is **her** photo album. (attributiv)*

oder

- substantivisch = alleinstehend mit Bezug auf das vorherige Nomen eingesetzt werden.

→ *This photo album is **hers**. (substantivisch)*

Personalpronomen (personal pronoun)	Possessivpronomen attributiv (possessive pronoun)	Possessivpronomen substantivisch (possessive pronoun)
I	my	mine
you (Singular)	your	yours
he, she, it	his, her, its	his, hers, its
we	our	ours
you (Plural)	your	yours
they	their	theirs

Vgl. auch Unit 1 Me and my job, Grammar box: Possessive Pronouns I

Practising grammar

Add the correct possessive pronoun.
1. Is this the Millers' house? No, I don't think so. … *Their* house isn't that large. The smaller one next door must be …
   Example: Their house isn't that large. The smaller one next door must be theirs.
2. Ronald is going to meet … wife Susan at 6 o'clock. *his*
3. Rose never leaves the house without … hat. *her*
4. Look, can you help me? I want to sort out these marbles. Which of these marbles are … / … marbles and which are … / … marbles ? The blue marbles are … / … and the blue and white ones are … / … (you / me) *your mine*
5. Mike is very glad to have a room of … own. *his*
6. Where is *my* football shirt, Mum? It's on *your* bed, freshly washed.
7. Over the past few years we were able to save some money and we bought a yacht last week. Look at the photo. This boat is … now. *ours*
8. John and Sheila have got a car each. The red sports car is *his* and the black one is *hers*.
9. Everyone in the family loves Rose's and James's old house. … *Their* garden is very large with a lot of old trees.

Families Unit 4

What is a typical family? – Four family portraits

A Look at these family pictures. Do they show typical families of today with their typical family members?

B Read the four family portraits on the next page and try to decide if any picture shows one of the families. Give reasons for your decision.

more generation family
extended family

Single-parent family

nuclear family
traditional family

Patchwork family

handwerk-technik.de

39

Unit 4 Families

Michael and Mary Miller with Elizabeth and Matthew

Michael Miller works as a mechanic in a Liverpool garage. Mary isn't working at the moment because six months ago she had her baby Matthew. But Mary is thinking of starting work again soon. "Today it's not such a problem to go to work as a mother of small children. I will look out for a good, well-trained childminder for Matthew as soon as he is twelve to fifteen months old, so that I can work at least at two days a week or maybe more. And in two weeks, our three-year-old daughter Elisabeth is going to attend the Tiny Tots nursery school for the first time. This will give me some time for myself." Mary and Michael live in a small semi-detached house in a new Liverpool residential area. "The house is quite small but it's enough for us and it's just what we can afford. Everything about us is small," Michael admits. "We have a small car, a small house with a small garden and a small dog called Tiny. I think we are a typical average family with an average lifestyle. But my dreams are big. Some time in my life I want to run my own garage and have a large house with a swimming pool."

Helen and Thomas Reilly with Susan, Anna, Jane and Ronald

Helen and Thomas Reilly live happily in an old farmhouse on the outskirts of Liverpool.
"I fell in love with our house at first sight. "It's large and there is enough space for three generations under one roof, for my husband and me, our children and their grandparents. Thomas's parents live with us. I think we are an old-fashioned family, a husband and wife with more than two children and with very traditional roles. My husband is the 'breadwinner' and I am the housewife. That sounds very traditional but I have always wanted an extended family with a lot of children. I was pretty sure that I wanted to give up my job and be a housewife for the sake of my children. Of course, all of our children go - or will go - to nursery school but I won't have a nanny or babysitter or send one of them to a childminder. I like the idea of looking after them myself and having a very close relationship with them, so that I can see how they grow and change every day."
Helen and Thomas now have four children, Susan, 6 years old, Anna, 4 years, Jane, 2 years and baby Ronald, 10 months old. "But that's not our complete family", Thomas tells us. "There are also Caesar, the dog, Ronnie and Willie, our two cats, Susan's dearly loved guinea pig Twiggy and, last but not least, Anna's tortoise Superman."

Sean and Carol Baker with Jason, Madeleine, Colin and Henry

Sean and Carol Baker married a year ago. Before their marriage they had known each other for a year. Their wedding photo shows them with their four children: Jason and Madeleine, 6 years old, Colin, 5, and finally Henry, 2 and a half. How is that possible? Well, the Bakers are a patchwork family. Sean was a widower when he met Carol. He lived alone with his children, Jason and Colin. When Carol's marriage broke up she was left alone to look after her children Madeline and Henry. Shortly after Carol and Sean were married the whole family moved into a large flat in an old Victorian house right in the city centre.
"We all needed a lot more room and quite some time to settle in," Carol explains. "At first it was very difficult for the children to get used to a new partner with their parent, to accept me as a 'new mother' and Sean as a 'new father'. Madeleine was extremely jealous. She didn't want to share me with Jason and Colin. There were a lot of quarrels between the children."
"We were thrown together but we grew close," says Sean. "In two weeks time Carol is going to have a baby. Then we will be a real patchwork family."
Right now, Carol cannot consider taking up a full-time job for the next three years – until the baby is old enough for nursery school. "Well, I think I will stay at home and look after the children and the house. I've got the chance to do some office work via computer to keep contact with the working world and earn a bit of extra money. And there is always the chance to have a babysitter or nanny here at home to look after the children now and then."

Samantha Foster with Roger and Mike

"If I didn't have my children I would be a very unhappy person", Samantha says.
She works as a language teacher in Liverpool and she brings up her two sons Roger, 7, and Mike, 5, alone. Two years ago she was divorced from her husband Leonard.
Samantha, Roger and Mike live in a small flat in Liverpool. Now and then Samantha's parents help her with the children and every other weekend they visit their father.
"Being a single parent isn't an easy life," Samantha says, "I can only work for a few hours a week, because I have to look after the children and the household. Time and money are always a problem and sometimes I miss a grown-up person to talk to."

Working with the text

A Answer the following questions on the texts. Always answer in full sentences.
1. Why isn't Mary Miller working at the moment?
2. What is Elizabeth going to do in two weeks?
3. What is so "very average" about the Miller family?
4. What does Helen mean when she talks about three generations under one roof?
5. Why does Helen call her family old-fashioned?
6. Why can't Carol think of taking up a fulltime job right now?
7. How does she try to keep contact to the working world?
8. Why was the new situation as a patchwork family difficult for the children?
9. What does Samantha think about being a single-parent family?

B Read the following sentences and fill in the gaps with words from the box.

> afford
> sake
> grown-up
> generations
> accept
> jealous
> space

1. The Millers live in a small house but it's exactly what they can …
2. The Reilly family doesn't live in the city centre. They live in a large old farmhouse with enough space for three … under one roof.
3. Helen Reilly gave up her job for the … of the children.
4. Carol and Sean Baker's children needed some time to … their father's and mother's new partner. Some of the children were …
5. As a single parent Samantha spends much time together with her sons but she would like to get together with a … person more often.

C Find these words in the family portraits.
1. something very normal and typical
2. not in the centre of the city, outside the city centre
3. argument, fighting with words
4. to work 8 hours a day

D Say why!
Complete the following sentences.
1. Mary Miller thinks it's no problem to go to work with small children because …
2. Helen does not like the idea of having a nanny or childminder for her children because …
3. As a mother of small children Carol has the chance to keep contact with the working world because …
4. Samantha thinks it isn't easy being a single-parent family, because …

Unit 4 Families

Working with language

Here are the four different family types presented in the texts. Make sure you understand their meaning. Work on the tasks.

nuclear family – traditional / extended family – patchwork family – single-parent family

Production

Hands-on tasks

A Give examples from the text which show you what family type the Miller, Reilly, Baker and Foster family is. Try to design a table. Present your table in class.

B Imagine someone asks you to explain what a patchwork or a nuclear family is. What would you answer? Sit together in pairs and write down a short explanation of each word.

C Now sit in small groups and work on the following tasks. *Interaction*

parent staying at home – grandparents – nanny – babysitter – childminder – nursery school

1. Sum up how the four families manage to make sure their children are looked after during a working day.
2. Discuss the various possibilities to make sure small children are looked after and make a list of advantages and disadvantages. Present your results in class, maybe on a poster.

Look at page 175 ("Wörter und Ausdrücke auf Englisch erklären") for help.

A … family consists of …	Eine … Familie besteht aus …
… is typical of a … family …	… ist typisch für eine … Familie
It is typical that a … family …	Es ist typisch, dass eine … Familie
You talk / one talks of a …. family when …	Man spricht von einer … Familie, wenn …
In a … family there are …	In einer …-Familie gibt es …
The expression … is used for a family with …	Der Ausdruck … wird für eine Familie mit … gebraucht

Childminders

Today, more and more women are trying to go back to work after having a baby. Those who do so have to find childcare, unless the father stays at home or there are grandparents who can look after the child. But for those who do not have those options, there might be a problem if the child is under three. Not every nursery school offers a place for under-threes, although more and more trained childminders offer vacancies especially for younger children.

Mary Miller has considered placing her son Matthew with a childminder. Since vacancies can be rare, she has already been looking out for a suitable place. Then, at her paediatrician's practice, she saw Esther Harper's poster.

OFSTED – What is it?
These letters stand for **Office For STandards in Education.** OFSTED is an independent group which inspects social and educational organisations and institutions. Every week, they carry out hundreds of inspections throughout England in schools, nursery schools or children's homes and report their results to the British government. They also publish their results on their website for everyone to read. OFSTED is meant to improve public services for children and young people and guarantee value for money. Private organisations and childminders can also apply for an inspection in order to convince parents of their good educational standards.

Families Unit 4

Looking for a childminder?
This is the right place for your child!

Esther Harper, OFSTED Registered Childminder, has a full-time vacancy, minding hours from 6 a.m. till 7 p.m. for children aged between 1 and 4 years.

I have …
- 8 years of experience with children (5 years as a trained nursery nurse in nursery school, 3 years as an independent childminder)
- completed certification courses for minding the under-threes
- First-aid certificates relevant to babies and young children
- completed certification courses for preparing healthy and vegetarian meals and snacks for babies and children

I offer …
- a safe home with a rich play and learning environment for your child, with a large play room offering a wide range of toys and play activities, nap room, child-size bathroom and kitchen facilities and an outdoor play area
- educational play to stimulate awareness of colours, shapes, sounds, tastes and textures.
- activities to develop coordination, for example by sorting activities
- memory-training games, singing, dancing, rhythmic and therapeutic exercises
- opportunities to develop linguistic competence through books, word games and imaginative play
- outings (forest or park days with picnic and activities)
- toddler swimming (assisted by 2 trained childminders)
- hand-eye coordination exercises especially for children under three
- potty-training
- nutritional weaning
- real-life experiences like cooking, shopping, gardening
- meals and snacks with healthy, organic food
- child behaviour management
- extra minding hours on request
- small groups with a maximum of 5 children

References available!
I'm regularly checked by OFSTED and have received an overall grading of GOOD.
For more information please contact:
phone 07400 851 851,
esther_harper_homeforchildren@yahoo.com

Working with the text

A Try to find these words from Esther Harper's poster.
1. a person who looks after children as a job
2. helping injured people
3. food without any meat
4. room where children and babies can sleep
5. playing not just for fun, play and games which help children to learn something
6. showing and teaching children social skills and manners, like welcoming people, table manners, coping with conflicts
7. certificates and papers which show your qualification

handwerk-technik.de

Unit 4 Families

B Mary Miller becomes interested in Esther Harper's poster and she phones her. Here is the phone call both had. It is mixed up. Try to reconstruct it.

Esther Harper
1. Esther Harper speaking.
2. Okay, I understand. But if you want to have a place earlier, you can rest assured that I'm the ideal childminder for you. I'm especially trained for babies, as you may have seen from my poster. I have certification especially for toddlers and babies.
3. I can perfectly understand your feelings. Well, just to make you feel sure about me, I'm a trained nursery nurse and a registered childminder. I have 8 years of experience and I'm regularly checked by OFSTED.
4. Yes, of course that's a good idea because vacancies for children under three years are sometimes difficult to find. But, why do you want to wait another six months? I have a vacancy for a baby right now.
5. Yes, of course, I can send you an information map with all my certificates and further information on my nursery.
6. Okay, see you on Wednesday, goodbye.
7. Thanks for your interest. First, I would like to know how old your child is.
8. I know you can't make a quick decision. But you don't have to hurry. I would like to offer you the chance to come to my nursery and see how I work.
9. Okay, we can meet next Wednesday at about 10 a.m. Is that okay?

Mary Miller
a) I want to go back to work, but in six months time - because I want to stay with my child in his first year.
b) Yes, the map would be a big help. But you see, as a mother it's always of great concern to make sure that your child is safe.
c) Well, my son Matthew is now 6 months old. I think at present he's too young for childminding. But I'm thinking of putting him with a childminder when he's 12 months old. I decided to start looking around early to make sure I find the perfect place for him.
d) Yes, that's exactly why I'm interested in a vacancy with you. But as a mother you know that I really want to be sure that my child is in good hands. So, do you have references?
e) Good morning Mrs Harper, my name is Mary Miller. I've got your poster from my paediatrician and I'm interested in one of your vacancies.
f) I read all that in your poster and it's great that welcome inspection, but I'm still indecisive.
g) That's a good idea. I could come on a Wednesday because my mother can babysit.
h) Yes, that's perfect.
i) Goodbye.

C Esther Harper tells Mary Miller that she is "the ideal childminder" for children under three. Looking at the poster, can you say why she is qualified for that group of children, especially babies?

Hands-on task

Interaction

At school, Sandra is asked to do a childminder placement. School told her to find a nursery which accepts under-threes. Sandra found out that Esther Harper is offering a placement, so she calls her and asks her questions about her nursery and about the work experience she can offer her with younger children. In small groups, work out a telephone dialogue between Sandra and Esther Harper. Present your dialogue in class.

Grammar box: Simple Past – Einfache Vergangenheit

- Das Simple Past beschreibt Vorgänge oder Handlungen, die in der Vergangenheit angefangen und ebenso in der Vergangenheit abgeschlossen wurden.
- Signalwörter: *yesterday, (one year) ago, in 2002, the other day, the day before yesterday, last (week), in those days, in the past*

Aussagen

	Regelmäßige Verben: 1. Verbform (Infinitiv) +ed
	like → liked
Ausnahmen	
	Bei Verben, die nach einem Konsonanten auf –y enden, ändert sich die Endung zu -i
	copy → copied
	Bei Verben, die auf einem betonten -er, -ir oder -ur enden, wird das -r verdoppelt
	prefer → preferred
	Nach kurzem, betontem Vokal (bei a, e, i, o, u) wird der Endkonsonant verdoppelt
	stop → stopped
	Unregelmäßige Verben: 2. Verbform (Past Tense)
	go → went
	fall → fell
	break → broke
Ausnahme	
	"To be" hat zwei Vergangenheitsformen: *was* und *were*

I	**was**	We	**were**
You	**were**	You	**were**
He, she, it	**was**	They	**were**

Verneinungen

Hilfsverben werden direkt verneint

was	→	wasn't
were	→	weren't
had	→	didn't have
could	→	couldn't
did	→	didn't

Vollverben werden mit *didn't / did not* verneint

liked	→	didn't like
copied	→	didn't copy
preferred	→	didn't prefer
went	→	didn't go
fell	→	didn't fall
broke	→	didn't break

Unit 4 Families

Work report

Sandra decided to do her placement at Esther Harper's nursery. Fill in the correct Simple Past form of the verb in brackets.

Yesterday … (1 be) the first day of my placement. My working day … (2 start) at 6 a.m. when Mrs Hollander … (3 bring) in her eight-month-old son Michael because she … (4 have) to start work very early that day. I … (5 make) a bottle for him because he … (6 cry) terribly when she … (7 bring) him in. She … (8 tell) me that she … (9 be) in a hurry and … (10 not have) the time to feed him. I … (11 sit) down with him quietly and when he … (12 calm) down, he … (13 drink) his bottle. After that, I … (14 change) his nappy and because he … (15 seem) to be tired again, I … (16 put) him to bed. Very soon, he … (17 fall) asleep.
Later, at 8 o' clock, Sandra, aged one year and three months, … (18 be) brought in by her grandmother and then, only ten minutes later, two-year-old Robert … (19 enter) the playroom with his mother. On Fridays, we only have three children, because the other two, Samira – 10 months – and Ronald – two years and six months – stay at home with their mother. Both children … (20 eat already) their breakfast at home. Mrs Harper … (21 want) me to take care of Robert while she … (22 do) some coordination exercises with Samira. Since we … (23 plan) to go on an outing and walk through the forest, I … (24 read) a picture book to him about forest animals. First, we … (25 have) a look at the picture and I … (26 ask) him about what he … (27 see) on the page and Robert … (28 be) able to answer most of my questions. Very soon, he … (29 begin) to tell his own little stories, so I was pleased that I … (30 succeed) in stimulating him to speak. I also … (31 prepare) all the bottles, meals and snacks for that day.
Shortly after lunch time, we all … (32 set) off for a walk through the forest. Before we … (33 go) out I … (34 make) sure that every child was dressed for a walk in the open. I … (35 help) Ronald to put on his weatherproof trousers and his rain cape because he … (36 cannot) manage it himself. Mrs Harper … (37 carry) Michael in a children's carrier and we … (38 take) our handcart with us for Sandra and Ronald to sit in. I … (39 collect) some leaves and other material from the forest for some handicraft activities and Robert … (40 join) in. When we … (41 come) back from our outing, the children … (42 nibble) some fruit snacks, the babies … (43 have) their bottles and I … (44 change) all the nappies once again. For the rest of the day, the children … (45 choose) their own play activities and games, while the babies … (46 spend) their time on their activity quilt. I … (47 supervise) and … (48 support) them in their play, for example I … (49 do) some finger games with the babies to train their coordination. At 6 p.m. the last parents … (50 fetch) their children.

Production

Hands-on tasks

A Have you already done a childminder placement? What kind of experience did you have? Write a work report about one typical day at your childminder.

B If you have not done a family placement yet, write about an experience you had as a babysitter in the past. How did you spend your time as a babysitter?

Families Unit 4

Grammar box: Questions in Simple Past – Fragen

Questions with "did"

Aussagen	Fragen	Antworten
I gained a lot of experience during my family placement.	**Did** you gain a lot of experience during your family placement?	Yes, I did. No, I didn't.

Wh-Questions

What	did	you do during your family placement?	Was?
Where	did	your placement family live?	Wo?
When	did	you start work?	Wann?
Why	did	you want to work in an extended family?	Warum?
Who		helped you to find a good family placement for you?	Wer?
How	did	you like your family placement?	Wie?

Practising grammar

After a three-week childminder placement Sandra gets back to college with her classmates. They are all interested in each other's experience. They ask Sandra about her childminder.

A Form Simple Past questions.
1. Where / you / do / your placement?
   Example: Where did you do your placement?
2. How many children / have / your childminder?
3. Esther Harper / give / you / some advice on working with children under three?
4. you / do / any outings?
5. Why / you / choose / Ester Harper's place?
6. you / manage / to write / all work reports?

B Here are some answers.
   Form the missing questions.
1. On her last day Sandra walked through the forest with the children. (What?)
   Example: What did Sandra do with the children on her last day?
2. Sandra read out a picture book to prepare her outing. (What?)
3. Sandra's working day started at 7 a.m. already. (When?)
4. At first the children reacted very shy. (How?)
5. It took Sandra about two to three days to establish good contact with the children. (How long?)
6. Sandra also went to the zoo with the children. (Where?)

handwerk-technik.de

47

Unit 4 Families

What makes up a family?

family member ['fæməli 'membə]	Familienmitglied
immediate family circle [ɪ'miːdjət 'fæməli 'sɜːkl]	engster Familienkreis
family parties ['fæməli 'paːtɪs]	Familienfeiern
circumstances ['sɜːkəmstənsɪs]	(Lebens-) Umstände

Who is who in Sandra Miller's family?

family tree ['fæməli triː]	Familienstammbaum
great-grandparents [greɪt-'grændpeərənts]	Urgroßeltern
great-grandfather [greɪt-'grændfaːðə]	Urgroßvater
great-grandmother [greɪt-'grændmʌðə]	Urgroßmutter
great-grandchild [greɪt-'grændʃɪld]	Urenkel
grandparents [grændpeərənts]	Großeltern
grandmother [grændmʌðə]	Großmutter
grandfather [grændfaːðə]	Großvater
grandchildren [grændʃɪldrən]	Enkelkinder
granddaughter [grænddɔːtə]	Enkelin, Enkeltochter
grandson [grændsʌn]	Enkel, Enkelsohn
mother [mʌðə]	Mutter
father [faːðə]	Vater
daughter [dɔːtə]	Tochter
son [sʌn]	Sohn
brother ['brʌðə]	Bruder
sister ['sɪstə]	Schwester
aunt [aːnt]	Tante
uncle ['ʌŋkl]	Onkel
niece [niːs]	Nichte
nephew ['nevjuː]	Neffe
cousin ['kʌzn]	Cousine, Cousin
husband ['hʌzbənd]	Ehemann
wife [waɪf]	Ehefrau
(to) be married to [bɪ: 'mærɪd tuː]	verheiratet sein mit
brother-in-law ['brʌðə-ɪn-lɔː]	Schwager
sister-in-law ['sɪstə-ɪn-lɔː]	Schwägerin

What's a typical family? – Four family portraits

childminder ['tʃaɪld,maɪndər]	Kinderbetreuer/in, Tagesmutter
well-trained [,wel'treɪnd]	gut ausgebildet
(to) attend [ə'tend]	besuchen (Kindergarten etc.)
semi-detached house [semi-dɪ'tætʃt]	Doppelhaushälfte
residential area [,rezɪ'denʃl 'eərɪə]	Wohngebiet
average ['ævərɪdʒ]	durchschnittlich, Durchschnitts-…
(to) admit [əd'mɪt]	zugeben
(to) run s.th. [rʌn]	etwas betreiben (ein Unternehmen)
(to) decide [dɪ'saɪd]	(sich) entscheiden
decision [dɪ'sɪʒn]	Entscheidung
marriage ['mærɪdʒ]	Ehe
(to) settle in ['setl ɪn]	sich einleben
jealous ['dʒeləs]	neidisch
quarrel ['kwɒrəl]	Streit
divorce [dɪ'vɔːs]	Scheidung
(to) be divorced [bɪ: dɪ'vɔːst]	geschieden sein
(to) be grown-up [bɪ: grəʊn-ʌp]	erwachsen sein
nuclear family ['njuːklɪə 'fæməli]	Kleinfamilie
extended family [ɪk'stendɪd 'fæməli]	Großfamilie
patchwork family [pætʃwɜːk 'fæməli]	Patchwork-Familie
single-parent family ['sɪŋgl-peərənt 'fæməli]	Familie mit einem Elternteil

Childminders

vacancy ['veɪkənt si]	hier: freier Betreuungsplatz
paediatrician's practice [,piːdiə'trɪʃəns 'præktɪs]	Kinderarztpraxis
independent [,ɪndɪ'pendənt]	unabhängig, selbstständig
play and learning environment [pleɪ ənd 'lɜːnɪŋ ɪn'vaɪə rən mənt]	Spiel- und Lernumgebung
nap room [næp ruːm]	Schlafraum
stimulate ['stɪmjʊleɪt]	anregen, stimulieren
shapes [ʃeɪps]	Formen
taste [teɪst]	Geschmack
texture ['tekstʃər]	Oberfläche
sorting [sɔːtɪŋ]	Auswahl-, auswählen
linguistic competence [lɪŋ'gwɪstɪk 'kɒmpɪtənts]	Sprachkompetenz
potty-training ['pɒti 'treɪnɪŋ]	Sauberkeitserziehung
nutritional weaning [njuː'trɪʃənəl wiːnɪŋ]	hier: Fläschchen-Entwöhnung
organic [ɔː'gænɪk]	biologisch
minding hours [maɪndɪŋ aʊərs]	Betreuungsstunden
on request [ɒn rɪ'kwest]	auf Nachfrage
overall grading [,əʊvə'rɔːl greɪdɪŋ]	Gesamtbewertung
inspect [ɪn'spekt]	inspizieren, überprüfen
educational standards [,edjʊ'keɪʃənl 'stændəds]	Erziehungsstandards

Unit 5 — Toys and games

Match the names and pictures of these toys and games

wooden blocks – Lego bricks – jigsaw puzzle – picture lotto – knight – castle – doll – puppet – clown – teddy bear – cuddly toy animal

Do you remember having a favourite toy when you were a child?
Which of these toys and games have you got in your nursery school?

Unit 5 Toys and games

Choosing toys for children

Fond memories of childhood usually bring to mind a favourite toy. A cuddly doll, colourful crayons or a special wagon are all childhood favourites.

Toys bring a great deal of joy to children, but they can also be valuable learning tools. Exploring, pretending and sharing are just a few of the important skills that children develop when they play.

Toys don't have to be expensive. Cardboard boxes in the backyard and measuring cups in the bathtub are favourites. But parents who wish to buy toys may find it helpful to know which ones to choose for children of different ages.

Birth to 18 months

Babies and infants learn about the world through their senses. They are interested in the sight, sound, smell, texture and the taste of things. They enjoy rattles, stacking toys, squeak toys, floating tub toys, books with rhymes and musical toys.

18 months to 3 years

These children are called toddlers. Objects or toys that they can squeeze, drop, poke, twist or throw are sure to give them delight. Toddlers also enjoy any toy that they can stack, pour, open, close, push or pull. A child of this age enjoys a tricycle or other ride-on toys, a wagon to get into, sandbox toys, balls, blocks of different sizes and shapes.

3 to 6 years

Preschool children learn by doing. From 3 to 6 years, children like to create play worlds.
They enjoy developing movement and communication skills. A child of this age enjoys dressing up and pretend play. For example they say: "Let's be mother and father".
Preschoolers like painting, drawing and building. Dressing-up clothes, pretend "props" like toy phones and puppets are big favourites.
Preschoolers are energetic and active. They need large balls to roll and throw, wagons to pull and tricycles to ride.

Toys and games Unit 5

Working with the text

A **True or false?**
Decide if these statements are true or false. Correct the false statements.
1. Most children have favourite toys.
2. Children's play is just for fun.
3. Children like expensive toys.
4. Small children love to throw things.
5. Preschoolers are too young to learn anything.
6. 4-year-old children get tired very soon.

B **Name toys that are good for**
a) exploring,   b) pretending,
c) sharing,   d) movement.

> Look at the toys from this text and page 49.
> You may also include toys from Unit 2 and 3.

C **Finish the following sentences.**
The meaning should be the same, but do not copy sentences from the original text.
1. Toys are not only for playing with …
2. Some parents want to know …
3. Sensory motor means …
4. The play of preschoolers is often …
5. Preschool children …
6. Pretending means …

Hands-on task

Give advice on toys `Interaction`
Some parents ask you about which toys to choose for their children. Tell them what children can do with the toys and why the toy is suitable for the age of their child.
Example:
My 3-year old daughter Alina loves being outside, she is very energetic.
You: there are a lot of toys that she'd enjoy. A ball could be a good choice, but also sandbox toys. Preschoolers like your daughter are very energetic and active, they need movement. So she can run around with the ball and play together with other children or you. Sandbox toys are good for building.

1. My grandson Paul is 2 years old. I need some toys for when he comes to visit me, but I don't have enough money to buy a lot.
2. My best friend has given birth to a little girl. What could be a toy for that age?
3. My son, two and a half years old, loves exploring and building. He is interested in everything new he can learn.
4. My daughter is 5 years old. She loves stories and acts them out.
5. My son Murat, 5, loves being with his best friend. What can I give him that he can share with his friend?
6. My granddaughter Sarah loves quiet activities. She is 4 years old.

Giving advice

You should / shouldn't buy …

It may be a good idea to (+ verb) …

Perhaps you can try …

Experts say that …

If your son / daughter enjoys …, you can give him / her …

With that toy, he / she can …

My advice is …

I advise you to (+ verb) …

Unit 5 Toys and games

Buying toys

Your nursery school playroom needs more toys for the home corner.
You and your colleagues have decided to have a child-size kitchen so that the 3- to 6-year-old children can pretend to cook and do housework. You have a budget of £50.

Interaction

Study the catalogue below and then decide which toys you want to order and why. Explain your choice to your classmates.

Example: "We decided to order the teatime set because we think they are good props. It is good for the interaction of several children playing together."

Reference	Item	Price	Reference	Item	Price
Ref: 257907	Teatime set teapot, cups, saucers, spoons, pretend cakes	£12.99	Ref: 420188	Vacuum cleaner	£9.99
Ref: 146900	Ironing board	£9.99	Ref: 019287	Kitchenette oven, sink, fridge in one block	£14.99
Ref: 005646	Vegetable set: Fruits and vegetables with knife and chopping board	£7.99	Ref: 597344	Set of pots and pans	£15.99
Ref: 341 297	Washing machine	£9.99	Ref: 146903	Iron	£4.99

These words and phrases may help you to explain your choice:

Phrases	Adjectives
We want / decided to order … because … We think that … In our opinion … … is better than … We prefer … to … … is more enjoyable to play with … is difficult / easy to clean / to handle / to store … helps the children pretending. … is a good prop for … … for playing alone / for interaction	pretty / ugly colourful useful / useless practical / impractical suitable / unsuitable stable / unstable **Hint:** **Look on page 54 Grammar box:** **Adjectives and Comparison.**

Working with the text

Filling in an order form
This is the fax order form for ordering your toys. Copy it and fill it in according to your choice.
Then read the order out aloud.

Reading numbers:
In numbers, 0 is pronounced as [ou], zero or nought.
Example: 35507 = three – double five – [ou] – seven.

`Production`

Send to:	The Toy Company		Fax: 0044-801-508 4509	
Item	Reference	Quantity	Price / Item	Price / Total
				Total:

Unit 5 Toys and games

> **Grammar box: Adjectives and Comparison** – Adjektive und ihre Steigerung
>
> | Adjektiv | Komparativ | Superlativ | Regel |
> |---|---|---|---|
> | young | younger | the youngest | Einsilbige Adjektive und solche, |
> | pretty | prettier | the prettiest | die auf –y enden, werden mit –er und –est gesteigert. |
> | tired | more tired | the most tired | Adjektive mit zwei und mehr |
> | expensive | more expensive | the most expensive | Silben werden meist mit more und most gesteigert. |
> | good | better | the best | Ausnahmen muss man gesondert |
> | bad | worse | the worst | lernen. |
> | much | more | the most | |
> | little | less | the least | |
>
> Mithilfe von Adjektiven und ihren Steigerungen lassen sich Vergleiche bilden.
> Dazu werden diese Konstruktionen verwendet: *(not) as ... as, -er / more / less ... than*
>
> *Jeff is 3 years old, Mary and Kathy are 4 years old and Tom is 6 years old.*
>
> *Tom is older than Mary and Jeff. Mary is older than Jeff, but younger than Tom.*
>
> *Tom is the oldest and Jeff is the youngest child. Mary is as old as Kathy, but not as old as Tom.*
>
> Achtung year / years: *Tom is 6 years old. He is a 6-year-old boy.*

Practising grammar

Form the comparatives and the superlatives of these adjectives. Then put in the most suitable form.

creative
old
young
active
expensive
energetic
interesting
valuable
good
colourful

This nursery school has 35 children of all ages. The (1)... toddler is 18 months old, the (2)... children are the preschoolers. They have a special room, a learning station which they find (3)... than the toddler room. All our children are very (4).... You can see that from the artwork over here. We think that children are (5)... if they can choose the materials for their artwork themselves. It is not so important that the material is very (6).... Coloured paper, cardboard and glue can be (7)... learning tools for the children. Even our toddlers love the (8)... crayons that we offer them.
Preschoolers are (9)... than toddlers. They like (10)... balls and wagons. But toddlers are as (11)... as preschoolers when exploring something new. We think that the (12)... toys are those that help children to learn about the world.

Toys and games Unit 5

Grammar box: Quantifiers – Mengenangaben

Zählbar	Nicht zählbar
many / a lot of toys (viele)	much / a lot of fun (viel)
few children (wenige)	little fun (wenig)
a few activities (einige)	a little time (ein wenig)
more games (mehr)	more time (mehr)
fewer rooms (weniger)	less work (weniger)

- Die Mengenangaben sind unterschiedlich, je nachdem, ob sie mit einem zählbaren oder einem nicht zählbaren Substantiv verwendet werden. *Many, few, a few, fewer*, stehen im Satz mit zählbaren Substantiven, *much, little, a little, less* mit nicht zählbaren Substantiven.

- *A lot of* wird häufig in bejahten Aussagesätzen verwendet, *much* und *many* in verneinten Aussagesätzen und Fragen. *A lot of* darf jedoch nicht in Kombination mit *very, too* und *so* benutzt werden.

- Fragen nach der Menge können mit den Fragepronomen *how much* und *how many* gebildet werden.

Practising grammar

A Put in a lot of / much / many / few / little.
1. Janet is very busy. She has very … free time.
2. Look at all these pictures! The children here really do … artwork.
3. Let's buy some toys. We have too … jigsaw puzzles.
4. We can give away some toys. We have too … play dough and too … skipping ropes.
5. How … tea sets shall we buy? Not too … because we don't have … money to spend.
6. I think Janet will be a good nursery nurse. She has … patience.
7. How … does the doll cost?
8. Oh, …, we can't buy it.

B Put in little / a little / few / a few.
1. There is no need to hurry. We have … time.
2. Have you ever been to the zoo? Yes, I've been there … times.
3. I don't think the children will enjoy this outing. There is only very … fun because there are … activities for them.
4. The playground is fun for preschoolers: there are … slides and swings, so they can be active.
5. Would you like some milk? Yes, …
6. Can we buy some new toys? Yes, I think so, we've got … money.
7. Murat likes his nursery school. He has … friends there.
8. I'm not very busy today. I have … to do.

Unit 5 Toys and games

Children, children, children

- **Babies** are very small children under twelve months. They have started to crawl but are not yet able to walk.
- Small children up to two years are called **infants** or **toddlers** if they have started to walk.
- Children from three years to school-age are called **preschoolers**.
- **School-age children** are at least five years old.

A Put the photos into the order of the descriptions.

B Which German words match the English terms?

Play with me

Games that make learning fun

Babies and infants

Roll and Go. For babies who are crawling, show them a soft ball or interesting toy. Roll it or place it a few feet away and encourage your baby to get it. You can place the toy
5 farther and farther away to motivate him to keep moving.

Peek-a-Boo! As the child approaches 6 to 9 months, you can start to play peek-a-boo.
10 Most babies really enjoy this game! In the game, the older player hides his / her face, pops back into the baby's view and says "Peek-a-boo!", sometimes followed by "I see you!"
15
Find It. As your infant approaches her first birthday, she might enjoy playing a "find it"-game with you. While she is in her high chair or sitting on the floor, show her one of her
20 favourite rattles or another small toy. Then cover it. Wait a moment to see if she reaches to uncover the toy. If she doesn't, show her where to find it. Games like this build babies' thinking skills.

Toddlers

25 **Feely Box.** You will need a cardboard box and some objects to hide in it. Cut a hole in the side of the box that is just big enough for the toddler to slide his arm into. Put a small object like an orange inside and ask your toddler to
30 put his hand in the box and try and work out what is in there, describing what it feels like as he goes along. Repeat with other objects!

Freeze! Toddlers and preschoolers love freeze
35 dancing. Play music and encourage the child to dance or move in whatever way she likes. Then tell her to stop when the music ends. This kind of activity builds listening skills.

Toys and games Unit 5

Preschoolers and school-age children

I spy with my little eye. Choose one item inside or outside the classroom or one from a set of flashcards, but don't say what it is. Start the game by saying: "I spy with my little eye … (something big, grey, beginning with C etc.). The other children make guesses by asking questions. You may only answer "Yes" or "No". The child who first guesses the item is the winner and can take your role in a new game.

Simon says. A group of children is lined up across from you. Tell the players that they should all obey you if you first say the words "Simon says". Players are out if they follow an instruction that doesn't begin with "Simon says", or if they fail to do what Simon says.
Begin by saying something like "Simon says, put your hands on your head." Check if everybody has put their hands on their heads. Give the next instruction, such as "Simon says, stand on one foot." Check and continue giving instructions.
Mix it up by giving instructions like "Raise your right hand" without the words "Simon says". Call out the players who have raised their hands. Play until one player is left, that person is the winner and can be Simon for the next round.

Hopscotch. Use chalk to draw a hopscotch pattern with eight squares on the ground and number them. Stand behind the starting line and toss your marker into square 1. Hop into square 2 and then continue hopping to square 8, turn around and hop back again. Pause in square 2 to pick up your marker, hop into square 1 and out.
A player must hop **over** any square where a marker has been placed.
Continue the game by tossing the marker into square 2 (next round: into square 3, and so on).
All hopping is done on one foot unless two squares are side-by-side. Then two feet can be placed down, with one foot in each square. A player is out
- if the marker fails to land in the proper square,
- if the player steps on a line,
- if the player loses balance and puts a second hand / foot down,
- if the player hops into a square where a marker is or
- if a player puts two feet down in a single square.

Hands-on tasks

A Group work `Interaction`
Decide in your group which of the games you want to work with. Work out how to play the game. Play the game together with your classmates: Use English only!

B One of your colleagues is interested in British games for children. Choose two of the games above and explain them in German.

`Mediation`

For more mediation: see page 184.

Unit 5 Toys and games

toy [tɔɪ]	Spielzeug
game [geɪm]	Spiel
wooden blocks ['wʊdn blɒks]	Bauklötze
bricks [brɪks]	Bausteine
jigsaw puzzle [dʒɪgsɔː 'pʌzl]	Puzzle
picture lotto ['pɪktʃə lotto]	Memory-Spiel
knight [naɪt]	Ritter
castle ['kɑːsl]	Schloss
doll [dɒl]	Puppe
puppet ['pʌpɪt]	Handpuppe
cuddly toy animal ['kʌdlɪ tɔɪ 'ænɪml]	Kuscheltier

Choosing toys for children

fond [fɒnd]	liebevoll
childhood ['tʃaɪldhʊd]	Kindheit
(to) bring to mind [brɪŋ tuː maɪnd]	ins Gedächtnis zurückbringen
crayon ['kreɪən]	Buntstift
car [kɑː]	Wagen
joy [dʒɔɪ]	Freude
valuable ['væljʊəbl]	wertvoll
learning tool ['lɜːnɪŋ tuːl]	Lernwerkzeug
(to) explore [ɪk'splɔː]	erforschen
(to) pretend [prɪ'tend]	so tun, als ob
(to) share [ʃeə]	teilen, gemeinsam spielen
skill [skɪl]	Fähigkeit
(to) develop [dɪveləp]	entwickeln
backyard [bækjɑːd]	Hof
measuring cup ['meʒərɪŋ kʌp]	Messbecher
bathtub [bɑːθtʌb]	Badewanne
(to) wish [wɪʃ]	wünschen
helpful ['helpfʊl]	hilfreich
infant, toddler ['ɪnfənt, 'tɒdlə]	Kleinkind
wagon ['wægən]	Waggon
sense [sens]	Sinn
sight [saɪt]	Anblick
sound [saʊnd]	Klang
smell [smel]	Geruch
(to) squeeze [skwiːz]	zusammendrücken
(to) drop [drɒp]	fallen lassen
(to) poke [pəʊk]	hineinstecken
(to) twist [twɪst]	verdrehen
(to) give delight [gɪv dɪ'laɪt]	Freude machen
(to) stack [stæk]	stapeln
(to) pour [pɔː]	gießen
(to) pull [pʊl]	ziehen
stage [steɪdʒ]	Phase
preschooler [ˌpriː'skuːleɜː]	Vorschulkind
props [prɒps]	Requisiten
energetic [ˌenə'dʒetɪk]	voller Energie

Buying toys

reference ['refrəns]	hier: Bestellnummer
item ['aɪtəm]	Artikel
saucer ['sɔːsə]	Untertasse
spoon [spuːn]	Löffel
ironing board ['aɪənɪŋ bɔːd]	Bügelbrett
fruit [fruːt]	Obst
vegetable ['vədʒtəbl]	Gemüse
knife [naɪf]	Messer
chopping board ['tʃɒpɪŋ bɔːd]	Schneidbrett
vacuum cleaner ['vækjʊəm 'kliːnə]	Staubsauger
oven ['ʌvn]	Backofen
fridge [frɪdʒ]	Kühlschrank
iron ['aɪən]	Bügeleisen
suitable [ˌsuːtəbl]	passend
stable ['steɪbl]	stabil

Play with me

(to) crawl [krɔːl]	krabbeln
(to) approach [ə'prəʊtʃ]	sich nähern
(to) pop back [pɒp bæk]	plötzlich zurückkommen
(to) freeze [friːz]	einfrieren
(to) encourage [ɪn'kʌrɪdʒ]	ermutigen
(to) guess [ges]	raten
(to) fail [feɪl]	nicht schaffen
(to) obey [ə'beɪ]	gehorchen

Unit 6 — Holidays around the year

Independence Day
Columbus Day
Halloween
Martin Luther King Day
New Year
Thanksgiving

Let's talk about holidays

All of these holidays are official holidays in the United States of America.
Which is which? Match the names with the pictures.
What do you know about these holidays?
If you haven't heard of them, can you guess what people celebrate on these occasions? Are there similar holidays in Germany?

Unit 6 Holidays around the year

Celebrating Halloween

Halloween is becoming more and more popular in Germany. Do you know where this custom comes from? Someone asked the nurses at the Wamego Kindergarten in
5 the USA about Halloween.
Here are their answers:

Sheila:
Halloween is one of my favorite* holidays. I
10 love the playful nature of this holiday with all its ghosts and goblins, parties, fun traditions and the smell of fall* in the air.

Annette:
15 One story says that on that day the spirits of all those who died the year before would come back looking for living bodies to possess for the next year. Naturally, the people who were still alive did not want to be possessed. So on
20 the night of October 31, villagers would dress up in all sorts of frightening costumes and noisily parade around the neighborhood* in order to frighten away the evil spirits.

Carol:
25 Today Halloween has turned into a funfilled holiday which focuses on things like skeletons, cemeteries and goblins. We celebrate it on October 31 in the USA, other English-speaking countries such as Great Britain and
30 Canada do the same.

Samantha:
When I was a child our favorite* tradition was to go trick-or-treating. Young children dress
35 up in costumes as ghosts, witches, monsters and go door-to-door saying "Trick or treat!" In other words, either you give me a treat or I will play a trick on you! So adults all hand out treats to the children. Treats are usually little
40 pieces of candy* or candy bars.

Pauline:
In the United States most homes also have a carved pumpkin, called a Jack-o-Lan-
45 tern, in front of the house. These pumpkins are hollow with a funny or frightening face carved into the pumpkin and lighted from the inside by candle.

50 [* AmE = American English]

Working with the text

A Study these words and explanations. Then match numbers and letters.

1 carve 2 Jack-o-Lantern 3 pumpkin
4 skeleton 5 ghost 6 goblin

a) to cut a face into the pumpkin
b) a small, ugly creature which enjoys causing trouble
c) the spirit of a dead person which appears again
d) a large, orange vegetable
e) the bone structure of a body without flesh
f) a carved pumpkin usually with a candle burning inside

B Answer the following questions.
1. Where does Halloween originally come from?
2. What were the spirits of the dead looking for?
3. How did people protect themselves against the ghosts?
4. Where is Halloween mostly celebrated in our time? On which day?
5. What do children do when they go "trick-or-treating"?
6. How are pumpkins used at Halloween?

Holidays around the year **Unit 6**

Preparing for Halloween in the classroom

Hands-on task

Choose one of the activities on the following pages and prepare it at home.

It's Halloween

It's Halloween! It's Halloween!
The moon is full and bright
And we shall see what can't be seen
On any other night:

Skeletons and ghosts and ghouls,
Grinning goblins fighting duels,
Werewolves rising from their tombs,
Witches on their magic brooms.

In masks and gowns we haunt the street
And knock on doors for trick or treat.
Tonight we are the king and queen,
For oh tonight it's Halloween!

Trick ... or treat

The people in this house were mean
When we asked for a treat
They did not give us anything
And chased us down the street

And so we soap their windows
And so we chalk their door
And so we think they'll never be
So nasty anymore

Unit 6 Holidays around the year

Performing a poem

How about performing the poems in class? Prepare the recitation of the two poems in groups. Imagine you have to recite them in front of a group of children in the nursery school and the children expect great things of you! Try to create some kind of Halloween atmosphere in the classroom. Maybe you could draw the curtains and light a candle? Bring a video camera if available or use your mobile phones and record your recitations.

For many people an important thing about Halloween is the chance to try out the craziest and funniest recipes, like this one – go ahead and try it!

Chocolate-coated Marshmallow Monsters

What you need:

marshmallows (if you can't get marshmallows, use "Mäusespeck", as there is not much difference)
lollipop sticks, 10 cm long
chocolate
black decorating gel for food

Stick 10 cm lollipop sticks into marshmallows and place them in the freezer for about 15 minutes until they are cold.
While the marshmallows are chilling, heat one cup of chocolate slowly on a low simmering heat in a double boiler, stirring constantly until the chocolate is completely melted. (If you do not have a double boiler you can use a metal bowl which is placed over a pot of hot water.)
Remove the marshmallows from the freezer and dip them lightly into the melted chocolate for a thin coating. To get a "mummy look" swirl them around a bit to give them layers of white. "Ghosts" should be dunked to make a little twisted peak on top. "Frankenstein" can be dunked with a spoon used to flatten the chocolate on top.
To let them cool use a block of styrofoam and stick them in. They won't take long to harden in the refrigerator. Afterwards you can add faces.

Use a small tube of black decorating gel with a small tip for that.
You can stick the Marshmellow Monsters into cellophane wraps to keep or just put them into your refrigerator ... but they will probably not be around for very long!

**Let's have a look at the vocabulary.
Which terms on the left and the right belong together according to the text?**

lollipop	to wrap
decorating	to dip
freezer	stick
cellophane	to chill
small	tip
coating	gel
constantly	to stir

Holidays around the year Unit 6

Making Creepy Crawlies

So easy, anyone can make them – and they really crawl …

What you need:

> square paper napkins
> black felt-tip pen
> lemons or oranges

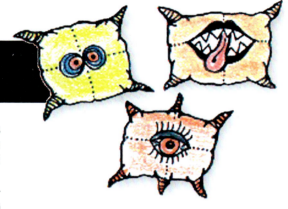

Unfold the napkin. Lightly draw one or two eyes in the centre. Or draw a mouth with sharp teeth all around. Try not to press down hard or you'll tear the napkin.
Twist each corner of the napkin to make a little leg. You can also pull out the centre of each side and twist it if you want to give your Creepy Crawly six or eight legs.
Put the Creepy Crawlies on the table, then slip a lemon or orange under them.
Push them along gently. As the fruit rolls, the Creepy Crawly will run along.

A Halloween poster

What you need:

> large paper (poster-size)
> scissors
> glue or glue stick
> felt-tip pens
> eraser, ruler
> (some) drawing talent

Work in groups. Prepare a poster which decorates your classroom and gives information about Halloween at the same time. Put pictures of witches, ghosts, pumpkins, children who go "trick-or-treating" or any other Halloween objects on it. Add text. Explain very shortly where the custom of Halloween comes from and what people actually do at Halloween. If you have access to the Internet, get additional information there. You can also try to find illustrations for your poster on the Internet. The rest is left to your imagination. Put up the results in class.

handwerk-technik.de

Unit 6 Holidays around the year

Working with language

Do you remember how to say an English date?
Here are some American holidays - read them out in class. Remember that in English there is a difference between a written date and the way you say it.

Example:
Halloween is on 31 October: "… on the thirty-first of October"
or: Halloween is on October 31: "… on October the thirty-first"

1. New Year's Day — 1 January
2. Martin Luther King's Birthday — 15 January
3. Mother's Day — 8 May
4. Independence Day — 4 July
5. Columbus Day — 12 October
6. Thanksgiving — 24 November
7. Christmas — 25 December
8. Labor Day — the first Monday in September (look it up in your calendar)

Holidays in the United States of America

Name	Date	Remarks
New Year's Day	1 January	Beginning of the year. It marks the traditional end of the "holiday season"
Martin Luther King Day	January, third Monday	Honours Dr. King, the famous civil rights leader
Presidents' Day	February, third Monday	Honours former U.S. presidents, especially President Washington and Lincoln
Memorial Day	May, last Monday	Honours soldiers who died fighting for the U.S.A.
Independence Day	4 July	Celebrates independence from Great Britain in 1776
Labor Day	September, first Monday	Celebrates the achievements of workers and marks the traditional end of summer
Columbus Day	October, second Monday	Honours Christopher Columbus, the discoverer of America
Veterans' Day	11 November	At 11 a.m. a moment of silence is held to remember all those who fought in the U.S. army
Thanksgiving	November, fourth Thursday	Day of thanks for the harvest. It marks the traditional beginning of the "holiday season"
Christmas	25 December	Christian holiday. It celebrates the birth of Jesus Christ

Grammar box: **Future** – Die Zukunft

Im Englischen gibt es hauptsächlich zwei Arten über Zukünftiges zu reden:

Die Zukunft mit *will*	**Die Zukunft mit** *going to*
will + Verb im Infinitiv	am / are / is going to + Verb im Infinitiv
Abkürzung: …'ll (I'll, you'll) Verneinung: won't **oder** will not Frage: Will you … ?	Abkürzung: I'm, you're, he's, she's, it's, we're, you're, they're Verneinung: not going to Frage: Am / Are / Is … going to …?
I think the weather will be hot in Italy. Der Satz drückt aus, was (vermutlich) geschehen wird.	*I'm going to sell my car tomorrow.* Eine Entscheidung ist getroffen worden.
Will you help me with my homework today? Hier ist die Rede von einem nicht näher bestimmten Zeitpunkt in der Zukunft. *I will make you a sandwich, you look hungry.* Spontaner Entschluss	*Carl is going to be a nurse.* Es ist seine Entscheidung, Erzieher zu werden. *Are you going to invite Julie to your party?* Plan bzw. Vorhaben
Die Zukunft mit *will* wird gebraucht, um • in allgemeiner Weise über zukünftige Ereignisse zu sprechen, • einen spontanen Entschluss zum Ausdruck zu bringen.	Die Zukunft mit *going to* wird gebraucht, um • über Pläne und Vorhaben zu sprechen, • über Dinge, die ganz bestimmt geschehen werden, zu sprechen. Oft ist dies verbunden mit einer genauen Vorstellung davon, wann etwas geschehen wird.

Practising grammar

A Will-future: Form complete sentences with the given elements.
1. The staff – to prepare a few things for the children
2. We – to carve out a pumpkin?
3. Some of the children – to perform a play
4. It – not – to take very long
5. We – not – to buy lots of sweets

B Form some more sentences: Now use the Going-to-future.
1. All the nurses – to dress up as witches
2. I – to talk about ghosts and goblins tomorrow morning
3. On Friday – everybody – to parade around the neighborhood
4. You – to wear your ghost costume tomorrow?
5. I think I – ask some of the mothers for help

C Decide what to use – 'will' or 'going to'?
1. Halloween … always … a children's holiday.
2. I … organise a Halloween party for the children next Saturday.
3. Maybe we … get a bigger pumpkin next year.
4. Carol … use all the marshmallows to make chocolate monsters.
5. We … work in groups this time, it's easier.
6. Oh, your goblin mask … certainly … frighten everyone!

Unit 6 Holidays around the year

Thanksgiving – the story

Discontent with the Church of England

In the early 1600s the government of England only allowed its citizens to belong to one church, known as the Church of England. As the English government had little tolerance for religious freedom, some people who wanted to make religion "pure" again left for Holland in 1609. The so called "Puritans" lived and prospered in Holland but they became worried when their children
5 started to speak Dutch and began to enjoy the Dutch way of life.

The voyage

So on September 6, 1620 the Pilgrims – as they were now called – and an unknown
10 number of crew members went aboard the ship "Mayflower" to travel to the "new world". The trip took many weeks. As the ship was made of wood the passengers could not build a fire, so the food had to be
15 eaten cold. Many of the passengers became sick and some died.

After they finally sighted land a meeting was held and an agreement was written. This agreement is called the famous "Mayflower
20 Compact" today.

The first winter

It was a long voyage and the Mayflower did not land at Plymouth, Massachusetts until
25 November 1620.

It was bad timing because it meant that the Pilgrims did not have time to grow food for the winter.

The first winter was extremely hard for
30 the new settlers. Freezing temperatures and snow made it difficult for the Pilgrims to construct their settlement. Out of the original group of Pilgrims only about half survived the first winter.
35

The Indians

On March 16, 1621 an Indian named Samoset arrived at the settlement and the Pilgrims were afraid until he called out "Welcome" in
40 English. Although the Pilgrims and Samoset had a difficult time communicating, he spent the night with them.

Samoset left the next day and returned a few days later together with an English-speaking
45 Indian named Squanto. He taught the Pilgrims how to hunt, fish and grow corn.

Holidays around the year Unit 6

The first Thanksgiving
Because of Squanto's help the Pilgrims had a very successful harvest in October 1621 with plenty of food for the winter. The Pilgrim's Governor William Bradford therefore proclaimed a day of celebration and thanksgiving some time in the middle of October. Squanto and many other Indians were invited to join in the celebration. This first Thanksgiving party lasted for three days.

Continuation of the celebration of Thanksgiving
The custom of celebrating when harvest time is over became an annual event in the following years. However, it was only in 1863 that President Abraham Lincoln officially proclaimed the last Thursday in November a national day of Thanksgiving.

Working with the text

A What do you learn about of the following words from the text? Explain them using the information you find in the text.
Example:
Church of England: In the early 17th century all people of Great Britain had to belong to the Church of England.
1. Pilgrims   2. Mayflower   3. Squanto   4. Thanksgiving

B Answer the questions on the text.
1. Why did the Puritans leave England?
2. What do we learn about their voyage across the Atlantic ocean?
3. Describe the difficulties the Puritans had in America.
4. What was the first meeting between Indians and white settlers like?
5. What do we learn about the first Thanksgiving?
6. Why do Americans still celebrate Thanksgiving today?

Hands-on tasks

A How do you celebrate Thanksgiving in your nursery school? Do you have any special decorations, games or activities? Talk to one of your classmates, together make a list and prsent your findings to the class.

B Find out and compare the dimensions of the Pilgrims' ship 'Mayflower' and those of a modern cruise ship. Find information about childcare on a modern cruiser.

C What do Americans usually eat at a Thanksgiving dinner? Do not just find out what they eat, but also how the food is prepared, who comes to this dinner plus any other information that seems interesting or relevant to you. Inform your class.

Unit 6 Holidays around the year

Independence Day [ˌɪndɪˈpendəns deɪ]	Unabhängigkeitstag
Thanksgiving [ˈθæŋksˌgɪvɪŋ]	Erntedankfest
holiday [ˈhɒlədɪ]	hier: Feiertag

Celebrating Halloween

(to) celebrate [ˈselɪbreɪt]	feiern
goblin [ˈgɒblɪn]	Kobold
fall (AmE; autumn = BrE) [fɔːl]	Herbst
spirits [ˈspɪrɪts]	Geister
(to) possess [pəˈzes]	besitzen, in Besitz nehmen
(to) frighten away [fraɪtn əˈweɪ]	verscheuchen
(to) focus on [ˈfəʊkəs ɒn]	sich konzentrieren auf
skeleton [ˈskelɪtn]	Skelett
witch [wɪtʃ]	Hexe
treat [triːt]	Süßigkeit, "Leckerchen"
(to) play a trick on s.o. [pleɪ ə trɪk ɒn]	jmd. einen Streich spielen
candy (AmE; BrE: sweets) [ˈkændɪ]	Süßigkeit
carved pumpkin [kɑːvd ˈpʌmpkɪn]	ausgehöhlter Kürbis
hollow [ˈhɒləʊ]	hohl

Preparing for Halloween in the classroom

(to) perform [pəˈfɔːm]	aufführen, vortragen
ghoul [guːl]	Geist, Erscheinung
tomb [tuːm]	Grab
broom [bruːm]	Besen
(to) haunt the streets [hɔːnt ðə striːts]	sich auf den Straßen herumtreiben
mean [miːn]	gemein, schäbig, knickerig
(to) chase [tʃeɪs]	(ver)jagen
(to) chalk [tʃɔːk]	mit Kreide bemalen
nasty [ˈnɑstɪ]	böse, gemein
recitation [ˌresɪˈteɪʃn]	Vortrag (eines Liedes etc.)
chocolate-coated [ˈtʃɒkələt-kəʊtɪd]	mit Schokolade überzogen
recipe [ˈresɪpɪ]	Kochrezept
lollipop sticks [ˈlɒlɪpɒp stɪk]	Lolli-Stiele
freezer [ˈfriːzə]	Gefrierschrank
mummy [ˈmʌmɪ]	Mumie
(to) swirl [swɜːl]	rühren
(to) dunk [dʌŋk]	(kurz) eintauchen
styrofoam [ˈstaɪrəfəʊm]	Styropor
refrigerator (kurz: fridge) [rɪˈfrɪdʒəreɪtə]	Kühlschrank
Creepy Crawlies [kriːpɪ krɔːlɪs]	ungefähr: 'Unheimliche Krabbler'
napkin [ˈnæpkɪn]	Serviette
glue, glue stick [gluː, stɪk]	Klebstoff, Klebestift

Thanksgiving – the story

discontent [ˌdɪskənˈtent]	Unzufriedenheit
pure [pjʊə]	rein, unverfälscht
(to) prosper [ˈprɒspə]	gedeihen, zu Wohlstand kommen
Indian (auch: Native American) [ˈɪndjən]	Indianer, Ureinwohner der USA
(to) grow corn [grəʊ kɔːn]	Mais anbauen
harvest [ˈhɑːvɪst]	Ernte
(to) proclaim [prəˈkleɪm]	proklamieren, verkünden
(to) survive [səˈvaɪv]	überleben

Unit 7 — Children from birth to three

Look at the infant and toddler equipment

A Match the words from the box to the pictures.

high chair – baby car seat / cradle – bottle with warmer –
pull toy animal – potty-training seat – cradle swing – walker – baby's changing unit
– baby cutlery – baby crib – rattle

B Answer the following questions.
1. Do you have any of this equipment for children under three in your nursery school?
2. Try to say what this equipment is used for.
3. What else do you need in order to take care of small children?
4. Does your nursery school accept under-threes? Think of reasons why some nursery schools do not offer care for this age group.

Unit 7 Children from birth to three

Caring for infants and toddlers

Does the care for infants and toddlers differ from the normal care for 4- and 5-year-old nursery school children? Here are some of the most important aspects:

Group size
Group care for children under 3 years of age requires a lot of attention. Caregivers have to build up a very close relationship with each baby. It takes a lot of time and consistent contact with the baby to build up the intimate relationship which every baby needs. And caregivers who want to work with small children need to have the same close relationship with the family. Only if family and caregiver know each other well, will the necessary bonding take place. For this reason, it is important that infant and toddler group sizes are small. A ratio of one adult to three children ensures that the caregiver has enough time for the attention and affection these children need. In addition, daily routine tasks such as feeding, bathing, changing nappies take a lot of time.

Crying
The caregiver has to understand and work with the babies' crying. It is their style of communication. Children tell us how they feel and what they need through their body language – by cooing, babbling and crying. Perhaps the baby wants a nappy change, a bottle, a nap or a hug. Caregivers have to understand and act on these signals.

One-to-one contact
Feeding, changing nappies, hugging and consoling cannot be dictated by a schedule. Caring for the under-threes cannot be planned in advance. The caregiver has to watch children closely and give them the attention they need. All the typical care-giving tasks need to be very affectionate one-to-one contacts.

Strict hygiene and safety
Babies in a group tend to be sick more often than they would at home. The caregiver should always follow strict hygiene rules when touching or handling baby fluids. Disinfecting toys and surfaces and frequent hand-washing should be daily routines. Infants want to explore their world. As soon as they begin to crawl and then walk, they seem to get into everything. That is why under-three-care must ensure that the infant and toddler environment is safe.

Talking to infants
Babies love to hear language and respond by making sounds. Throughout the first two years, children are attaching meaning to words. They understand a lot more than they can say. Therefore, caregivers should use daily routines as wonderful opportunities to talk. They should name new toys, sounds, tastes, activities, equipment and sing songs to them. The caregiver should always find ways to stimulate language production by, for example, reading aloud from books and talking about them as a daily routine. As well as toys, there should be a variety of elementary books for infants and toddlers.

Regular training
In addition to language exposure, infants and toddlers need basic potty-training and also encouragement to sit up and to drink and eat on their own.

Stranger anxieties

Since infants and toddlers develop a very intense relationship with their family and caregiver, they often start crying and feeling miserable when their parent or caregiver leaves or when a stranger enters the nursery. For this reason, childcare should generally remain in the hands of one caregiver.

Working with the text

A All these statements are false.
Find text passages which show that they are false.
1. Infant and toddler groups can have up to ten children.
2. Daily routine care is one of the quickest tasks in looking after infants and toddlers.
3. All babies cry very often and therefore a caregiver should ignore this crying.
4. A caregiver for under-threes should work to a regular schedule which children have to get used to.
5. Babies stay healthier in a group.
6. When their time has come toddlers start to talk. They do not need extra stimulation.
7. As toddlers just start using language, reading out books is not an activity for them.
8. Small children are always very open to every person.

B Finish the following sentences.
1. The care of and contact with a baby is …
2. Infants and toddlers need close and one-to-one contact with the caregiver because …
3. Caregivers must be very attentive because …
4. Caregivers should use any chance to …
5. Infants and toddlers need regular training to …
6. Babies' crying is a signal that …
7. Caring for infants and toddlers …

Hands-on task

Production

"Taking care for infants and toddlers is just a very normal routine job like any other job."
What is your opinion? Write about 80 to 100 words.

Unit 7 Children from birth to three

Working with language

Analysing infants' and toddlers' body language: For those who care for children from birth to three, it is important to understand their body language, such as crying and laughing, in order to get information on how they feel.

Crying can have different meanings. What does the child's facial expression tell you? Is there eye contact or not? Is the child searching for it or avoiding it? What about kicking the feet? This can show interest. Barriers with arms and legs may show unwillingness. A lot of children touch the part of their body which is important to them at the time, like rubbing eyes when tired or touching the forehead while thinking about something.

Look at the photos and the children's body language. Say what mood the child is in and what the relevant body signs are. What do they tell you? Use the words from the word box below.

Words describing moods
confused – awake – lively – interested – angry – tired – astonished – dissatisfied – satisfied – fast asleep – unwilling – contented – discontented – stubborn – surprised – bright – alert – sad

Words describing body activities
raise – cross – open – close – shut – build up barriers – kick – rub – smile – look angry – widen – touch – avoid – search for – be active – move strongly – stay calm – sit / lie still

Children from birth to three Unit 7

The care environment for children under three

What should places for infants look like?

There are basic rules for laying out a room to achieve a baby-friendly environment. In their first years of development, children need to have interesting things to watch, reach for or touch, things to get support from while learning to walk, safe areas to crawl and roll, all kinds of equipment and toys to stimulate the child's senses, as well as areas for rest. All these aspects should be part of the baby-friendly environment. It should be safe and there should not be too much stimulation, such as bright lights, too many children, constant noise or too many things lying around which overwhelm the infant.

What about Esther Harper's crèche? Janet is visiting the place before starting her childminder placement. When she enters the main group room she sees three children. At first glance, the room seems to be much the same as in every nursery school.

But at a second glance Janet notices small differences. She sees two sofas and lots of small mattresses to rest on and there is also a quiet corner for children who need a break separated from the group room by a curtain. Janet hears Esther Harper's soft voice talking while she is caressing a child sitting on a sofa. One child is sitting in a walker trying to move forward. The other one is lying in a cradle swing fast asleep. There are three high chairs and extra spaces with a soft safety floor to crawl on. She sees two walkers and two activity centres on a quilt, one to lie under and the other to sit in. A small climbing frame area is also carpeted with a soft safety floor. Here she sees large pillows, carpeted steps, wooden boxes to crawl through and two cradle swings. In one door frame there is a bouncing cradle.

As in any other nursery school, there are small tables and chairs and also some shelves. At the back of the group room there is a small kitchen to prepare dinners. All furniture is equipped with corner protections. The wall sockets have covers, too. The place offers all kinds of toys but the floor is not covered with them. Toys with which children are not playing, as well as games, materials for painting and books are kept on shelves. Looking at the books, Janet finds out that there are quite a number of elementary ones made of plastic, cloth or heavy cardboard, some with a sound animation. There is only one picture per page, showing familiar things like a dog, a ball, a baby and an apple.

The walls are very neat and there are no children's paintings, artwork or seasonal decoration. There is only one large decoration of a tree, birds and flowers. The light is dimmed down to a warm light. The place has one more separate sleeping area. There is a baby's changing unit, a bathroom with normal-sized facilities but with two potty-training seats, a baby bathing tub and an extra changing unit.

Unit 7 Children from birth to three

Working with the text

Fill in the missing words taken from the text.
There are (1) … rules which a childminder should think of when laying out a (2) … environment. There should be a lot of (3) … things for children to watch, reach for and touch, but also child-size equipment for toddlers to get (4) … from while learning to walk. But there is one important rule for a nursery: there should not be too much (5) …. This would (6) … the infant. While it is important to (7) … a child's senses, there should also be areas where children can get some (8) …. Of course, all areas should be (9) … because children crawl around and they should not run a risk of being injured. A (10) … with a (11) … to separate it from the group room gives an opportunity for children to take a break. Spaces where children are active should be carpeted with a (12) …. All safety standards should be followed, for example (13) … for furniture or (14) …. There should also be a good choice of toys and games for children but also some (15) … books for the smallest.

Hands-on tasks

Production

A Does Esther Harper's crèche provide a baby-friendly environment?
To answer this question, sum up all the different things available there.
Sit in pairs and fill in the mind map below.

B Compare your results in class and discuss them. The word box below gives you some help.

> I think the nursery is baby-friendly / safe / appealing / pleasant / appropriate for infants
> … because it offers … / it follows … / it gives children the chance to …
> There are enough … like …
> The place is safe … because …
> But there is / are … missing
> There should be more opportunities for the child to …

Interaction

C Imagine you are going to open your own crèche. The children you will be looking after are Tom (7 months), Brandon (9 months), Helen (one year and 2 months) and Ronda (2 and a half years). How would you equip a room for those children? What extra rooms and areas would you like to have for them? Sit in small groups and draw a plan. Present it in class.

Children from birth to three Unit 7

Training and learning in crèches

After Janet's first day with Esther Harper, she gives her some advice on how to work with infants and toddlers.

Esther: Okay, all the children are asleep. We can sit down for a while and talk about the special care small children need. I've already seen you've had some training in basic care like changing nappies, feeding and cooking meals …

Janet: Yes, we had courses at school and I also did a first-aid training course.

Esther: That's good. Those are the basics. But we should also try to stimulate the child's language and physical skills.

Janet: Yes, that's what we're doing in our nursery school placements as well. We plan all kinds of activities but I'm unsure about under-threes because the youngest child in my nursery school is already 3 years and 2 months old. There are no children three or below.

Esther: Well, it's not that much different. The only thing you have to bear in mind is that most of the children are at the beginning of developing language and physical skills. You should encourage the child to talk, but remember they can't repeat sentences – and some can't speak at all. You might start by making animal noises. And, as with any other older child, keep on talking to the toddler, saying new words all the time. Finger puppets and finger games are also perfect to teach sounds and words. If you sing a rhyme combined with finger puppets or fingers, so much the better!

Janet: Yes, that's what I do. At nursery school I also like to read aloud from picture books.

Esther: You can do that with our children too, but you can't read out the whole story from a picture book. You should start with elementary books. Toddlers can learn when they point at pictures and answer your questions, such as "Where is the dog?" and so on. Soon the child will give you the word and later small sentences. That's how we start with little children.

Janet: I sometimes do role plays after reading a book to my nursery school children. But I know the little ones here can't do that.

Esther: Well, you can start with some imaginative play like handling a baby doll as a real child or imitating daily routines like feeding, bathing and rocking to sleep. These are small role plays which they will be able to imitate.

Janet: Tomorrow I'd like to do an activity with the toddlers. What do you suggest?

Esther: Maybe you could start with fine motor skills. All toddlers love to work with paint. You could take tempera paint and let them paint with their palms on paper. Or if the weather is nice, go outside and encourage them to play with water. We have some large buckets and plastic cups, ladles, sieves and sponges. The sandbox is also a good activity. There are lots of toys for digging, sifting and building. Toddlers like water and sand. They are perfect materials to exercise their muscles and train coordination.

Janet: I thought I might stay inside and do some active games to exercise their gross motor skills. I think I'll use the mattresses and the climbing frame – and boxes to climb on, crawl through, jump over or balance on.

Esther: That's a great idea. The children will love to do that. You could play music and tell an active story. It's a good idea to combine language and motor skills. But do as you like!

Unit 7 Children from birth to three

Working with the text

A Answer the following questions.
1. What is Janet already trained in?
2. Why is she unsure about children under three?
3. What does someone working with smaller children have to bear in mind?
4. How should Janet try to start developing language skills?
5. What can she do instead of doing a role play?
6. What does Esther Harper suggest she might do outside with the children?
7. What does Janet plan to do with the children the next day?

B Janet wants to remember all the ways of training small children's language and exercising their motor skills, so she takes down some keywords in a table. Fill in this table from what you learnt in the text and your own experience.

Skills	Ways to train / activities
Language	• finger games • …
Fine motor skills	• forming shapes with play dough • …
Gross motor skills	• going on an outing to the playground • …

Hands-on task

Interaction

Michael, 8 months   *Samira, 10 months*   *Sandra, 1 year*   *Ronald, 2 years*   *Robert, 2 years*

These are the children Esther Harper cares for. Sit in groups and work out activities to train language and exercise motor skills. Make sure your activities fit the children's age group. Present your suggestions in class.

Children from birth to three Unit 7

Grammar box: Reported Speech – Indirekte Rede

Steht der Einführungssatz für die wörtliche Rede in einer Zeitform der Vergangenheit, so ändert sich die Zeitform in der indirekten Rede.

Direct Speech / Direkte Rede	Reported Speech / Indirekte Rede
Statements – Aussagesätze **Present Tense** Esther Harper said, (= Einführungssatz) „I **prepare** the bottles for the children in the small kitchen."	→ **Past Tense** Esther Harper said (that) she **prepared** the bottles… Der Aussagesatz kann mit *that* eingeleitet werden. Für *said* können ebenso *told*, *mentioned* genutzt werden. Ein indirekter Befehl wird mit "to" oder "not to" + Infinitive (= Grundform) gebildet.

Achtung!
Weitere Verschiebungen bei Orts- und Zeitangaben: today → that day, now → then, tomorrow → the next / following day, here → there, this → that, these → those

---

Practising grammar

A **Janet wants to use some indirect speech in her work report. So she has to transform Esther Harper's direct statements into reported speech.**
Example: Esther Harper said: "Michael's mother fetches him an hour later."
Esther Harper told me that Michael's mother fetched him an hour later.
1. You don't need to make the breakfast for the children.
2. I do finger games with Samira to exercise her fine motor skills.
3. Tempera paint is the best paint to stimulate toddlers to work with colours.
4. Toddlers like to paint with their palms, an activity which exercises their fine motor skills.
5. Ronald already speaks three-word-sentences.

B **Here are some more of Esther Harper's sentences. Put them into reported speech. Bear in mind the changes in time and place expressions in some of them.**
1. Robert's mood is different today.
2. He often starts crying and seems to be sad.
3. I like to work with these crayons, because they are large and better for small children's hands.
4. Today you can do some outdoor activities with sand or water.
5. You can now start to encourage the smaller children to repeat short sentences.
6. This is a real good book with finger games and nursery rhymes.
7. Most of these rhymes I know by heart.
8. When you know them by heart, you can do them with the children whenever there is a chance.
9. For tomorrow, I suggest you sing some of the rhymes with the group.

Unit 7 Children from birth to three

Children from birth to three

high chair [haɪ tʃeər]	Hochstuhl
cradle [ˈkreɪdl]	Wiege
potty-training seat [ˈpɒti ˌtreɪnɪŋ siːt]	Töpfchentrainingssitz
baby's changing unit [ˈbeɪbis ˈtʃeɪndʒɪŋ ˈjuːnɪt]	Wickeltisch
baby crib [ˈbeɪbi krɪb]	Kinder-/Babybett
consistent [kənˈsɪstənt]	beständig
intimate [ˈɪntɪmət]	eng, intim
caregiver [ˈkeəˌgɪvər]	pflegende Person
bonding [ˈbɒndɪŋ]	Bindung
(to) ensure [ɪnˈʃɔːr]	versichern, sicher stellen
affection [əˈfekʃən]	Liebe, Zuwendung
affectionate [əˈfekʃənət]	liebevoll
body language [ˈbɒdi ˈlæŋgwɪdʒ]	Körpersprache
nappy (BrE) [ˈnæpi]; diaper (AmE) [ˈdaɪpər]	Windel
(to) coo [kuː]	gurren
(to) babble [ˈbæbl]	plappern, lallen
(to) hug [hʌg]	umarmen
(to) console [kənˈsəʊl]	trösten
schedule [ˈʃedjuːl]	(Zeit-)Plan
in advance [ɪn ədˈvɑːnts]	im Voraus
under-threes [ˈʌndər θriːs]	Unter-Dreijährige
(to) be sick [sɪk]	(sich) erbrechen
hygiene rules [ˈhaɪdʒiːn ruːls]	Hygieneregeln
baby fluids [ˈbeɪbi ˈfluːɪds]	Körperflüssigkeiten des Babys
(to) disinfect [ˌdɪsɪnˈfekt]	desinfizieren
frequently [ˈfriːkwəntli]	häufig
(to) respond to [rɪˈspɒnd]	antworten, reagieren auf
(to) attach to [əˈtætʃ]	hier: verbinden mit
(to) stimulate [ˈstɪmjʊleɪt]	anregen, stimulieren
stimulation [ˌstɪmjʊˈleɪʃən]	Anregung, Stimulierung
language production [ˈlæŋgwɪdʒ prəˈdʌkʃən]	Sprachproduktion
elementary book [ˌelɪˈmentəri bʊk]	Elementarbilderbuch
stranger anxiety [ˈstreɪndʒər æŋˈzaɪəti]	Angst vor Fremden, "Fremdeln"
miserable [ˈmɪzərəbl]	unglücklich, traurig
facial expression [ˈfeɪʃəl ɪkˈspreʃən]	Gesichtsausdruck
barriers [ˈbæriərs]	Barrieren
unwillingness [ʌnˈwɪlɪŋnəs]	Unwille, Ablehnung
(to) rub [rʌb]	reiben
forehead [ˈfɔːhed]	Stirn
mood [muːd]	Stimmung
confused [kənˈfjuːzd]	verwirrt
awake [əˈweɪk], alert [əˈlɜːt]	wach, aufgeweckt
contented [kənˈtentɪd], satisfied [ˈsætɪsfaɪd]	zufrieden
discontented [ˌdɪskənˈtentɪd], dissatisfied [ˌdɪsˈsætɪsfaɪd]	unzufrieden
stubborn [ˈstʌbən]	stur
bright [braɪt]	hier Stimmung: erfreut
(to) avoid [əˈvɔɪd]	vermeiden

The care environment for children under three

(to) lay out (a room) [leɪ aʊt]	gestalten (einen Raum)
baby-friendly [ˈbeɪbi-frendli]	"babyfreundlich", angemessen für Babys
support [səˈpɔːt]	hier: Halt
(to) equip with [ɪˈkwɪp wɪð]	ausstatten mit
(to) overwhelm [ˌəʊvəˈwelm]	überwältigen, überschütten
quilt [kwɪlt]	Decke
crèche [kreʃ]	Krippe, Einrichtung für Unter-Dreijährige
carpeted [ˈkɑːpətɪd]	(mit Teppich) ausgelegt
bouncing cradle [ˈbaʊntsɪŋ ˈkreɪdl]	Babywippe
rubber [ˈrʌbər]	Gummi
protections [prəˈtekʃəns]	hier: Sicherungen (z. B. Schutzkappen)
wall socket [wɔːl ˈsɒkɪt]	Steckdose
appealing [əˈpiːlɪŋ]	ansprechend
appropriate [əˈprəʊpriət]	angemessen, passend

Training and learning in crèches

imaginative play [ɪˈmædʒɪnətɪv pleɪ]	Fantasiespiel, nachahmendes Spiel
(to) rock to sleep [rɒk to sliːp]	in den Schlaf wiegen
fine motor skills [faɪn ˈməʊtər skɪls]	Feinmotorik
gross motor skills [grəʊs ˈməʊtər skɪls]	Grobmotorik
tempera paint [ˈtempərə peɪnt]	Tempera-/Deckfarbe
palm [pɑːm]	Handfläche
ladle [ˈleɪdl]	Kelle
sieve [sɪv]	Sieb
(to) dig [dɪg]	graben
(to) sift [sɪft]	sieben
active story [ˈæktɪv ˈstɔːri]	Bewegungsgeschichte

Unit 8 — Nursery school and kindergarten abroad

At an American kindergarten in Wamego, Kansas

In other countries work at a nursery school or kindergarten is sometimes very different from the way we do things. Here is an example from a kindergarten in Kansas, U.S.A., where children learn reading, writing and mathematics.

1 The librarian encourages interest in literature through reading with the children

2 Children act out stories

3 Children like to listen to stories on the computer

4 Other children prefer listening to audio books

Working with the pictures

A Describe what the librarian in picture 1 is doing.
B What are the children and the librarian in picture 2 probably doing?
C What about you?
  1. Do you read books to children in your nursery school? What sort of books do the children like best?
  2. What do you think of children using computers and other media to listen to stories?
  3. Are there any children in your nursery school who have already started learning to read and write?

Unit 8 Nursery school and kindergarten abroad

At a British nursery school

The Village Kindergarten
LINCOLN, Great Britain

The Village Kindergarten has been open since September 2000 and has built a reputation for quality childcare in the area. Registered for only 26 places (six babies under 2 years
5 and twenty 2- to 5-year-olds), our nursery has been a small friendly unit with a family-style atmosphere. The babies have their own "protected" area, with toys and cots for naps, but join the older children as much as possible
10 for activities and at every mealtime.

There are creative or "messy" areas, a quiet book corner and a role play area that can be a baby-room, a café or hairdresser's, depending on the topic that week.

15 Upstairs the older children are encouraged to join in maths and literacy activities. With a large library of books and basic computer games there is plenty of choice to help each child develop at their own speed. On the basis of our philosophy which encourages active learning through play we use lots of interactive games and activities to keep learning fun!

20 At Village Kindergarten we also think it is very important to help the children to develop social skills, preparing them for the more formal environment at school. Table manners and thinking of others, taking turns and sharing, potty-training and dressing independently are all part of growing up. And sometimes all this is really difficult to learn when you're a toddler! Each child is allowed to grow and develop at their own speed. We encourage them to learn while keeping their interest and let them
25 enjoy their childhood as well as help them to achieve their milestones in life.

Working with the text

A Write a short summary of this text in German.

Mediation

B Answer the following questions.
1. What age groups are welcome at the Village Kindergarten?
2. Name the different areas of the nursery.
3. How can the nursery team separate younger and older children?
4. Name the activities for older children in the text.
5. How do the staff "keep learning fun"? (line 18)
6. Which are the "social skills" (line 20) that children develop at Village Kindergarten?
7. Is the Village Kindergarten rather like a German nursery school or is it different? What is your opinion? Find arguments from the text.

Working with language

A Fill in the missing words.
Small children have a special (1)... area. There is a (2)"..." area for creative activities. There are (3)... for the babies when they need a nap. Table (4)... are important, too. An important social skill is (5)... with others what you have. Children are allowed to develop at their own (6)... .

B Find opposites of these words.

line 6: small	line 9: possible	line 15: upstairs	line 22: (to) dress
line 9: older	line 12: quiet	line 71: active	

Hands-on tasks

A Plan a "messy area"
1. Write a list of ten things that belong in a "creative, messy area" (see line 12 of the text). If you don't know the exact words try to describe what you mean.
2. Draw a picture on a (poster-size) sheet of paper showing your "messy" area. Add the words you have found. Hang the poster up in your classroom.

B Talk about your ideas

Production

Read the text about the Village Kindergarten once again. Pick five ideas or activities that seem especially interesting or important to you. Make a list. Write down just one keyword or key expression for each idea.
Now imagine it's Open Day at the British nursery. All the nurses in the nursery are asked to tell the visitors and parents what they personally like about their work there. Take your five-point list and inform the parents. Speak in complete sentences.
*Example: On your list you find **"naps"** – you say:* "In our nursery children can have a nap when they feel tired."

C Internet activities
Use the Internet to find out more about reading and writing in nurseries and kindergartens. Find (English!) websites that promote early reading and writing activities. What arguments can you find for teaching very young children how to read and write?
Make a PowerPoint presentation from your findings and inform your class.

D What do you personally think of teaching nursery children how to read and write? Write a comment.

Unit 8 Nursery school and kindergarten abroad

The terms kindergarten and nursery school

What people in Germany call "Kindergarten" has quite different names in English-speaking countries. The following text explains the most common terms.

In the **United States of America** the German expression "kindergarten" usually refers to the first
5 level of official education in the K-12 educational system. ("K-12" means "from kindergarten to 12th grade".) Kindergarten is usually placed inside an elementary school. Many private businesses in the U.S.A. name their day-care businesses "kindergarten" or "kindergarden".

Great Britain: In England and Wales many children attend "nursery schools" or "nursery classes"
10 which belong to primary schools. The first year is often called "reception class". In addition, some parents send their children to private nursery schools. In Scotland the most common word for the first level is "nursery".

The **Australian** word is "preparatory grade" (commonly called "grade prep"
15 or "prep") which is the year before the first grade of school. In the Australian state of New South Wales, however, it is called "kindergarten".

Kindergarten establishments in **Germany** are for preschool children of all ages. They are often run by churches, city or town administrations.
20 Kindergartens in Germany are not a part of the school system as they are in the U.S.A.

Working with the text

A Copy this table and fill in the information you find in the text above.

Country	United States of America	Great Britain: England, Wales	Great Britain: Scotland	Australia
1st year of education is called				

B How much does childcare cost?
1. What do people have to pay for one month at a local nursery in your city or town?
2. Use the Internet to find out childcare costs in other countries. What are the monthly fees for childcare for example in Great Britain, in the United States of America and in Australia? Find at least one example.

Hands-on task

Find information on the Internet about the following topics.
1. What is an "elementary school"? (line 6)
2. Where is "Wales" (line 9) and where is "New South Wales" (line 16)?
3. Find the names of the capitals of the English-speaking countries mentioned in the text.
4. Which are the "English-speaking countries" in the world? (line 1)

Grammar box: **Present Perfect** – Das Perfekt

Das Present Perfect bildet man mit

> **have + Verb in der 3. Verbform (past participle) (bei he / she / it: has)**

- Bei regelmäßigen Verben wird die 3. Verbform gebildet, indem an das Verb *–ed* gehängt wird.
    work → worked, play → played

- Achtung Schreibweise:
    tidy – tidied
    study – studied (aber: play – played)
    stop – stopped
    plan – planned (vgl. auch Unit 4)

- Bei unregelmäßigen Verben ist die 3. Verbform in Listen der unregelmäßigen Verben zu finden (vgl. Seite 191).
    been, seen, written, made, held

I			started
we	**have**		finished
you	(Kurzform: 've)	(Verneinung: haven't)	walked
they			prepared
			gone
he / she / it	**has**		written
somebody	(Kurzform: 's)	(Verneinung: hasn't)	eaten
Bill, Jane			been

- **Signalwörter:** Häufig wird das Present Perfect mit Signalwörtern wie *since, for, just, ever, never, so far* gebraucht.

- Man verwendet das Present Perfect, um Handlungen in der Vergangenheit zu beschreiben, die Auswirkungen auf die Gegenwart haben bzw. noch andauern, oder die zu einem Ergebnis in der Gegenwart führen.
    Oh, I have lost my keys! (A minute ago they were still in my pocket!)
    They have bought a new car. (Look, it's outside the house!)
    The guests have gone home. (So now we can start tidying up.)
    She has cleaned her shoes. (Now they look almost new.)

- **Wichtig:** Formal entspricht das englische Present Perfect dem deutschen Perfekt …
    I have eaten – Ich habe gegessen
    I have gone – Ich bin gegangen
    … das heißt aber nicht, dass die beiden Zeiten auch gleich verwendet werden! Wo im Englischen das Simple Past benutzt wird, verwendet man im Deutschen häufig das Perfekt (vgl. auch Unit 4):
    I went to school for ten years – Ich bin zehn Jahre zur Schule gegangen.

Unit 8 Nursery school and kindergarten abroad

Practising grammar

A Find the right form of these verbs using the Present Perfect.
Example: you – to speak: You have spoken.

1. I – to break
2. he – to drive
3. you – to discuss
4. we – to forget
5. they – to bring
6. John – to stop
7. the children – to paint
8. the head nurse – to think

B Answer the questions in the Present Perfect. Use the verbs in brackets.
Example: Where is Paul? – He … (to go out – just) – He has just gone out.

1. I can't find my keys. Where are they? Someone … them. (to take)
2. Do you know this nursery? Yes, but I … its name. (to forget)
3. Do you like this story for children? Yes, I … it to them. (to read)
4. We … it. (to illustrate – already)
5. Where is Claudia? She … shopping. (to go)
6. No, I …. (not to unpack - so far)
7. Wait a minute, I think I … them on the sideboard. (to see – just)

C Write sentences using the Present Perfect.
Make the first part of the sentence positive and the second part negative.
Example: The children have finished (to finish) their breakfast, but they haven't gone (not – to go) outside.

1. The children … (to tidy away) the toys but they … (not – to tidy up) the kitchen.
2. The children … (to finish) the book but they … (not – to act out) the story.
3. They … (to match) letters but they … (not – to learn) the alphabet song.
4. Martha … (to find) rhymes but she … (not – to finish) her poem.
5. I … (to show) the children the new books but we … (not – to read) them together.
6. We … (to look) at the pictures but I … (not – explain) the text.
7. My colleague Claudia … (to come back) from shopping but the others … (not – to arrive).

D Translate these sentences into English.
1. Warst du schon einmal in einem englischen Kindergarten?
2. Ich habe noch nie mit DUPLO gespielt.
3. Wart ihr schon draußen? Das Wetter ist so schön!
4. Habt ihr die Bücherecke aufgeräumt?
5. Steve war schon immer ein schwieriges Kind.

Nursery school and kindergarten abroad Unit 8

A daily report

Below is a report about Matthew Brown, a boy from the "Tiny Tots" nursery school.
These are the things he has done today.
Make complete sentences about Matthew's activities using the Present Perfect.

Example: Today Matthew … (to play) with … (Peter, Paul and Mary).
             Today Matthew has played with Peter, Paul and Mary.

Tiny Tots
Daily report

Name: *Matthew Brown*

Date: *24th May 20 ..*

Today I … (to enjoy) playing with / in
DUPLO ✗ / the home corner / cars and trains ✗ / jigsaw puzzles
Today Matthew …

I … (enjoy) reading picture books / comic books ✗
He …

For lunch I … (to have)
maccaroni and cheese ✗ / sausages and chips
For lunch he …

For tea I … (to have)
cheese and toast / crackers and jam ✗
For tea Matthew …

I … (to make) progress in
maths / reading / painting / story telling ✗
He …

Toileting progress: I … (to use) 1 ✗ / 2 / 3 nappy (nappies) today
He …

Today I … (to start) painting with *water colours*
Today Matthew …

General information: *Matthew … (to be) fine today*
Matthew …

Special remark:
Could Matthew please have some more nappies?
Thank you – Tom

(When Matthew's mother reads Tom's remark, she says:
"But I … (always – to put) lots of nappies into his bag!")

Unit 8 Nursery school and kindergarten abroad

At an American kindergarten in Wamego, Kansas	
library ['laɪbrəri]	Bücherei
librarian [laɪ'breərɪən]	Bibliothekar/in, Person, die für die Bücherei verantwortlich ist
(to) act out [ækt aʊt]	darstellen, vorspielen
audio book [ɔːdɪəʊ bʊk]	Hörbuch
At a British nursery school	
reputation [ˌrepjʊ'teɪʃn]	Ruf
care [keə]	Betreuung
quality childcare ['kwɒlətɪ tʃaɪld keə]	Kinderbetreuung auf hohem Niveau
cot [kɒt]	Liege
messy area ['mesɪ 'eərɪə]	unordentlicher Bereich, wo Kinder Dinge liegen lassen dürfen
upstairs [ʌpsteəz]	im oberen Stockwerk
literacy activities ['lɪtərəsɪ æk'tɪvətiːs]	Leselern-Aktivitäten
social skills ['səʊʃl skɪlz]	soziale Fertigkeiten, Sozialkompetenz
table manners ['teɪbl 'mænəz]	Tischmanieren
independent(ly) [ˌɪndɪ'pendənt]	selbstständig, unabhängig
(to) promote [prə'məʊt]	fördern, unterstützen
(to) achieve [ə'tʃiːv]	erreichen
milestone [maɪl stəʊn]	Meilenstein, Ziel
Open Day ['əʊpən deɪ]	Tag der offenen Tür
The terms kindergarten and nursery school	
grade [greɪd]	Klassenstufe
elementary school [ˌelɪ'mentərɪ skuːl]	Grundschule
day-care business [deɪ-keə 'bɪznɪs]	Firma, die sich (gegen Bezahlung) um Kinder kümmert
reception class [rɪsepʃn klɑːs]	Eingangsklasse, erstes Jahr
preparatory grade [prɪ'pærətərɪ 'greɪd]	Vorbereitungsklasse, Vorschulklasse
preschool children [prɪ-skuːl 'tʃɪldrən]	Kinder im Vorschulalter
city/town administration ['sɪtɪ/taʊn ədˌmɪnɪ'streɪʃn]	Stadtverwaltung
A daily report	
cracker ['krækə]	Keks, Cracker
toileting progress ['tɔɪlɪtɪŋ 'prəʊgres]	Fortschritte bei der Sauberkeitserziehung

Unit 9 — Being ill

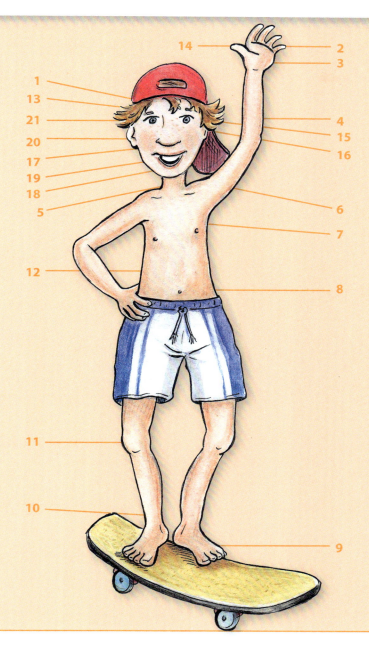

Match these parts of the body to numbers 1 – 21:

head – arm – hand – finger – thumb – leg – knee – foot – tummy – navel (belly button) – chest – shoulder – throat – eyes – ears – nose – mouth – teeth – hair – cheek – forehead

What do children often say when they feel ill?
How can you see that somebody is ill?

handwerk-technik.de

Unit 9 Being ill

Signs that children are not feeling well

When Janet arrives at nursery school one morning there are some children with a cold: a boy has a runny nose and a girl is coughing. So she talks with Sarah about illnesses in children.

Sarah: Small children are not able to say that they feel ill or what is hurting. Therefore, nursery nurses must be able to see when children are starting to feel unwell. Children often get symptoms quickly. A child who seems perfectly well in the morning, may have a headache and a high temperature in the afternoon - or vomit.
Janet: How can we tell that children are becoming ill?
Sarah: There are physical signs of an illness coming. There may be rings around the children's eyes and they may be sleepy. Their skin can be very pale or they have flushed cheeks.
Janet: And how can I see that in a child with a darker skin tone?
Sarah: There are some signs of illnesses that look different depending on children's skin tones. Light-skinned children may look paler than normal, but black or Asian children may look grey or have dark rings under their eyes.
Janet: Do poorly children also behave differently?
Sarah: They often have no appetite. They are quieter than usual or they don't want to join in. They cry more easily, are more irritable or they cling to the nursery nurse. Sometimes they go back to sucking their thumbs and other babyish behaviour. If you know the children in your group well, it can help you to see that children are not their usual selves: for example, a child who is normally a good eater is not feeling hungry, or children who normally put on their clothes themselves are asking for help with dressing. These may be signs that the child is feeling poorly.
Janet: And what can we do if a child is ill?
Sarah: Most children need their parents to be with them when they do not feel well, so nursery nurses should contact them. Calling a doctor is necessary if the child is getting worse very quickly.
Janet: And what else can we do?
Sarah: Young children pick up infections easily, so that it is very important that nurseries are as hygienic as possible.

Working with language

A Find 3 other words that mean 'ill'.

B Find the noun that belongs to 'ill'.

Working with the text

Answer these questions:
1. Why is it important to understand the signs of coming illnesses?
2. Fill the signs of coming illness in the following chart:

Physical signs	Behaviour
rings around the eyes	sleepy

3. What is special about children with different skin tones?
4. Why is it important to know the children well?
5. What must the nursery nurse do if a child is ill?

A phone call to Nora's mother

Nora Brown, 4 years old, is a very lively child. She is active, enjoys exercise and has a good appetite. Normally, as soon as she arrives in the morning she starts playing with the other children.
Today she is different: when she arrives this morning she seems a little bit sleepy but after a while she is her usual self and joins in with the other children's play. But two hours later Janet sees that Nora has not eaten her sandwich for breakfast. Next, Janet observes that the girl has stopped playing, that she has gone to the quiet corner and has started to suck her thumb. Now Janet sees that Nora's cheeks are flushed. She walks over to her, puts one hand on her forehead and feels that she has a temperature. She can also see a rash starting around the girl's neck. Janet decides to call Nora's mother who is still at work. She thinks that it's the best for her to come and pick up her daughter.

Janet: Tiny Tots, Janet Smith speaking. It's about your daughter, Mrs Brown. I think she's ill. I think you should come and pick her up.
Mrs Brown: But she was all right this morning, perhaps a bit sleepier than usual, but that sometimes happens, doesn't it?
Janet: Yes, in the beginning she was like every day. But she hasn't eaten her breakfast and you know how hungry she always is in the morning.
Mrs Brown: Yes, that's true …
Janet: Soon after that she went to the quiet corner and stayed there for an hour. She has cuddled up with her teddy bear.
Mrs Brown: You know, it's a bit difficult for me to leave the office at the moment … we're so busy. Have you taken her temperature yet?
Janet: No, I haven't. But I've just felt her forehead and I think she's quite hot. Her cheeks look flushed and also a rash has started around her neck, so I really think you'd better come.
Mrs Brown: Oh yes, that sounds really bad. I'll leave work immediately. But you know that it'll take half an hour to get to the nursery school. Is that alright?
Janet: Of course, Mrs Brown, don't worry. Nora will be very happy that her mother's coming.
Mrs Brown: All right. I think I'll take her to the doctor straight away. Bye, Janet.
Janet: Bye, Mrs Brown.

Working with the text

Answer these questions on the text in your own words.
1. What is Nora's usual behaviour like?
2. What is the first symptom that she shows?
3. What other symptoms does she have?
4. When does Janet decide to call Nora's mother?
5. Why does Nora's mother not want to come at once?
6. What does the mother decide then, and why?

Unit 9 Being ill

Hands-on task

Interaction

Making a phone call to parent

Read about Aliye's morning in the nursery school.

> Aliye Kassem, a girl of 5 years, arrives at 8:30 a.m. at your nursery school. Her father explains to you that Aliye did not want to have breakfast at home, which she normally enjoys. The little girl, however, says that she feels alright.
> For the next two hours you observe her but you cannot see any difference in her. Then all of a sudden Aliye becomes very pale and starts vomiting.

A What are Aliye's symptoms?

B What do you think is best for Aliye: being collected by her parents or staying on?

C Work with a partner. Prepare a phone call to Aliye's father and present it to the class.

Poorly children, worried parents

Parentsnet.org is one website where worried parents can get advice from other parents. These are two postings:

> My healthy, happy child has been ill five times since he started a new nursery three months ago. He gets better and is back for a week, then catches something else and is back at home for a week at least each time.
> I know children will catch things when they go to nursery, but is this normal? As a result we have had an awful family time of flu, ear infection and chicken pox.
> Do you think I should speak with the nursery?
> *A very worried parent*

> Yes, it is absolutely normal for children starting nursery school to pick up everything as they build up their immune systems. But I am not a doctor and if you are worried you should see yours with your child. Do you think the nursery might have problems with their hygiene?
> *Another parent*

Working with the text

A What is the parent worried about?

B Why might hygiene be the problem?

C What children's diseases can you see in the photos?

Hygiene in a nursery school

Hands-on task

Production

Imagine you work in that nursery school which has a lot of hygiene problems.
The nursery teacher asks you to write down some rules on a poster to hang it up in the nursery.

A First identify the hygiene problems in this nursery.

A nursery or a bad dream?

One morning you enter your nursery and this is what you see:
The floor seems clean but under the breakfast table there are breadcrumbs.
What about the table? Nobody has cleared away the leftovers from breakfast, and in the middle of all that mess two children are sitting and doing a puzzle. From the jam on their fingers you can see clearly what they had for breakfast. You look a bit more closely, and yes, there is also jam on the floor. A boy is throwing banana and orange peel into the bins. Who's eating the fruit? You look around and you see some pieces of oranges and bananas right on the carpet in the block area. The children who are eating them are building something with Lego bricks at the same time. Some of the bricks look greasy and smeared. On the carpet there are also some used paper tissues. Who has used them? Oh yes, it's the boy with the runny nose. He's got a cold.
There is an unpleasant smell in the room. Perhaps from the washroom? You take a look but everything is alright there. The toilets and washbasins are clean, there is a fresh towel for every child. Maybe the bins? It seems they haven't been emptied and cleaned for days.

B Think of rules with the help of the hygiene procedures below.
Example:
Always clear the table after each meal.

Item	Hygiene procedure
Toys and play equipment	Sterilise regularly.
Dishes and cutlery	Wash in hot water, sterilise for babies.
Tables	Wipe with a clean cloth every time they are used, disinfect regularly.
Worktops	Wipe with a clean cloth.
Toilets, handbasins, sinks	Clean regularly. Check toilets frequently during the day.
Bins	Empty bins frequently. Wash out bins every day.
Floors	Clean floors regularly. A disinfectant should be used.

C Create your poster and write down the rules.

Unit 9 Being ill

Grammar box: Plural – Mehrzahlbildung

Regelmäßige Plurale enden auf –s

a flower → some flower**s**; one place → many place**s**; one toy → two toy**s**
Achtung Rechtschreibung: -**es** folgt nach den Konsonanten –**s**, -**sh**, -**ch**, -**x**:
bus → bu**ses**; dish → di**shes**; church → chur**ches**; box → bo**xes**
auch: potato → potato**es**; tomato → tomato**es**

Betontes -**y** am Wortende wird zu -**ies**:
baby → bab**ies**; party → part**ies**

-**f**, -**fe** am Wortende wird zu -**ve**:
shelf → shel**ves**; knife → kni**ves**

Unregelmäßige Plurale enden nicht auf –s

one m**a**n → two m**e**n;   one woman → two wom**e**n
a child → some child**ren**
one f**oo**t → two f**ee**t   one t**oo**th → several t**ee**th
a **mouse** → some mi**ce**
one **sheep** → two **sheep**   one **fish** → many **fish**

Grammar box: Present Perfect – Das Perfekt (Fortsetzung)

In vielen Fällen entspricht das **Present Perfect** dem deutschen Perfekt:
I've just washed my hands.   *Ich habe gerade meine Hände gewaschen.*

In zwei Fällen wird das **Present Perfect** jedoch anders verwendet, als es dem deutschen Sprachempfinden entspricht:

- **Present Perfect und Gegenwart**
  For und *since* in der Bedeutung "seit" werden im Englischen mit **Present Perfect** verwendet, im Deutschen mit der Gegenwartsform.
  Dabei wird *for* mit einem Zeitraum, *since* mit einem Zeitpunkt verwendet
  (*since 10 o'clock, for two hours*).
  Auch die Fragen *how long …?* und *since when …?* werden mit **Present Perfect** gebildet.

  Tom has worked here for two years.   *Tom arbeitet seit zwei Jahren hier.*
  Nora has had a temperature since 10:30 a.m.   *Nora hat seit 10:30 Uhr Fieber.*
  Since when have you been here?   *Seit wann bist du hier?*
  How long has she been ill?   *Wie lange ist sie schon krank?*

- **Present Perfect und Vergangenheit**
  Enthält der Satz eine Zeitangabe der Vergangenheit, dann darf kein **Present Perfect** verwendet werden. In diesem Fall steht eine Form des **Past Tense** (vgl. Unit 4).
  Fragen mit *when ..?* werden ebenfalls mit **Past Tense** gebildet.

Vgl. auch Unit 8, Grammar box: Present Perfect

Working with language

A Put *for* or *since* into the sentence parts.

1. … two weeks
2. … yesterday
3. … last Tuesday
4. … half an hour
5. … half an hour ago
6. … 2 o'clock
7. … 12th August
8. … ten years
9. … I was young
10. … 2008

B When Nora's mother comes to pick up her sick daughter she asks Janet a lot of questions.
Form groups of two and ask and answer these questions.
After you have finished, swap the roles of Janet and Nora's mother.

Example: How long / Nora / feel bad? (breakfast time)
Mrs Brown: How long has Nora felt bad?
Janet: She has felt bad since breakfast time.

1. How long / Nora / be really unwell?   (two hours)
2. Since when / she / be off-colour?   (all morning)
3. Since when / Nora / be in the quiet corner? (11 o'clock)
4. How long / she / have this high temperature? (30 minutes)
5. How long / she / cuddle up with her teddy bear? (one hour)
6. Since when / the girl / have / this rash?   (quite some time)
7. How long / there / be / these symptoms?   (a short time)
8. Since when / her behaviour / be different ? (nearly all morning)
9. How long / you / observe / Nora?   (three hours)

C Complete the following text with verbs in the Simple Past or Present Perfect.

Janet … (1 work) with the Tiny Tots for half a year now. When she … (2 start) six months ago she … (3 be) very anxious. She … (4 not know) then whether she … (5 can) cope with a group of 25 children. The first days … (6 be) quite difficult. She … (7 try) to join in with the other nursery nurses. After a few days she … (8 know) most of the daily routines in the nursery. School … (9 be) also quite difficult at the beginning. But her classmates … (10 be) very friendly.
Now she … (11 already become) friends with some of them and they … (12 help) her to feel good during the classes.
When Janet looks back now she sees that she … (13 already / learn) a lot. She … (14 have) a lot of new experiences, and best of all, she … (15 always / enjoy) working with children. So she is sure that her idea of being a nursery nurse … (16 be) a good one from the beginning.

Unit 9 Being ill

The first-aid box

Every nursery should have at least one first-aid box.
It should be out of reach of the children but easily accessible to adults so you can treat at once. Major injuries, however, need medical attention!
If you are not sure, call for medical help.

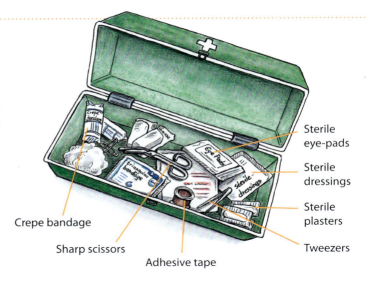

Sterile eye-pads
Sterile dressings
Sterile plasters
Tweezers
Crepe bandage
Sharp scissors
Adhesive tape

Injury	Treatment	Check for …
Grazed skin	Rinse the wound with clean water. Allow to heal in the air.	
Bruises and trapped fingers	Apply cold pack.	Run a hand gently over the limb to check that nothing feels lumpy which might be a sign of a fracture.
Bump to the head, e.g. falling over or running into another child	Apply cold pack.	Vomiting or headaches – these could indicate concussion.
Nose bleed	Tip the head forward. Pinch the soft part of the nose just below the bridge. Put cold pack on the neck.	Seek medical attention if the bleeding continues for more than 30 minutes.
Insect stings	Try to remove the sting but don't squeeze it. Put on a cold pack to reduce the swelling.	Medical help is needed if the sting is in the mouth or if the child starts to look ill. Some children are allergic to stings.
Cuts and wounds	Apply direct pressure to the wound with a clean pad. Tie a bandage around the pad firmly but not too tightly. With small wounds a sterile plaster may be enough.	Wounds to the face, especially near the eyes, need medical attention.

Being ill Unit 9

Small accidents and injuries

These are just some accidents that happen in nursery school:

1 Asif Latifi fell from the climbing frame in the playground of the nursery and bumped his knee and his head. After some time says he says he feels sick. It is 3 p.m.

2 Shortly after 1 p.m. Nora Brown is cutting out shapes.
Suddenly you hear her cry and see blood on her left thumb.

3 A wasp has stung Jason Miller during an outing to the pet zoo.
You know that he is allergic to wasp stings. It is 10 o'clock in the morning.

A Work with a partner, then present your thoughts to the class.   *Interaction*
1. Which parts of your first-aid box do you need for the injuries above?
2. Do you need medical help in any of these cases?
3. Explain how to treat these children using the information above.

B The information on minor injuries could be a useful part of the first-aid box of your nursery. Write out a German version.   *Mediation*

By law all accidents, major or minor, must be recorded in workplaces in Great Britain.

Accident Report

Name: Jamie Gray
Date and time: 1:25 p.m. 29 August 20...
Where: playground
What happened: splinter in the little finger of his left hand
Injuries: splinter
Treatment: splinter taken out, washed under tap
Medical aid sought: /

Person dealing with accident: Janet Smith
Parent's signature: M. Gray

A Answer these questions.
1. What was the accident in the report on the left?
2. Why must you write in the name of the person dealing with the accident?
3. Why do parents have to sign the report?

Production

B Write accident reports for the children Asif, Nora and Jason from the top of the page.

Production

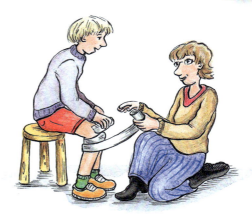

handwerk-technik.de

Unit 9 Being ill

head [hed]	Kopf
thumb [θʌm]	Daumen
leg [leg]	Bein
knee [niː]	Knie
tummy ['tʌmi]	Bauch
navel ['neɪvl], belly button ['beli bʌtən]	Bauchnabel
chest [tʃest]	Brust
shoulder ['ʃəʊldə]	Schulter
throat [θrəʊt]	Kehle, Rachen
cheek [tʃiːk]	Wange
forehead ['fɒrɪd]	Stirn

Signs that children are not feeling well

sign [saɪn]	Zeichen
cold [kəʊld]	Erkältung
runny nose ['rʌni nəʊz]	laufende Nase
poorly ['pɔːli]	kränklich
(to) cough [kɒf]	husten
illness ['ɪlnɪs]	Krankheit
(to) hurt [hɜːt]	weh tun
(to) feel unwell [fiːl ʌnwel]	sich unwohl fühlen
behaviour [bɪ'heɪvjə]	Verhalten
sleepy ['sliːpi]	schläfrig
skin [skɪn]	Haut
irritable ['ɪrɪtəbl]	reizbar
flushed [flʌʃt]	gerötet
(to) cling to s.o. [klɪŋ tuː]	sich an jmd. hängen
(to) suck thumb [sʌk θʌm]	Daumen lutschen
(to) vomit ['vɒmɪt]	sich erbrechen
headache [hed eɪk]	Kopfschmerzen
depending on [dɪ'pendɪŋ ɒn]	abhängig von
skin tone [skɪn təʊn]	Hautfarbe
light-skinned [laɪt-skɪnd]	hellhäutig
self (sg.), selves (pl.) [self, selvz]	das eigene Selbst
(to) feel poorly [fiːl 'pʊəli]	sich elend fühlen
temperature ['temprətʃə]	Temperatur, Fieber
rash [ræʃ]	Hautausschlag

Poorly children, worried parents

(to) catch [kætʃ]	hier: eine Krankheit bekommen
flu [fluː]	Grippe
chicken pox ['tʃɪkɪn pɒks]	Windpocken
ear infection [ɪər ɪn'fekʃən]	Ohrenentzündung
hygiene ['haɪdʒiːn]	Hygiene

Hygiene in a nursery school

(to) wipe [waɪp]	(ab-)wischen
cloth [klɒθ]	Tuch, Lappen
worktop [wɜːk tɒp]	Arbeitsplatte
regularly ['regjʊləli]	regelmäßig
frequently ['friːkwəntli]	häufig
handbasin [hænd 'beɪsn]	Handwaschbecken
breadcrumbs [bredkrʌms]	Brotkrümel
leftover [left 'əʊvə]	Rest
peel [piːl]	Schale
greasy ['griːzɪ]	verfettet, fettig
smeared [smɪəd]	verschmiert
paper tissue ['peɪpə 'tɪʃuː]	Papiertaschentuch
unpleasant [ʌn'pleznt]	unangenehm
towel ['taʊəl]	Handtuch

The first-aid box

first-aid box [fɜːst-eɪd bɒks]	Erste-Hilfe-Koffer
adhesive tape [əd'hiːsɪv]	Klebeband
dressing ['dresɪŋ]	Wundauflage
eye pads [aɪ pædz]	Augenauflagen
tweezers (nur pl.) ['twiːzəz]	Pinzette
scissors (nur pl.) ['sɪzəz]	Schere
plaster ['plɑːstə]	Pflaster
crepe bandage ['kreɪp 'bændɪdʒ]	Mullbinde
grazed [greɪzd]	abgeschürft
(to) rinse [rɪns]	ausspülen
wound [wuːnd]	Wunde
(to) heal [hiːl]	heilen
bruise [bruːz]	Bluterguss
trapped [træpt]	eingeklemmt
cold pack [kəʊld ˌpæk]	Kühlpad
limb [lɪm]	Glied
lumpy [lʌmpi]	klumpig
fracture ['fræktʃə]	Bruch
bump [bʌmp]	Beule
concussion [kən'kʌʃn]	Gehirnerschütterung
nose bleed [nəʊz bliːd]	Nasenbluten
(to) pinch [pɪntʃ]	zusammendrücken
(to) seek medical help [siːk 'medɪkl help]	ärztliche Hilfe holen
sting [stɪŋ]	Stich
swelling [swelɪŋ]	Schwellung
(to) be allergic to sth. [bɪ ə'lɜːdʒɪk tuː]	allergisch gegen etwas sein

Unit 10 — Food and drink for children

What can you see in the pictures?

Which of these foods are good for children?
What is breakfast in a German nursery school like?

Unit 10 Food and drink for children

Give them a good start: breakfast

One morning, while Janet is having breakfast before going to college, she reads the newspaper. One article catches her interest:

Give them a good start: breakfast

"You are what you eat", they say. And everybody knows that children who eat breakfast perform better at school than those who don't.

I was surprised, therefore, to read in new statistics that 48 per cent of inner-city children never eat
5 breakfast. Why?
Is it because the parents don't have enough money? But the cost of a slice of bread – better than nothing – is not very high.
Is it because the parents are too lazy? They can't get themselves out of bed? And what about the children who have probably been watching television till late the night before?
10 Or is it perhaps that we are frightened of our children and can't face the breakfast battle? And if it is a battle the question is "Do our children actually enjoy breakfast?" If the answer is "no", then we must do something!
My husband likes a typical English breakfast with eggs, bacon, sausages, tomato and black pudding. But my children moan about a cooked breakfast and want those coloured cereal packets with gifts
15 inside the box.
Cereals contain many vitamins and it does not take a lot of time to fill a plate with crunchy morsels and pour some milk over them.
But children are not the only breakfast dodgers.
We all know the adult who, for different reasons, starts the day with only a cup of coffee, hastily
20 gulped down before rushing off to work.
As far as I am concerned, I have happy memories of thick slices of fresh bread or a croissant, dipped into a bowl-size cup of milky French coffee. Toast and jam is another favourite breakfast. I think breakfast is important to keep me from feeling hungry at work and running out of energy.
As for the children – let's make sure breakfast doesn't go out of fashion.
25 We can set the alarm clock five minutes early – and we can all eat our way to a more energetic start into the day.

Food and drink for children Unit 10

Working with the text

A **True or false? Correct the false statements.**
1. 25 % of inner-city children never eat breakfast.
2. The author's children like a cooked breakfast.
3. Bread is too expensive.
4. Parents are a good example to children.
5. Children don't want to eat cereals.

B **Comprehension: Answer the following questions about the text.**
1. Why is breakfast important? Give several reasons.
2. What are the reasons why some children don't have breakfast?
3. What different food options for breakfast are mentioned in the text?
4. Why are cereals a good choice for children's breakfast?
5. What can we do to make sure that children get a good breakfast?

C Write a short summary of the newspaper article in German for your colleague. **Mediation**

D What do you have for breakfast? Translate the following sentences into English.

> Ich esse immer eine Scheibe Brot mit Butter und Marmelade. Dazu trinke ich eine Tasse Kaffee.

> Ich trinke nur schnell einen Orangensaft, bevor ich zur Schule hetze. Ich habe nicht genug Zeit.

> Mein Frühstück besteht aus Cornflakes und Obst.

> Ich lieb meine Rice Krispies!

> Ich esse ein Brötchen mit Salami und trinke Milch.

> Am Morgen mag ich noch nichts essen. Das ist zu früh!

And what about you?

> …

handwerk-technik.de

Unit 10 Food and drink for children

A balanced diet

Later that day at school Janet learns something about healthy food for children. Her teacher Mrs Shotton brings several cereal packets into the class. Janet is happy that she read the newspaper article because she knows more than her classmates, Stacey and Celine.

Mrs S:	Have a look at these packets. Do you have cereals for breakfast?
Stacey:	Oh yes, I have a bowl of cereals every morning.
Mrs S:	And why do you eat it?
Stacey:	I don't know. My mother often buys them, that's why I eat them. If we don't have cereal at home, I eat something else.
Celine:	Cereals are delicious, especially the Honey Pops. My little sister loves them.
Janet:	Cereals contain many vitamins.
Mrs S:	Yes, very good Janet. You are absolutely right. Is this the reason why they are so popular?
Janet:	I think it is handy to prepare a bowl of cereal for breakfast. But I think it starts in the supermarket. If the packaging is colourful, it will be very attractive to children. And if there is a free gift inside, children will tell their parents to buy the packet.
Mrs S:	Excellent. But do you think cereals are good for breakfast?
Celine:	Yes, of course. Why not? Vitamins are good, aren't they?
Mrs S:	Do cereals only consist of vitamins? Have a look at this package of Rice Krispies.
Stacey:	(reads from the package) Rice, sugar, salt, glucose-fructose syrup, malt flavouring, niacin, iron, vitamin B6, riboflavin (B_2), thiamin (B_1), folic acid, vitamin B_{12}.

Celine:	Wow! I didn't know that there are so many different ingredients inside. Do children need all those things?
Mrs S:	Well, if you don't know, we will find out! Has anybody already heard of the term "a balanced diet"?
Janet:	I think it has something to do with the energy we need. I also read something about nutrients.
Mrs S:	Yes, your body needs nutrients. If you don't eat enough, for example, your body will soon stop working. At different times in our lives our bodies need different amounts of nutrients. If we want to give our body all the nutrients that it needs, we will have to eat different foods. That's a balanced diet: a diet that consists of different foods and therefore provides all the nutrients. By the way, which nutrients do you know?

Stacey:	Vitamins … and fat.
Celine:	I know something about protein. Oh, and there are some minerals. Iron is a mineral, isn't it?
Janet:	What about carbohydrates, sugar for example?
Mrs S:	Thank you, well done. You can add water to the list of nutrients. But water does not give us energy. Only carbohydrates, fat and protein provide energy. What do children need energy for?
Janet:	I read this in the newspaper this morning: a good breakfast keeps you from feeling hungry and from running out of energy. And children who eat breakfast perform better at school.
Mrs S:	True. Those children can concentrate better because the brain needs energy as well. Another reason is that they need energy to move and play.
Stacey:	But how much energy and nutrients do children need?
Celine:	And if children have cereals for breakfast, will they get the energy and nutrients they need?
Mrs S:	Well, let's find the answer to these questions. There are tables to tell you how much energy a child needs per day. It depends on the age of the child of course. If you open your books, you will find a list on page …

Working with the text

A Match up the two halves of the sentences.

1. If we don't have cereals at home today,
2. If the packaging is colourful,
3. If you don't know,
4. If you don't eat enough,
5. If we want to give our body all the nutrients that it needs,
6. If you open your books,
7. And if children have cereals for breakfast,

a) will they get the energy and nutrients they need?
b) we will have to eat different foods.
c) I will eat something else.
d) you will find a list on page …
e) children will tell their parents to buy the packet.
f) your body will soon stop working.
g) we will find out.

B Comprehension: Answer the following questions according to the text.

1. Why are cereals so popular?
2. What is meant by the term "a balanced diet"?
3. Which six nutrients are mentioned in the text?
4. Which factors influence the amount of energy a child needs?
5. What does a child need energy for?

Hands-on tasks

A Look at different cereal boxes.
Are those cereals healthy?
Compare the amount of nutrients they offer.
Compare them to the amount of nutrients a child needs.

B What does the packaging look like?
Find reasons why the packaging looks inviting to children.

Unit 10 Food and drink for children

> **Grammar box: Conditional sentences (Type I)** – Bedingungssätze (Typ I)
>
> | If you eat too much sugar, | you will get bad teeth. |
> | If you don't eat a balanced diet, | you will not get all the necessary nutrients. |
> | **Simple Present** | **Will-Future** |
>
> - Wenn die Bedingung als möglich oder wahrscheinlich angesehen werden kann, dann verwendet man **Simple Present im if-Satz** und **Will-Future im Hauptsatz**.

Practising grammar

A Put the verbs in brackets into the correct tense.
1. If children … (to eat) regularly, they … (to get) enough energy.
   Example: If children eat regularly, they will get enough energy.
2. If a newborn baby … (to get) enough milk from its mother's breast, it (not to need) a bottle.
3. If a baby … (to want) some food, most of the time it … (to start) crying.
4. If babies … (to swallow) too much air, it … (to make) them sick.
5. If you … (not to use) clean bottles when feeding, bacteria … (to be) in the food.
6. If fathers … (to help) feeding the baby, they … (to feel) included.
7. If your baby … (not to drink) all the formula in the bottle, you … (to have) to throw away the unused portion — never save it for later.
8. Some mothers … (to feel) guilty if they … (not to breastfeed).

Achtung: Der Hauptsatz kann auch vor dem if-Satz stehen.

> **Grammar box: Conditional sentences (Type II)** – Bedingungssätze (Typ II)
>
> | If you gave a baby some chocolate, | it would become ill. |
> | If I were you, | I would not eat so much chocolate. |
> | **Simple Past (= Past-Tense-Form)** | **Conditional I (= would + Verb in Infinitiv-Form)** |
>
> - Wenn die Bedingung als unmöglich oder unwahrscheinlich angesehen werden kann, dann verwendet man **Simple Past im if-Satz** und **Conditional I im Hauptsatz**.

B Put the verbs in brackets into the correct tense.
1. If you … (to give) newborn babies cow's milk, they … (to become) ill.
2. If I … (to be) you, I … (not to give) a baby solid foods in its first months.
3. If babies … (to be able) to hold a bottle, they … (to drink) on their own.
4. If breast milk … (to cost) money, the price … (to be) very high.
5. If all parents … (to buy) formula milk, breastfeeding … (not to be) necessary.
6. Janet says: "If I … (to be) a father, I … (to help) my wife to look after the baby."
7. If ice-cream … (to be) stored at room temperature or in a warm area, bacteria … (to grow) quickly.
8. If a nursery nurse … (to have) a bad personal hygiene, she … (not to be) allowed to work with food (or with children).
9. If Muslims … (to eat) pork, they … (to break) the rules of their religion.
10. If children … (not to like) cereal, nobody … (to buy) them.

Breast or bottle? The importance of milk

For the first months of their lives the only food that babies need is milk, either from their mothers' breast or from a bottle.
Breastfeeding. The National Health Service and the World Health Organisation/WHO recommend that you exclusively breastfeed your baby for the first six months. They will tell you that "breast is best". Breast milk contains all the ingredients a baby needs in the right proportions and at the right temperature. To produce enough milk the mother needs to eat a balanced diet with healthy nutrients and some extra calories. She also needs to drink a lot – but no alcohol, because whatever a mother eats or drinks passes directly into the bloodstream, then into the breast milk and finally into the baby. Breastfeeding has a positive effect on the baby's and the mother's health. Breast milk is easy for the baby to digest and it contains antibodies which help to protect the baby from infections. Breastfeeding also gives a mother a special feeling of closeness to her baby. In addition, breastfeeding can help mothers to return to their pre-pregnancy weight more quickly. Breastfeeding only works well if the mother is happy to do it and there are no medical problems. It is not always easy and some mothers say that it can sometimes hurt because their breasts get sore.
Bottle-feeding. An alternative is to bottle-feed. You can use pumped breast milk or formula milk. You cannot give cow's milk to babies because it is too difficult to digest. There are many different types of formula milk depending on the age and weight of the child or the ingredients. They usually come in powdered form. Formula milk has to be mixed with boiled water according to the instructions on the box. Some people say that formula milk is convenient. Other people think it is unnecessary if the mother has enough milk and they say that formula milk can never be as good as breast milk.
Solid foods. You can start to introduce solid foods into the baby's diet when the baby is around 6 months old. This is called 'weaning'. You gradually combine solid foods with breast or formula milk because milk alone no longer provides enough nutrients for the baby's growth. You should try different foods, one at a time. They should be sieved or puréed, so that the baby can swallow them without chewing or choking. You should start with simple foods that babies can easily digest, such as vegetables, cereal or rice. Weaning should not replace milk completely. Never stop breastfeeding abruptly! Children should be breastfed for at least their first year of life.

Working with the text

A Rules about bottle-feeding a baby: Match up the two halves of the sentence.

1. If you prepare a bottle,
2. If you do not use hygienic equipment,
3. If the milk in the bottle is too cold,
4. If the milk in the bottle is too hot,
5. If the baby swallows air while feeding,
6. If you keep the baby in an upright position,
7. If the baby does not burp after a while,

a) the air will rise above the milk and find its way out of the body.
b) you can gently rub or pat its back to get the wind up.
c) the baby can become ill.
d) it can make them feel uncomfortably full or give them pain and they need to burp.
e) you must read the instructions on the box.
f) you must cool it by holding it under water.
g) you can put it in a bowl of warm water.

B Breast or bottle?

1. Find arguments for and against breast-feeding in the text.
2. Find arguments for and against bottle-feeding in the text.
3. Do some Internet research and find more arguments for and against both options.
4. Write an essay about: "Breast is best – a perfect way to give babies a good start."

Unit 10 Food and drink for children

Planning meals for children

Janet is starting her new work experience in a nursery school. Of course she gets to know the children first but after breakfast her colleague Sarah gives her a guided tour of the premises. She explains everything that is important. Now they are in the dining-room.

Sarah: Well, this is the dining-room. Here the children have breakfast and lunch. We particularly look after the children's food. We want them to get a balanced diet.
Janet: Yes, I know. We talked about a balanced diet and all the nutrients at school.
Sarah: Well, then you will know that children need different groups of food that are particularly good for children, such as milk, vegetables, eggs, some meat and fish. We try to provide a healthy mixture of these foods.
Janet: I see. And what about drinks?
Sarah: Look at the trolley over there. Children who are thirsty can always get something to drink. We offer water because it's pure and quenches the thirst. We don't allow sweet and sugary drinks in here.
Janet: Yes, our teacher Mrs Shotton says that sugary drinks can cause tooth decay and spoil the children's appetites.
Sarah: She's absolutely right. Sometimes we offer fruit juice but we dilute it with water because the juices are too acid. We also offer milk, for example in the afternoon.
Janet: Do you have a menu?
Sarah: Yes, of course, look here, this is this week's menu:

	Monday	Tuesday	Wednesday	Thursday	Friday
Menu					
Breakfast	milk, cereals with banana, toast	milk, porridge, apple	milk, yoghurt, toast	milk, cereals, toast	milk, cereals, toast
Lunch	maccaroni and cheese, broccoli, fruit salad, water	chicken nuggets, chips, mushy peas, yoghurt, water	bean and sausage stew*, bread rolls, fresh peach, water	fried fish, rice salad, strawberry mousse, water	pancakes with fruit filling, water
Mid-afternoon	diluted fruit juice, cheese and biscuits	milk, fruit scone	diluted orange juice, rice crackers	banana milk shake	hot chocolate, dried fruit mix (raisins, apricots)

Janet: What is the asterisk for?
Sarah: Oh yes, this is important. There are children of different cultures and religions in our nursery school, for example Muslims. They don't eat pork. And some Muslims will only eat meat if the animal has been killed in a certain way by specialist butchers. The asterisk means that we have to pay attention and serve something different to them.

Food and drink for children Unit 10

Janet: That's very complicated, isn't it?

Sarah: Once you get to know the children better you will know who eats what and who doesn't. If you are not sure about something, please check with us. We like to respect religious customs.

Janet: Our teacher says that we have to be careful about allergies because some children are allergic to certain types of food. Especially nuts can make the children choke.

Sarah: Absolutely! It's always important to check with parents if there are any foods or drinks that children shouldn't be given. We have a list in the office … Last year we had a child here who suffered from coeliac disease. The girl wasn't able to eat foods with gluten in them. Gluten is found in cereals such as wheat, oat, barley and rye. So everything that was made with flour – for example, ordinary bread or biscuits – was not permitted. This meant a lot of extra work. We had to prepare separate food for her.

Janet: What about the meals on the menu? Do you prepare them as well?

Sarah: No, we don't. We prepare breakfast and the afternoon snack. But as far as lunch is concerned we get it delivered. It is ready-cooked and comes in containers. We only need to distribute it and sometimes help the children eat it. Would you like to see our small kitchen?

Working with the text

A Comprehension
1. What kinds of drinks do they serve in the nursery school? Why?
2. What kinds of food do Muslims not eat?
3. What is the problem with nuts?
4. What is coeliac disease?
5. Do they prepare lunch themselves?

B Which of these things are correct when you plan a meal for children? Why? Why not?
1. Use a lot of fruit and vegetables.
2. You have to respect religious customs.
3. Don't use gluten in your meals.
4. A meal should provide all nutrients.
5. You should offer sugary drinks.
6. You have to pay attention if there are children with allergies.
7. Cook all the meals yourself.
8. Use meat every day.

C Analysing the menu
1. Compare the nursery's menu with the general rules of a weekly diet.
2. Explain which nutrients can be found in this menu. Which foods contain them?

The balance of good health
- 2 to 3 servings of meat or poultry as a main dish a week
- 1 to 2 servings of fish
- 1 to 2 meals containing pulses
- 1 to 2 meals made of grain
- not more than 2 to 3 eggs a week
- 3 to 5 servings of fruit or vegetables a day
- up to 3 servings of milk or yoghurt a day

Unit 10 Food and drink for children

Hands-on tasks

A What drinks are offered to the children at your workplace?
B Most nursery schools have a plan for the food they serve to the children at lunch. Get the plan for one week from your workplace and present it in class.
C Are there children who need a special diet in your nursery school? Report to the class.
D Design a poster to inform parents about good or bad foods for children aged 3 – 5 years.

> For more information on how to create a poster see page 189.

Making meals fun

At school Janet learns about the tasks of a nursery nurse. The following text is in her book:

One of our roles in caring for children may be to introduce them to new foods. Trying out new foods is a learning opportunity for children and may help them to develop tastes for other foods. Mealtimes should be fun and enjoyable. Children are more likely
5 to eat when they feel happy and relaxed.
The way food is served and presented to children is important. We can present food in a variety of ways to help children enjoy mealtimes:
- Cut out food into interesting shapes or small pieces, e.g. cut
10 pizza into stars and triangles, carrots into small sticks.
- Arrange food on plates to make pictures.
- Give food special names, e.g. Jungle Kebab with dip, Funny Face Pizza, Power Sandwich.
- Allow children to serve themselves.
15
When children feel involved, they are more likely to say that they like a new sort of food. Children can help by preparing, cooking or serving the food.

The teacher gave the class the following task:
"Choose a suitable recipe which you can prepare with children in your nursery school. Produce an information sheet to explain the recipe to children and to enable them to do most of the preparing by themselves."
Janet's first thought was to prepare muffins. Children love muffins. It does not take long to bake them and they are not too complicated to prepare. Another aspect is that you don't need many different ingredients, so muffins are not too expensive.
At home she looked up a recipe and suddenly realised: "Children can't read – how am I to explain the recipe to them!?"

Food and drink for children Unit 10

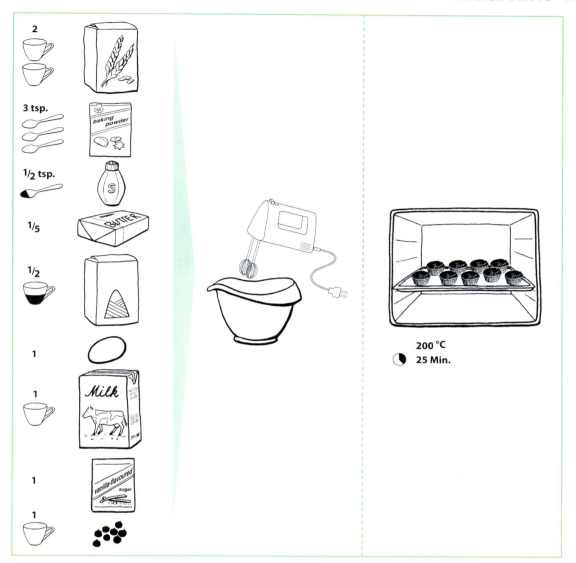

Working with the text

Comprehension
1. Why should mealtimes be fun?
2. How can food be presented in an attractive way to children?
3. What is the reason for letting children help prepare food?
4. What are the important aspects in choosing a suitable recipe for children?

Hands-on task

Production

Imagine it was your task to bake or cook something together with children.
Choose a recipe and explain it to them by using pictures. Why did you choose this recipe?

Unit 10 Food and drink for children

Baking muffins

Janet is at the nursery school. She wants to put into practice what she has planned at school. Three of the children, Lisa, Marie and Matthew, want to help her to bake muffins. Together they look at the poster she created.

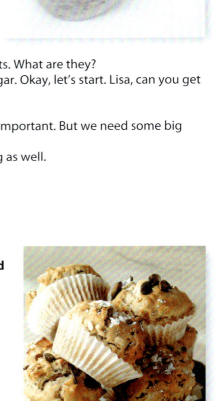

Janet:	Well, what do you see on the poster?
Lisa:	I can see some foods.
Janet:	Yes, they are the ingredients that we need for the muffins. What do we need?
5 Marie:	I can see some milk and some sugar.
Lisa:	Some flour and an egg.
Matthew:	I can't see any chocolate. I want chocolate muffins.
Janet:	Today, we are going to prepare blueberry muffins. Can you see some blueberries in the picture?
Matthew:	Yes, but I don't like blueberries. I want some chocolate flakes.
Lisa:	I like blueberries. I want some blueberry muffins.
Janet:	Do we need any more ingredients?
Marie:	Yes, we need some salt and there are some sachets. What are they?
Janet:	They are baking powder and vanilla-flavoured sugar. Okay, let's start. Lisa, can you get some bowls from the cupboard?
20 Lisa:	Which bowls? The red or the blue ones?
Janet:	You can take any bowl you like. The colour is not important. But we need some big bowls, not the small ones.
Matthew:	Is there anything I can do? I want to do something as well.
Janet:	Yes, you can fetch some aprons …

Working with the text

A Comprehension
Copy the table and list all the expressions with some and any from the text.

some	any
some foods	any chocolate

Interaction

B Finish the conversation between Janet and the children.

108 handwerk-technik.de

Food and drink for children Unit 10

Grammar box: Some and Any

	Man benutzt *some*
I need some milk. *We need some blueberries.*	• mit unzählbaren Nomen wie Butter, Milch, Zucker, Zeit etc. • mit Nomen im Plural
	Man benutzt *any*
Is there any milk left? *We don't have any baking powder.*	• in Fragen • in negativen Aussagesätzen
	Man benutzt *some*
Could you give me some sugar, please? *Would you like some tea?*	• in höflichen Anfragen oder wenn wir etwas anbieten • in Fragen, die vermutlich mit "Ja" beantwortet werden
	Man benutzt *any*
Can you help me to bake some muffins? *You can take any biscuit you like.*	• in positiven Aussagesätzen, wenn es mit der Bedeutung "jeder beliebige" benutzt wird

Grammar box: Zusammengesetzte Wörter mit Some und Any

	Man benutzt *something/anything*
There is something wrong with the oven. *Is there anything I can do?* *There isn't anything I can do.*	• im Sinne von „etwas" in Aussagesätzen • im Sinne von „irgendetwas" in allgemeinen Fragen (falls Antwort „ja" erwartet, dann something) • im Sinne von „nichts" in negativen Aussagesätzen
	Man benutzt *someone/somebody* bzw. *anyone/anybody*
There is someone/somebody at the door. *Is there anyone/anybody you would like to call?* *There isn't anyone/anybody who thinks of me.*	• im Sinne von „jemand" in Aussagesätzen • im Sinne von „jemand" in Fragen • im Sinne von „niemand" in negativen Aussagesätzen
	Man benutzt *somewhere/anywhere*
I would like to be somewhere else. *Is there anywhere you would rather be?* *I can't find the baking powder anywhere.*	• im Sinne von „irgendwo" in Aussagesätzen • im Sinne von „irgendwo" in Fragen • im Sinne von „nirgendwo" in negativen Aussagesätzen

Practising grammar

A Decide whether to use some or any.
1. There's … milk left in that glass.
2. Haven't you got … time for children?
3. I need … strawberries. I want to make jam.
4. Will … fruit be good for making jam?
5. Would you like … cake?
6. She wanted … chocolate but there wasn't … left.
7. Do you have … idea where the mixer is?
8. Are there … recipes that you particularly like?
9. I'm going to buy … eggs.
10. Oh, I can't pay. I haven't got … money.

B Decide whether to use somewhere/anywhere, something/anything, someone/anyone etc.
1. I lost my key. Has … found it?
2. Excuse me, but there's … .in your hair.
3. Do you live … near Liverpool?
4. Healthy food? I don't know … about it.
5. Can't you play … else?
6. I am thirsty, can I have … to drink?
7. I haven't heard … about Janet lately.
8. I would like to be … else.

Unit 10 Food and drink for children

Give them a good start: breakfast

(to) perform [pəˈfɔːm]	hier: leisten, arbeiten
(to) face [feɪs]	ins Auge sehen, konfrontiert werden mit
black pudding [blæk ˈpʊdɪŋ]	Blutwurst
(to) moan [məʊn]	stöhnen
cereals [ˈsɪərɪəlz]	Zerealien, Getreideflocken
crunchy [krʌntʃɪ]	knusprig
morsels [ˈmɔːslz]	Häppchen, Bissen
dodgers [dɒdʒəz]	Drückeberger
(to) gulp [gʌlp]	hinunterschlingen, herunterschlucken

A balanced diet

packaging [ˈpækɪdʒɪŋ]	Verpackung
(to) consist of [kənˈsɪst]	bestehen aus
ingredients [ɪnˈgriːdɪənts]	Zutaten, Inhaltsstoffe
flavouring [ˈfleɪvərɪŋ]	Aroma
balanced diet [ˈbælənst ˈdaɪət]	ausgewogene Kost, ausgewogene Ernährung
nutrients [ˈnjuːtrɪənts]	Nährstoffe
carbohydrates [ˌkɑːbəʊˈhaɪdreɪts]	Kohlenhydrate
(to) provide [prəˈvaɪd]	bereitstellen, versorgen mit

Breast or bottle? The importance of milk

(to) recommend [ˌrekəˈmend]	empfehlen
(to) digest [daɪˈdʒest]	verdauen
pre-pregnancy weight [priː-pregnəntsi weɪt]	Gewicht vor der Schwangerschaft
sore [sɔːr]	wund
according to [əˈkɔːdɪŋ tuː]	gemäß, in Anlehnung an
depending on [dɪˈpendɪŋ ɒn]	abhängig von, je nach...
(to) choke [tʃəʊk]	würgen, ersticken

Planning meals for children

guided tour of the premises [ˈgaɪdɪd tʊə ɒv ðə ˈpremɪsəz]	eine Führung durch die Räumlichkeiten
trolley [ˈtrɒlɪ]	Teewagen, Servierwagen
(to) quench the thirst [kwentʃ ðə θɜːst]	den Durst löschen
(to) dilute [daɪˈljuːt]	verdünnen
mushy peas [ˈmʌʃɪ piːz]	Erbsenpüree / -brei
stew [stjuː]	Eintopf
asterisk [ˈæstərɪsk]	Sternchen
(to) spread [spred]	verteilen, ausbreiten, streuen
customs [ˈkʌstəms]	Sitten, Gebräuche
coeliac disease [ˈsiːlɪæk dɪˈziːz]	Zöliakie; Sprue (med.)
wheat [wiːt]	Weizen
oat [əʊt]	Hafer
barley [ˈbɑːlɪ]	Gerste
rye [raɪ]	Roggen
(to) be permitted [bɪ pəˈmɪtɪd]	erlaubt sein
(to) prepare [prɪˈpeə]	zubereiten
delivered [dɪˈlɪvəd]	angeliefert
ready-cooked [ˈredɪ-kʊkt]	vorgekocht
(to) distribute [dɪˈstrɪbjuːt]	verteilen, verbreiten
poultry [ˈpəʊltrɪ]	Geflügel
pulses [pʌlsɪz]	Hülsenfrüchte

Making meals fun

opportunity [ˌɒpəˈtjuːnəti]	Gelegenheit, Möglichkeit
shapes [ʃeɪps]	Formen
triangles [ˈtraɪæŋglz]	Dreiecke
involved [ɪnˈvɒlvd]	beteiligt, einbezogen
(to) enable [ɪˈneɪbl]	befähigen, aktivieren

Baking muffins

sachet [ˈsæʃeɪ]	Tütchen
apron [ˈeɪprən]	Schürze

Unit 11 — Family problems

Sometimes people have got a problem which they think they cannot solve alone or which they don't want to talk over with someone in the family. Some people write a letter to the "agony aunt" of a newspaper or magazine and hope to receive an answer. Here is part of a letter which Claire from Glasgow wrote because she feels very upset and wants some good advice.

> Dear Meg,
>
> My husband and I have been married for 10 years now. I am 35 and my husband is 37. We are parents of three lovely children: seven, four and three years old. I love my children very dearly and I would do anything for them. I really want them to be happy and for us all to live together in harmony – but now I don't know what to do.
> I am afraid that I may have to do something which will destroy our family life. I'm desperate and think my life is falling apart. 10 years ago I met my husband and we fell in love. We married and raised a family. Our life was normal and happy but now everything has changed ...

What information can you get about Claire's family situation so far?

How does Claire feel?
Can you imagine what kind of problem the family might have?
What might the end of the letter look like? Finish the letter and compare it with your classmates' letters.

Unit 11 Family problems

Searching for help – letters to the agony aunt

Dear Meg

Every week the column with a heart

This is how Claire's letter continues:

… After 10 years I feel that we are drifting apart. There are lots of quarrels between my husband and me. I feel that he can't understand my feelings and interests and sometimes I can't stand his behaviour. We have an argument nearly every day! At first I tried to hide everything from the children – but now we even shout at each other in front of them. My husband can get so furious sometimes. Our children are suffering because of the situation. Our son Mike has developed some learning problems in school. Anne's nursery nurse told me that our daughter has become very withdrawn and timid in nursery school and that our smallest daughter Jean cries a lot, even if nothing serious has happened.
We can only keep the peace if we keep out of each other's way.
But I don't want my married life to be like this. I think our life has become a misery. Sometimes I believe that divorce is the only solution to our problems but then I also feel that I can't live without my husband. What can I do?

Meg says:
Your husband is certainly as unhappy and confused as you are. He shouts at you, doesn't he? This shows that he is desperate himself. Husband and wife sometimes have these conflicts. Don't worry, they can be solved.
When things are peaceful, try to talk to him calmly. Try to explain how you are feeling and try to find out why his behaviour has changed. You must alter the situation because your children are suffering.
But if you feel that your love for your husband has totally gone, you should think of divorce because you can't go on quarrelling in front of your children forever! A tense atmosphere like this is more harmful for your children than divorce. Your children are old enough to understand what is going on and if you gently explain to them what is happening, they will be able to understand.

Do you have a problem? Write to dear Meg:
Daily News, PO Box 84, 1 Liverpool Street, London E 1 SBZ or
e-mail letters@daily-news.co.uk

Family problems Unit 11

Working with the text

A How does Claire's letter end?
Here are some false statements about what Claire wrote.
Can you correct them?
1. They had their first problems shortly after their wedding.
2. They have some quarrels now and then.
3. So far they have been able to hide their disturbed relationship from the children and lead a happy family life with them.
4. Her husband's quarrelling and behaviour never go too far.
5. Their quarrelling does not have any impact on the children.
6. Claire does not want a divorce because she believes that keeping the family together comes first.
7. Claire feels that her love for her husband has totally gone.

B Below you find a summary of Claire's letter. Fill in the missing words.

hide
understanding
agony aunt
misery
marriage
divorce
husband
desperate
interests
quarrels
suffering

Claire writes a letter to the (1)… because she is having some problems with her (2)… . After ten years of (3)… she feels that her husband has no (4)… of her feelings and (5)… . They have lots of (6)… which they cannot (7)… from the children any more. As the children seem to be (8)… because of the family situation, Claire believes that their life is a (9)… . She has even thought of (10)… as a solution to the problem. But she is also (11) … because she thinks she cannot live without her husband.

C Have a closer look at the family's problem and answer the following questions.
1. What kind of feelings and worries does Claire have? Describe them.
2. What influence does the situation have on the children?
3. How would you describe Claire's feelings and attitude towards divorce?
4. What does Meg think of divorce? What else does she suggest doing?
5. What would you advise Claire to do? Give reasons for your suggestions.

Unit 11 Family problems

Aggression in the family

Here are two more letters to the agony aunt, both telling of disturbed family situations.

Aggressive father and husband

Dear Meg,
I'm married to a dictator.
My husband wasn't like this when we met 14 years ago but now he's destroying
5 our family. I am a 40-year-old with twin daughters. We were a happy family and my husband was a loving father till last year. When he was made redundant his behaviour changed. Now it's getting worse. He has
10 become very aggressive and rude towards all three of us. He doesn't use physical violence, but he bullies us. He shouts over almost nothing and his language is foul and abusive. My two children often feel deeply
15 embarrassed and intimidated. And it hurts me to see my 5-year-olds suffering. If I say something, he forbids me to open my mouth until he's in a good mood again.
Most of the day he sits in front of the
20 television and drinks lots of beer. When he has had too much it's terrible for us. The stress is making me ill but I have to be strong for the kids. How can I change our situation?

Rosalind from Stafford

A boy at a defiant age

25 Dear Meg,
Our 5-year-old son Mike has become a major problem for us. His aggressive behavior puts a strain on all of us. If I call him in for supper, when he is
30 playing outside, he shouts and storms at me. We have terrible rows and he is really abusive, swearing and kicking out in anger at me – although he does not really make contact. These situations
35 have become the norm. First we thought it was just a defiant phase but lately it has become worse. Since his little sister was born six months ago he has had some kind of aggressive outburst
40 almost daily. If I say "No" to him, he goes mad. He can't control his temper. Once he even hit his little sister.
What's the matter? Is he just nervous or hyperactive? Might there be a vitamin
45 deficiency in his diet?

Susanna from Oxford

Family problems Unit 11

Working with the text

A Briefly sum up the main problem of each letter in just one sentence.
Use the following sentence pattern:

> The first / second letter deals with a husband / a boy … who …

B Now have a closer look at the letters and say whether these statements are true or false. Correct the false statements.
1. Rosalind's husband has always been a very dominant person who behaves aggressively towards his children.
2. Her husband's behaviour changed when he lost his job.
3. Sometimes it even gets to the point where he uses physical violence.
4. Her husband's constant outbursts have a bad impact on the children.
5. Rosalind has had some serious and intensive discussions about the problem with her husband.
6. Her husband spends his days doing useful things.
7. Mike only abuses his mother verbally.
8. His attacks are only directed at his mother, never at anyone else.
9. His aggressive attacks increased when his little sister was born.

C Answer the following questions on the letters.
1. How did the behaviour of Rosalind's husband change? Describe it.
2. How do Rosalind and her children suffer from her husband's aggressive behaviour?
3. What could be the reason for his aggression?
4. How does the boy Mike behave towards his mother?
5. Why might Mike behave in this aggressive way? Try to think of reasons.

Hands-on task   `Mediation`

Translate the following sentences into English.
1. Es gibt immer Konflikte in der Familie.
2. Manchmal können Eltern einen Streit nicht vor den Kindern verbergen.
3. Eltern machen sich Sorgen um ihre Kinder.
4. Leute, die einer Kummerkastentante schreiben, hoffen eine Lösung für ihre Probleme zu finden.
5. Kinder leiden unter einer angespannten Atmosphäre.

Unit 11 Family problems

Hands-on tasks

A Do you think it's a good idea to write a letter to the agony aunt? Or should people look for help elsewhere? Discuss your attitude towards letters to agony aunts.

Interaction

If you need help, look at the useful phrases in the box below.

In my opinion one should / shouldn't …	Meiner Meinung nach sollte jemand / sollte jemand nicht ….
To my mind it's a problem / it's not a problem to …	Meiner Meinung nach ist es ein Problem / kein Problem …
I don't see a problem in … because …	Ich sehe kein Problem darin …, weil …
I think it is understandable that … because …	Ich denke es ist verständlich, dass …, weil …
In his / her place I would also … / I would prefer to … because …	An seiner / ihrer Stelle würde ich auch … / würde ich es bevorzugen …, weil …
I would never … because …	Ich würde niemals …, weil …
It is always bad to … because …	Es ist immer schlecht zu …, weil …
It's not bad to … because …	Es ist nicht schlecht zu …, weil …

B Take over Meg's role and answer one of the letters.

Production

Again there are useful phrases in the box below.

I advise you to …	Ich rate Ihnen …
Before you … (do something)	Bevor Sie …
That depends on …	Das kommt darauf an …
I don't think you should …	Ich denke, Sie sollten nicht …
You should discuss your problems / doubts with …	Sie sollten Ihre Probleme / Zweifel mit … diskutieren …
If you feel … you will have to …	Wenn Sie fühlen, dass …, dann müssen Sie …
This is for you to decide …	Das müssen Sie entscheiden …
It is obvious that …	Es ist offensichtlich, dass …
It might be better if you … (+ Simple Past)	Es könnte besser sein, wenn …
The right thing to do is ….	Das Richtige zu tun, ist …
Don't hesitate to …	Zögern Sie nicht …
Take the first step and …	Machen Sie den ersten Schritt und …
It is always better to …	Es ist immer besser zu …
In any case, why don't you …	In jedem Fall, warum … Sie nicht …
What are you waiting for?	Worauf warten Sie?
Now the time has come to …	Jetzt ist die Zeit gekommen, um …

Family problems Unit 11

Grammar box: **The Passive** – Das Passiv

Aktiv

My family	supports	me. (Present Tense)	Meine Familie unterstützt mich.
My family	supported	me. (Past Tense)	Meine Familie unterstützte mich.
Subjekt	Verb	Objekt	

Passiv

I	am supported	by my family. (Present Tense)	Ich werde von meiner Familie unterstützt.
I	was supported	by my family. (Past Tense)	Ich wurde von meiner Familie unterstützt.
Subjekt	Verb	Objekt	

Aktiv	Passiv
He **intimidates** the children.	The children **are intimidated**.
He **intimidated** the children.	The children **were intimidated**.
Claire **leaves** John.	John **is left** by Claire.
Claire **left** John.	John **was left** by Claire.

- **Bildung:** am / is / are + 3. Verbform → Passiv in Present Tense
  was / were + 3. Verbform → Passiv in Past Tense

- **Beachte:** Am Ende des Satzes kann das Subjekt mit der Präposition *by* (= by-agent) angehängt werden. Dieser "by-agent" wird jedoch nur genannt, wenn dies für den Satz Bedeutung hat. *This letter was written **by** Claire.*

Practising grammar

Change these active sentences into passive sentences.
Decide whether you add a by-agent or not.

  Example: Susanna wrote **a letter to the agony aunt** yesterday morning.
      A letter to the agony aunt was written by Susanna yesterday morning.
1. Claire told **John** that she wanted to leave him.
2. Mike even hits **his little sister**.
3. Her husband opens **all of her letters.**
4. Rosalind thinks that her husband's aggressive behaviour destroys **their family**.
5. Rosalind's husband bullies **the children**.
6. Meg gives **Claire** some good advice.
7. They publish **Meg's advice column** every day.
8. Mainly women write **letters to the agony aunt**.
9. She asked **her mother** for help.
10. People ask **Meg** a lot of questions.

Unit 11 Family problems

A child suffers

A Read the info on child abuse and make sure you understand what the different forms of child abuse are. You can work with a partner and / or use a dictionary for help.

B Look at these different cases and find out what kind of abuse these children suffer from. Give reasons for your opinion. Find sentences which describe each type of abuse.

Case 1: He comes to her during the night when everyone is asleep. He walks carefully and slowly but his footsteps wake her up before he lies down on the bed beside her. "It's just a game," he says. "It's our secret, don't tell anybody about it."

Case 2: "Mummy says she has to work because Dad left us. Jimmy and I are alone when she's at work. We play or watch TV and try not to be too loud because of the neighbours. Sometimes I'm hungry and thirsty. Jimmy cries a lot. He's always very frightened when Mummy doesn't come home at night and we have to stay on our own."

Case 3: "It's not Dad's fault, it's my own fault. I'm just too clumsy. I'm always doing something wrong, dropping things or getting in his way. Things like that put him in a rage."

Case 4: "No one hits me. It's something else. I can't really explain why I feel so sad. At home it's difficult sometimes and school is hell. Everyone is constantly picking on me; Mum, Dad, my elder brother and sister and my classmates as well, telling me to shut up and calling me a moron, an idiot … things like that."

What is child abuse?

The word refers to any kind of mistreatment a child or teenager has to suffer. Most often the child is mistreated by a grown-up person such as a parent, an aunt or uncle, another relative, a neighbour or sports trainer.
Sometimes the person is not much older but stronger, for example a classmate, brother or sister who bullies a younger one.
These examples show that abuse can affect any child.
But there is one thing which is very typical about sexual abuse. The child is usually abused by a person he or she depends on or at first trusted. It can be a parent or a relative but also a friend of the family or neighbour who at first seems to show some interest in the child's life and problems. In reality this person is only interested in his or her own abnormal needs.
There are different forms of child abuse and quite often a child has to endure more than just one. The following list summarises each type:

Physical abuse
- Hitting a child in such a way that the child is injured

Sexual abuse
- Misusing a child as a sexual partner

Neglect
- Not giving a child what he or she needs (for example food and clothes)
- Leaving a child on his / her own

Emotional abuse
- Bullying and intimidating a child verbally
- Denying a child affection

Family problems Unit 11

Why didn't we react?

Janet and Susan, who are working at the "Rainbow Nursery School", are outside with their group of children. Something has happened to Raymond, a child in Janet's group. Read the dialogue and find out what happened to him.

Janet: Did you hear about Raymond?
Susan: Yes, Helen told me about him yesterday. It's a great shock, isn't it? Do you know any more details?
Janet: Well, yes and no. He's in hospital and his left arm is fractured. Neighbours must have heard some kind of row going on. Finally someone called the police. That's what his mother told me in tears on the phone. But she wasn't very clear about what had actually happened. She just told me it was some kind of accident and that his father hadn't really meant to hurt him.
Susan: Do you really believe it was just an accident?
Janet: No, not any more. I can't get Raymond's face out of my mind. He's always been a very timid boy. Now it's quite obvious what was going on. The first thing I noticed was that he always wore a long-sleeved sweater with a long-sleeved shirt even on hot days. Once I wanted him to take them off because they were soaked with sweat. But he didn't really want to and then when I lifted his sweater I saw some bruises on his back. The same day I asked his mother how he got them. 'Well,' she said, 'he's a bit clumsy. He fell off a chair.'
Susan: And was there anything else?
Janet: Yes, but I wasn't really sure about what was going on. One day I saw that he had some bruises just as if someone had grabbed him around his wrists. But when I asked his mother again she said, 'Just a little fight with his older and stronger brother. You know how boys are, don't you?'
Susan: What did you do then?
Janet: I told Helen about it and we decided to keep a closer eye on Raymond. We noticed that he was becoming more and more timid. He often tried to keep his distance from the group and he didn't speak a lot. Once we sat in a circle and I asked the children to tell us about how they had spent their last Sunday in the family. At first he didn't want to tell us anything at all. Then he started stammering.
Susan: How did the other children react?
Janet: They began laughing at him but I was able to make them stop. It was a difficult situation.
Susan: Didn't they include him in their games?
Janet: Let's just say the other children did not really like playing with him. Quite often Raymond sat at the table all alone. I think the children found him no fun to play with. He started crying very easily and was always afraid of doing something wrong. He kept on asking me, 'Can I do that?' 'Is that all right?'
Susan: Those seem to be quite clear signs, don't you think?
Janet: Yes, everything was becoming very obvious. We had some serious discussions with his mother but she always gave us some kind of explanation. And we didn't find any more bruises so we thought perhaps there really was nothing going on. Now everything has become very clear. I can't understand why we didn't react.

Unit 11 Family problems

Working with the text

When Raymond came into the nursery school with bruises on his back and wrists Helen, the head of the nursery school, and Janet decided to make notes on Raymond's data sheet about everything important they had noticed.

A Only the first entry is a full sentence. Transform the keywords on the data sheet into full sentences and complete the entries.

B Write down the missing entry from May 11th.

Rainbow Nursery School

Surname: Johnson
First name: Raymond
Date of birth: January 11th, 20..
Parents: Mary and Jonathan Johnson
Address: 3 Oak Lane, Liverpool
Other family members: one older brother, 7 years old
Commencement: March 1st, 20..

Special notes:

March 15th 20..	Raymond has got some bruises on his back. His mother says he fell off a chair.
April 1st 20..	bruises – wrists – mother – say – fight with brother –
April 8th 20..	all children sit in circle with other children – talk about Sunday family activity – first Raymond not speak – then start stammering
May 2nd 20..	Raymond – start crying – several times – during play
May 7th 20..	Raymond – be afraid of doing something wrong – keep on asking … ?
May 11th 20..	…

Family problems Unit 11

C Match the first and second parts of the sentences according to the text.
1. Janet received information …
2. Raymond's left arm is fractured … c
3. Because of the trouble going on in Raymond's home … d
4. Raymond's mother told Janet on the phone … a
5. Janet began to disbelieve the mother's explanations … h
6. Raymond was very timid and cried a lot … b
7. It was very strange …f
8. Janet was first concerned that there was something going on …
9. Janet was unable to find out about Raymond's homelife … j
10. Now Janet feels ashamed … e
    a) … that it was just bad luck, as his father did not mean to hurt him. 4
    b) … and for those reasons the other children didn't often play with him. 6
    c) … and Janet believes it happened because his father beat him. 2
    d) … a neighbour called the police. 3
    e) … because she didn't react. 10
    f) … that Raymond always wore a long-sleeved sweater with a long-sleeved T-shirt. 7
    g) … that something serious had happened to Raymond. 1
    h) … because she had noticed bruises on Raymond's back and wrists before. 5
    i) … when she saw bruises on Raymond's back. 8
    j) … because he didn't want to talk about it and started stammering. 9

D Answer the following questions.
1. Why do some people not react even if it is quite clear that a child has been mistreated? Can you think of reasons?
2. Why do parents beat their children? What could be reasons?

Hands-on task

Production

After what happened to Raymond, Helen and Janet discuss his case with their colleagues to decide on procedures for future cases. Sit in small groups and take over Janet's role. Then prepare a poster with typical "warning signals" for child abuse. Present your poster in class for discussion.

For information how to create a poster look at page 189.

Unit 11 Family problems

(to) solve (a problem) ['sʌlv (ə 'prɒbləm)]	(ein Problem) lösen
solution [sə'lu:ʃn]	Lösung, Problemlösung
agony aunt ['ægənɪ ɑ:nt]	Kummerkastentante
advice; (to) advise [əd'vaɪs, əd'vaɪz]	Ratschlag; raten
(to) destroy [dɪ'strɔɪ]	zerstören
(to) be desperate ['despərət]	verzweifelt sein
(to) fall apart [fɔ:l ə'pɑ:t]	auseinander fallen
(to) raise a family [reɪz ə 'fæməlɪ]	eine Familie gründen, ernähren
(to) compare [kəm'peə]	vergleichen

Searching for help – letters to the agony aunt

(to) drift apart [drɪft ə'pɑ:t]	sich auseinander bewegen
(to) stand s.th. [stænd]	etwas ertragen
behaviour; (to) behave [bɪ'heɪvjə, bɪ'heɪv]	Verhalten; sich verhalten
argument ['ɑ:gjʊmənt]	hier: Streitgespräch
furious ['fjʊərɪəs]	(sehr) wütend
(to) suffer ['sʌfə]	leiden (to suffer from a disease = an einer Krankheit leiden)
withdrawn [wɪð'drɔ:n]	zurückgezogen
timid ['tɪmɪd]	ängstlich, verängstigt
serious ['sɪərɪəs]	ernst, ernsthaft
peaceful [pi:sfʊl]	friedlich
married life ['mærɪd laɪf]	Eheleben
confused [kən'fju:zd]	verwirrt
(to) worry ['wʌrɪ]	sich Sorgen machen
calm [kɑ:m]	ruhig
(to) alter ['ɔ:ltə]	verändern
totally ['təʊtəlɪ]	völlig, ganz und gar
tense atmosphere [tens 'ætməsfɪə]	angespannte Atmosphäre
(to) quarrel ['kwɒrəl]	streiten
gently ['dʒentlɪ]	hier: vorsichtig, sanft
disturbed relationship [dɪ'stɜ:bd rɪ'leɪʃnʃɪp]	gestörte Beziehung
attitude towards ['ætɪtju:d tə'wɔ:dz]	Einstellung zu
(to) suggest [sə'dʒest]	vorschlagen
suggestion [sə'dʒestʃn]	Vorschlag

Aggression in the family

twins [twɪnz]	Zwillinge
(to) be made redundant [bɪ meɪd rɪ'dʌndənt]	gekündigt werden
rude [ru:d]	unhöflich, grob
(to) hit [hɪt]	schlagen
physical violence ['fɪzɪkl 'vaɪələns]	körperliche Gewalt
(to) bully ['bʊlɪ]	jmd. tyrannisieren
foul [faʊl]	hier: unflätig
abusive [ə'bju:sɪv]	beleidigend
(to) intimidate s.o. [ɪn'tɪmɪdeɪt]	jmd. einschüchtern
nevertheless ['nevəðəles]	trotzdem, dennoch
row [raʊ]	Streit
(to) abuse [ə'bju:z] verbally ['vɜ:bəlɪ]	hier: beleidigen
(to) swear [sweə]	fluchen
norm [nɔ:m]	Normalität, Regel
outburst [aʊtbɜ:st]	Ausbruch
temper ['tempə]	Wesen, Naturell, hier: Wut
deficiency [dɪ'fɪʃnsɪ]	Defizit, Mangel
(to) have an impact on [hæv æn 'ɪmpækt ɒn]	einen Einfluss haben auf
elsewhere ['elsweə]	woanders

A child suffers

child abuse [tʃaɪld ə'bju:z]	Kindesmissbrauch
mistreatment [mɪ'stri:tmənt]	Misshandlung
(to) be abused [bɪ ə'bju:zd]	missbraucht werden
(to) be mistreated [mɪ'stri:tɪd]	missbraucht, misshandelt
case [keɪs]	Fall
secret ['si:krɪt]	Geheimnis
(to) be frightened [bɪ fraɪtnd]	ängstlich sein
fault [fɔ:lt]	Fehler
clumsy ['klʌmzɪ]	ungeschickt
rage [reɪdʒ]	Zorn
(to) pick on s.o. [pɪk ɒn]	herumhacken auf jmd.
moron ['mɔ:rɒn]	(Umgangssprache) Schwachkopf, Depp
(to) depend on [dɪ'pend ɒn]	abhängig sein von
(to) trust in [trʌst ɪn]	vertrauen in
abnormal needs [æb'nɔ:ml ni:dz]	abnormale Bedürfnisse
(to) endure [ɪn'djʊə]	ertragen, erleiden
(to) injure ['ɪndʒə]	körperlich verletzen

Child abuse

physical abuse ['fɪzɪkl ə'bju:z]	körperliche Misshandlung
sexual abuse ['seksjʊəl ə'bju:z]	sexueller Missbrauch
neglect [nɪ'glekt]	Vernachlässigung
emotional abuse [ɪ'məʊʃənl ə'bju:z]	emotionaler Missbrauch
denying s.o. affection [dɪ'naɪŋ ə'fekʃn]	jemandem Zuneigung verweigern

Why didn't we react?

fractured ['fræktʃəd]	gebrochen
actually ['æktʃʊəlɪ]	eigentlich, tatsächlich
it's obvious [ɪts 'ɒbvɪəs]	es ist offensichtlich
long-sleeved [lɒŋ-sli:vd]	langärmelig
soaked with sweat [səʊkd wɪð swet]	triefend vor Schweiß
bruises [bru:zɪz]	blaue Flecke
(to) grab around [græb ə'raʊnd]	umgreifen
wrists [rɪsts]	Handgelenke
(to) stammer ['stæmə]	stottern, stammeln
data sheet ['deɪtə ʃi:t]	Datenblatt, Karteikarte
entry ['entrɪ]	Eintrag
ashamed [ə'ʃeɪmd]	beschämt

Unit 12 — Children with special needs

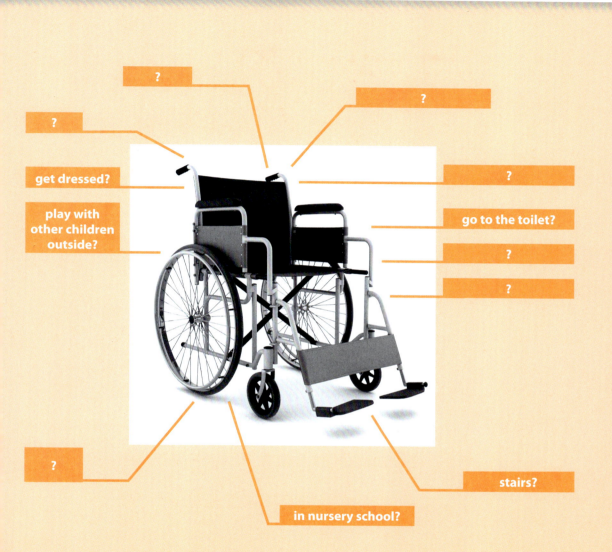

- get dressed?
- play with other children outside?
- go to the toilet?
- stairs?
- in nursery school?

This is Andrew's wheelchair

Andrew is five years old and because of a birth defect he is a bit different. He suffers from cerebral palsy and has to sit in a wheelchair. Because of brain damage he has intellectual and language difficulties.
Andrew is a child with special needs.
What could be a problem for him?

Unit 12 Children with special needs

Andrew McArthur – a child with special needs

Katherine McArthur is Andrew's mother. Andrew, who suffers from a physical and mental disability, attends an integrated nursery school class at Windham Integrated Nursery School in Manchester. Katherine, who is the chairman of the Manchester Needy Child Fund, helps other parents to cope with their child's special needs. She recommends that parents send their children to integrated nursery school classes. She also wants to raise money for these classes. In an interview she explains why.

Reporter: Mrs McArthur, in the brochure of the Needy Child Fund you say that it's normal to be different and that you don't accept the word disability.

Katherine: Yes, I don't think of my child Andrew as disabled. He is just different. He has special needs but he's a normal person with his own personality. Everyone has got their own personality and this is his. He may sit in a wheelchair and perhaps his ability to take things in may be limited but he has a wonderful smile and a terrific sense of humour.

Reporter: But it's difficult to believe that you can lead a normal life with Andrew.

Katherine: I feel that we lead a very, very normal life. You get used to the situation. When you meet other people they often say, 'What a burden! How can you bear it?' But our life is as normal as any other life. Of course we had to adapt our household to Andrew's special needs. The fact that he is sitting in a wheelchair is just one of many things which may cause a problem. But we have our daily routines. Andrew needs special care and attention but this has become very normal for us.

Reporter: Quite often people don't know how to treat someone with special needs or they have problems speaking to or even being with a disabled person.

Katherine: Yes, that's a pity. Sometimes people stare at Andrew – most often grown-ups. Children just look at him and ask why he is sitting in a wheelchair. It's not disgust they feel, but real interest. I tell them openly about Andrew. When they know everything about his special needs they treat him like any other child. That's how I would like everyone to react. Openness is the best for all of us!

Reporter: Has Andrew got a sister or a brother? How do they cope with his special needs?

Katherine: Andrew's sister is two years older. Well, sometimes there were moments when she complained and said: "It's not fair! Why always Andrew first?" But it's wonderful to see her together with Andrew. She fully accepts him as her brother and she loves him dearly.

Reporter: Is this the reason why you support integrated nursery school classes?

Katherine: Yes, absolutely! Andrew attends an integrated class at Windham Integrated Nursery School. The experience there is positive and enriching. Such groups teach the children to accept other people as they are. It's always a real pleasure watching the children playing together. For this reason I want the Needy Child Fund to support integrated nursery schooling.

Children with special needs Unit 12

Working with the text

A Answer the following questions on the text.
1. Katherine says her son isn't disabled. How does she describe his situation?
2. Why does she feel that her family leads a very normal life?
3. How do people – grown-ups and children – react to Andrew?
4. How does Andrew's sister cope with his special needs?
5. What is an integrated nursery school class?
6. Why does Katherine want to support this kind of schooling?

B Find phrases in the text which mean the same as the following phrases.
1. Andrew can't move and he has an intellectual deficit.
2. Andrew lives with a disability.
3. They had to change their household so that Andrew can live in it with all his disabilities.
4. Some people don't know how to behave towards someone who is disabled.

C Now it's your turn. Explain in your own words what Katherine wanted to express with the following phrases.
1. Andrew is a normal person with his own personality. (line 17 / 18)
2. It isn't disgust they feel, but real interest. (line 35 / 36)
3. Openness is the best for all of us. (line 38)

Hands-on task   Interaction

Katherine talks about adapting their home to Andrew's special needs. What kind of adaption could this be? How do you have to change a normal household so that Andrew can live in it? Sit in groups and work out your adaptation plan for his home. Present your suggestions in class.

Here are some keywords which might help:

(to) alter / design s.th. to fit the needs of the disabled	behindertengerecht umbauen / umgestalten
(to) equip with	ausstatten mit
adapted to the needs of the disabled	behindertengerecht
sanitary facilities	Sanitäranlagen
accessible for wheelchairs	rollstuhlgerecht
ramp, wheelchair ramp	Rollstuhlrampe
liftAufzug	
sick-bed	Krankenbett
invalid chair	Krankenstuhl
invalid toilet seat (raised toilet seat)	Krankentoilettensitz
automatic opening / close	automatisches Öffnen / Schließen
(to) remove obstacles	Hindernisse aus dem Weg schaffen

Windham Integrated Nursery School

Windham Integrated Nursery School is situated on the outskirts of Manchester. Our school building dates from 1910 and is a building of great warmth and character which has been modernised, extended and improved over time.

We believe that all children should be treated with respect and openness. All of them should be supported according to their different personalities and different needs. Children are just not the same – but they should have the same opportunities. For this reason we support integrated nursery classes, which are best examples of our central idea: **inclusion.** This means that we welcome all children, able-bodied as well as children with a special need.

The majority of our children (around 60 %) are children with special needs. The nursery is staffed with nursery nurses who are especially trained for children with special needs and who are supported by health professionals such as occupational therapists, speech therapists and physiotherapists.

At Windham Integrated Nursery School your child will find every help and support to develop physically and intellectually. We want your child to build up all the skills he or she needs to become more independent and to enjoy life.

For this reason we offer your child ...

■ **a safe and well-equipped surrounding**

The integrated nursery school consists of three separate classes but our classrooms are semi-open which means that the classes share a central area in the building.
The outside play area is well-equipped and attractive. We always take special care that every area and playing equipment meets the special needs of our children and that everything is safe. For example, you will find a special climbing apparatus for children with special needs and all kinds of special equipment that support physical activity. Our play area is especially designed to develop imaginative and mental skills.

■ **a young team of professional health workers**

Our staff is well-trained and can give your child all the health care according to his or her needs.

■ **close contact with all our health workers**

We provide parents with all the information and support they need. For this reason we have an advisory team that every parent can consult at any time.

■ **close contact with other parents**

Much of the information that will be helpful to you is in the hands and heads of other parents like yourself. For this reason we organise parents groups which you can join.

■ **small classes**

Our classes are limited in number because we think that every child needs intensive care and attention.

Children with special needs Unit 12

Hands-on task

The topic "children with special needs" aroused your interest.
Surfing the Internet you found Windham's homepage.
Give a short summary of its main ideas in German to inform your colleagues about it.

Working with the text

A Here is what one parent heard about Windham Integrated Nursery School by hearsay. All of these statements are wrong.
Correct them.
1. Windham only offers places to children with special needs.
2. The school mainly concentrates on children who suffer from cerebral palsy.
3. Windham classes are of normal size – just like in any other nursery school.
4. The school building is equipped with the usual nursery school equipment.
5. The nursery school has separate classrooms for every group and an outside play area.

> **Inclusion – what is it?**
> The principle of inclusion in childcare means that all children attend and benefit from the same childcare programme. Nursery schools working with this idea make sure that no one is excluded because of their special needs. The idea behind all this is friendship, non-discrimination and participation of all children. Inclusion means to establish a childcare system without any kind of exclusion. Diversity is seen as a chance for everyone to gain valuable experience.

B There are also some parents who read Windham's brochure but still can't understand some of its expressions. Explain in your own words what the following phrases mean.
1. line 8: All children "should be supported according to their different personalities and different needs"
2. line 42/43: The "playing equipment meets the special needs of (the) children"
3. line 61: "advisory team"
4. line 65/66: Much of the helpful information is "in the hands and heads of other parents"

C Some parents wonder about Windham's central idea. Looking at the info box above, try to explain in your own words what the word inclusion means and how Windham tries to make it work. Have a look at the vocabulary and translate the info box "Inclusion" first to make sure you understood its meaning.

Information on the topic

birth defect	Geburtsfehler	hearing loss	Gehörverlust
paralysis	Lähmung	hearing impairment	Gehörstörung
(to) be paralysed	gelähmt sein	(to) be deaf	taub sein
malfunction	Fehlbildung	visual loss	Sehverlust
malfunction, deformation	Missbildung	visual impairment	Sehstörung
cerebral palsy	spastische Lähmung	speech/language impairment	Sprachfehler
brain damage	Gehirnschaden	cleft palate	Gaumenspalte
Down Syndrome	Down-Syndrom	autism	Autismus
dyspraxia	Motorikstörung		

127

Unit 12 Children with special needs

Windham regularly opens its doors for those parents who want to apply for a place for their child but who are still unsure.
Here is what Mrs Betty Palmer, head of Windham, tells one of the parents on their tour of the house.

Mr Hornby: "My son Robin has to sit in a wheelchair. What problems will there be for him in your nursery school? Very often when we take him out to visit public places he can't get inside because no one had thought about the needs of paralysed people."

Mrs Palmer: "Don't worry, Mr Hornby, I can reassure you that our school is perfectly adapted to the needs of your child. Every room can be reached by wheelchair. We have wheelchair ramps and a lift. So I'm sure there won't be any problems for Robin. You will see in a minute."

Mr Hornby: "Glad to hear that. There is something else I would like to know …"

Hands-on task

Production

Here are some more questions parents asked on that tour.
Now take over Mrs Palmer's role and try to answer them on the basis of what you learnt from the brochure.
Choose one parent's question and write down your advice in detail.

Tom Miller

"Our son Michael was born with a cleft palate and for this reason he has communication difficulties.
Will there be opportunities for him to improve his language skills?"

Mary Taylor

"John suffers from dyspraxia and he needs professional physical exercise.
Do you have trained people who can take special care of children like John?"

James Scott

"Six months ago our daughter Sheila had a serious accident.
Now she is paralysed and has to sit in a wheelchair.
The situation is new to us and of course very hard. I think we mostly need good advice because sometimes the whole situation is too much for us. Do you offer consultation hours or possibilities to exchange experience with other parents?"

Roberta Major

"I'm a bit worried. Our son Lucas suffers from a birth defect and he has physical and mental difficulties.
We know from our situation at home that he needs a lot of attention.
How can you make sure he receives the attention and care he needs?"

Children with special needs Unit 12

Grammar box: Who – which – that

Andrew, **who** suffers from cerebral palsy, visits one of the integrated nursery school classes at Windham.	**Who** → für Personen • im nicht notwendigen Relativsatz (= nach who steht eine Zusatzinformationen, die für das Verständnis des Hauptsatzes entbehrlich ist) • Der who-Satz wird durch Komma abgetrennt.
The majority of the children at Windham, **which** was established in 1910, are children with special needs.	**Which** → für Gegenstände • im nicht notwendigen Relativsatz (s. o.) • Der which-Satz wird durch Komma abgetrennt.
This is the woman **who / that** works as a physiotherapist.	**Who / that** → für Personen • im notwendigen Relativsatz (= nach who steht eine Information, die für das Verständnis des Satzes unentbehrlich ist) • Der who-Satz wird <u>nicht</u> durch Komma abgetrennt.
This is the nursery school **which / that** offers integrated nursery school classes.	**Which / that** → für Gegenstände • im notwendigen Relativsatz (s. o.) • Der which-Satz wird <u>nicht</u> durch Komma abgetrennt.

Practising grammar

Here is Mrs Palmer on her tour of the house with some parents. Fill in *who* or *which*.

Mrs Palmer: I'd like to welcome you here in our entrance hall (1)… dates from 1910. As you can see there is a wheelchair ramp (2)… makes it possible for those children (3)… can't walk to get around the whole building. There are also some lifts (4)… are at the back of the hall.
Parent A: Is it possible to see the classroom (5)… my daughter is going to be based in soon?
Parent B: Yes, I'd also like to see my son's classroom and I'd like to meet the nursery nurse (6)… will be in charge of his group.
Mrs Palmer: No problem, we will arrange everything for you. Perhaps we could do a tour of the house first and see our outside play area (7)… is also very interesting because there you will find some equipment (8)… is especially designed for children with special needs. That way you will see everything. And then you will have the opportunity to meet the whole staff team and speak to everyone (9)… is of interest to you.
Parent C: Is it true that you are the only nursery school (10)… offers integrated nursery school classes here in Manchester?
Mrs Palmer: Yes, that's true. And I don't want to show off but you won't find another nursery school in Manchester (11)… is as well-equipped and as well-staffed as ours. Everyone (12)… works for us is especially trained to give your child the best health care he or she needs.
Parent D: What do we have to do to apply for a place at your nursery school?
Mrs Palmer: Well, that's a very complicated question (13)… I would like to answer later. First of all, let's go on our tour of the house (14)… you will surely enjoy.

Unit 12 Children with special needs

Choosing toys for children with special needs

Look at the following text and fill in *which* or *who*.

Much of the nursery school equipment can be used by both children (1)… suffer from special needs and those (2)… are able-bodied. Sometimes things must be adapted to allow children with special needs to join in with play. A child (3)… has difficulties gripping objects can be offered a sponge for a ball play. A sponge is very light and easy to hold. A child (4)… suffers from visual impairment may need a bell inside a ball in order to be able to catch it. It's always important to provide children, especially those with special needs, with a wide range of objects (5)… help to develop their sensory experience.
These examples show that it takes time and careful consideration to choose a toy for a special needs child.

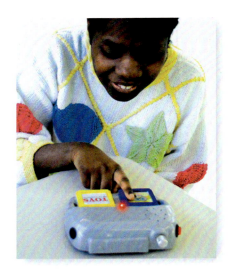

Before you buy a toy, think of the following questions:

Sound:
Do you need a toy (6)… makes a noise because your child suffers from visual loss? Does the sound have a positive effect?

Sensory:
Does the toy have features (7)… will attract the child's interest? Would a child like to touch them? A blind child might enjoy holding and exploring a toy (8)… has a texture or a smell. Children with hearing loss will need a light (9)… can be activated by touch. Those with visual loss should be able to activate a sound.

Touch:
What does the toy feel like – soft, hard, smooth, rough, cuddly? Does it feel pleasant so that the child, (10)… started playing with it, will like to go on exploring it? For those (11)… have grasping problems: is the toy easy to hold and release?

Size:
Children with dyspraxia may not be able to grip objects (12)… are too small or too large. An object (13)… is too large might not fit on the lap tray of a wheelchair.

Here is a good example:
"Learn your face!" is a toy (14)… is designed for many needs. The toy is easily activated because every part of the face is the appropriate size and can be touched easily. Every part turns on a light and plays a message when it is pushed. In addition the toy can be fixed to a lap tray or to the wall.

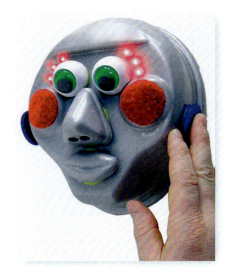

Children with special needs **Unit 12**

Working with the text

Fill in the missing words from the text.

Today there is a wide range of toys. Most toys can be used by all children, those with a special need and those who are (1) …. Good toys help children to develop their (2) …. For this reason toys for children with a special need should make use of the senses a child can use. Children with a (3) … need some kind of visual signal, like a (4) … which the child activates by (5) …. Those who suffer from a visual loss need a toy which makes some kind of (6) …. It's also important how a toy feels like, the texture of a toy should always be (7) …. Children with a grasping problem need a toy which they can (8) … and (9) … easily. For example, those children can be offered a (10) … instead of a ball. Too large toys are also a problem for children who sit in a (11) … because they might not fit on their (12) ….

Hands-on task

`Production`

Look at the following children and their special needs.
On the basis of the text and what you have learnt about toys in unit 5, what kind of toy would you suggest for them? Give some advice.

Theresa, 5 years old
Theresa suffers from brain damage which causes mental and physical difficulties.
She needs some time to understand how a toy works and she is very slow in movement.
Her grip isn't firm.

James, 3 years old
James has serious dyspraxia which means that he still can't walk.
He only crawls. He also suffers from visual impairment.

Cedric, 5 years old
Cedric has to sit in a wheelchair. He suffers from cerebral palsy.
Because of a malfunction of his right arm he isn't able to move and use it.

Unit 12 Children with special needs

wheelchair [wiːltʃeə]	Rollstuhl
child with [tʃaɪld wɪθ] special needs [ˈspeʃl niːdz]	Kind mit einem besonderen Bedürfnis, behindertes Kind
intellectual difficulties [ˌɪntəˈlektjʊəl ˈdɪfɪkəltɪs]	intellektuelle Schwierigkeiten
language difficulties [ˈlæŋgwɪdʒ ˈdɪfɪkəltɪs]	Sprachschwierigkeiten
cerebral palsy [ˈserɪbrəl ˈpɔːlzɪ]	spastische Lähmung

Andrew McArthur – a child with special needs

integrated nursery school class [ˈɪntɪgreɪtɪd ˈnɜːsrɪ skuːl klɑːs]	integrative Kindergartengruppe (Gruppe mit behinderten und nicht behinderten Kindern)
chairman [ˈtʃeəmən]	Vorsitzende, Vorsitzender
(to) bear s.th. [beə]	etwas ertragen
(to) recommend [rekəˈmend]	empfehlen
(to) raise money [reɪz ˈmʌnɪ]	Geld aufbringen
(to) be disabled [bɪ dɪsˈeɪbld]	behindert sein
disability [dɪsəˈbɪlətɪ]	Behinderung, Unfähigkeit
ability [əˈbɪlətɪ]	Fähigkeit
(to) be able to [bɪ ˈeɪbl tuː]	fähig sein zu
personality [ˌpɜːsəˈnælətɪ]	Persönlichkeit
(to) be limited [bɪ lɪmɪtɪd]	eingeschränkt sein
sense of humour [sens ɒv ˈhjuːmə]	Sinn für Humor
What a burden! [wɒt ə ˈbɜːdn]	Was für ein schweres Schicksal!
(to) withstand [wɪðˈstænd]	standhalten, durchhalten
(to) adapt [əˈdæpt]	anpassen
adaptation [ædæpˈteɪʃn]	Anpassung
special care [ˈspeʃl keə]	besondere Pflege, Fürsorge
(to) stare at s.o. [steə æt]	jmd. anstarren
disgust [dɪsˈgʌst]	Entsetzen, Ekel
(to) treat s.o. [triːt]	jmd. behandeln
openness [ˈəʊpənəs]	Offenheit
(to) complain [kəmˈpleɪn]	sich beschweren
(to) support [səˈpɔːt]	unterstützen
enriching [ɪnˈrɪtʃɪŋ]	bereichernd
intellectual deficit [ˌɪntəˈlektjʊəl ˈdefɪsɪt]	intellektuelles (geistiges) Defizit, Mangel
physical disability [ˈfɪzɪkl ˌdɪsəˈbɪlətɪ]	körperliche Behinderung
mental disability [ˈmentl ˌdɪsəˈbɪlətɪ]	geistige Behinderung

Windham Integrated Nursery School

(to) be situated [bɪ ˈsɪtjʊeɪtɪd]	sich befinden
(to) modernize [ˈmɒdənaɪz]	modernisieren
(to) extend [ɪkˈstend]	erweitern
(to) improve [ɪmˈpruːv]	verbessern
majority [məˈdʒɒrətɪ]	Mehrheit
(to) be staffed with [bɪ stɑːft]	mit Personal besetzt
health professionals [helθ prəˈfeʃnls]	Fachkräfte im Pflegebereich
occupational therapist [ˌɒkjuːˈpeɪʃnl ˈθerəpɪst]	Beschäftigungstherapeut/in
speech therapist [spiːtʃ ˈθerəpɪst]	Sprachtherapeut/in
physiotherapist [ˌfɪziəʊˈθerəpɪst]	Physiotherapeut/in
(to) become [bɪˈkʌm] independent [ˌɪndɪˈpendənt]	unabhängig/ selbstständig werden
well-equipped [welˈɪkwɪpt]	gut ausgestattet
semi-open [semɪˈəʊpən]	halb offen
(to) meet [miːt]	hier: entsprechen, gerecht werden
climbing apparatus [ˈklaɪmɪŋ ˌæpəˈreɪtəs]	Kletterapparat
imaginative [ɪˈmædʒɪnətɪv]	fantasievoll
imaginative skill [ɪˈmædʒɪnətɪv skɪl]	Vorstellungskraft
health care [helθ keə]	Gesundheitspflege
advisory team [ədˈvaɪzərɪ tiːm]	Beratungsteam
by hearsay [baɪ hɪəseɪ]	vom Hörensagen
unsure [ʌnʃʊə]	unsicher
reassure [ˌriːəˈʃʊə]	hier: beruhigen
(to) show off [ʃəʊ ɒf]	angeben

Inclusion – what is it?

inclusion [ɪnˈkluːʒən]	Aufnahme, hier: Inklusion
(to) benefit from [ˈbenɪfɪt frɒm]	Nutzen ziehen von, profitieren von
(to) exclude from [ɪkˈskluːd frɒm]	jmd. ausschließen von
exclusion from [ɪkˈskluːʒən]	Ausschluss von
participation [pɑːˌtɪsɪˈpeɪʃən]	Teilnahme, Beteiligung
diversity [daɪˈvɜːsɪtɪ]	Vielfalt

Choosing toys for children with special needs

able-bodied [ˈeɪblˈbɒdɪd]	nicht behindert
(to) grip [grɪp]	greifen
sponge [spʌndʒ]	Schwamm
bell [bel]	Klingel, Klingelton
wide range [waɪd reɪndʒ]	weites Angebot
sensory [ˈsensərɪ]	sensorisch, mit den Sinnen
consideration [kənˌsɪdəˈreɪʃn]	Überlegung
noise [nɔɪz]	Geräusch
effect [ɪˈfekt]	Wirkung
(to) activate [ˈæktɪveɪt]	aktivieren, auslösen
by touch [baɪ tʌtʃ]	durch Anfassen
smooth [smuːð]	glatt
rough [rʌf]	rau
cuddly [ˈkʌdlɪ]	anschmiegsam, knuddelig
(to) release [rɪˈliːs]	hier: loslassen
lap [læp]	Schoß
lap tray [læp treɪ]	Tablett, das sich am Rollstuhl befestigen lässt
(to) fix [fɪks]	fixieren, befestigen
(to) crawl [krɔːl]	kriechen

Unit 13 — Story time, rhyme time

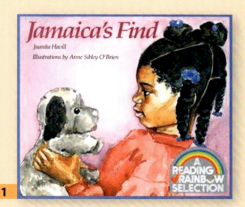

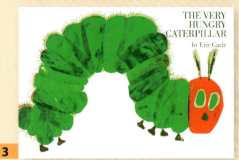

Look at these covers of different English children's books

Do you know any of them? In English or in German?
What might they be about?

handwerk-technik.de

Unit 13 Story time, rhyme time

Books and stories for children

Books are not only sources of information but also of great pleasure to most children. Listening to stories, sharing books with adults as well as curling up in a chair with a book can help children to escape and develop their imagination.

Sharing a book that is about other children in similar circumstances can help children. They may enjoy the story and then feel ready to talk about how they are feeling. For example there are books about children who have lost a parent.

Images and words in books can be very powerful. This means that we have to make sure that we show positive and non-discriminatory images. We need to make sure that they do not stereotype any group of people. For example, not all grandmothers have grey hair, sit in rocking chairs and knit. When choosing a book we need to look carefully for hidden messages. Do men always do the driving? Do girls always need rescuing? Are there any black or Asian people in positive roles?

This is a list of some kinds of books:

- **Picture books:** There are mostly pictures, very little text.

- **Pop-up books:** When you open them a tri-dimensional object pops up, e.g. a human body.

- **Feely books:** The different pages are made from different materials: hard, soft, hairy, sandy etc. materials. They are very good for the sensory development of children.

- **Factual books:** They give information about a special topic, e.g. animals, ships, seeing a doctor.

- **Dual-language books:** Two children with different home languages can share the same book. They help children understand that there are different languages and different ways of seeing the world.

- **Big books:** They can be shared with groups of children.

- **Story books:** These are collections of longer stories in one book. In Britain, the stories of Winnie-the-Pooh have been favourites with children for generations.

Working with the text

A **Find words and expressions in the text to fit these definitions.**
1. reading or looking at a book together with somebody
2. the living situation somebody has
3. to give a fixed idea of a particular type of person which is often not true in reality
4. ideas behind a text that you cannot see at first glance
5. the development of feeling, hearing, tasting, seeing and smelling

B **Explain these words and expressions from the text in English.**
1. curling up (line 2)
2. to escape (line 3)
3. non-discriminatory (line 16)
4. dual-language (line 40)

C **Think and talk about the following questions.**
1. Men who always do the driving, girls who always need rescuing: what are the hidden messages?
2. Imagine that all the books in your group are about happy nuclear families, all of them 'typically German'. Is there a hidden message in that as well? Say why or why not.
3. Go back and have a look at the book covers on page 133. What kind of books might they be?

Mediation

D **The nursery school teacher in your group is interested in what British nursery nurses learn about children's books. Summarise the most important points in German for her.**

Organizing a reading-aloud activity

Before you start
Think about these points: how many children will take part? Do you need any props? Do you need a chair circle? How do you want to introduce the story? Do not forget to practise, so that you can read fluently.

While reading
Vary your voice. This will make your reading easier to listen to and understand. Different characters in the story may have different voices. If you read more slowly or more quickly, you may build up suspense.
Spend some time looking at the cover and illustrations. Talk about the cover together and ask the children to predict what will happen.
Find ways to make the story an ACTIVE rather than a passive experience. In some stories that repeat the same text on each page, the children can become a part of the story experience. Children will often anxiously wait for their part! You can ask children what they think will happen next.
Hold the book so that the child or children can see the pictures while you are reading. Even though it might be difficult, this is important because children use the pictures to understand, remember and retell a story.

After reading
Think about a follow-up activity. Encourage the children to talk about the book. They may make drawings or create role plays in which they experiment with and explore the themes of the book.

For mediation: see page 184.

For giving feedback in class: see page 185.

Unit 13 Story time, rhyme time

When are you coming back?

When Little Bear heard the letter falling on the doormat one morning, he jumped out of the bed where he was lying with Mummy Bear and Daddy Bear. He raced downstairs, picked the letter up off the doormat and with a big jump he was back in bed. "How nice to have you back," said Mummy Bear, snuggling him. "I always come back, don't I?" smiled Little Bear.

"Oh dear," said Daddy Bear as he read the letter. "What's the matter?" asked Mummy Bear. "Uncle Bear has broken his leg. He wants you and me to come and help him out for a couple of days." "And me!" said Little Bear. Daddy Bear hugged him. "You must stay here, safe with Granny Bear."

Mummy Bear and Daddy Bear packed their bags while Granny Bear made breakfast. "When are you coming back?" asked Little Bear. "The day after tomorrow," replied Mummy Bear. "How long is that?" asked Little Bear. "That's two times sleeping," said Mummy Bear. "That's very long," said Little Bear, "and I still don't know how long that is."

"Look here, Little Bear," said Mummy Bear, "I'll give Granny Bear three suits for you to wear: a blue one, a yellow one and a red one. Today you put on the blue suit and this is the first day. Then you sleep. And when you wake up again you put on the yellow suit. That's the second day. When you sleep in the evening of the second day and wake up the next morning you put on the red suit. When you are wearing the red suit we'll be back home soon."

It started to snow. Little Bear and Granny Bear watched the world outside turn white. "We'll be able to make a snow den later," said Granny Bear. Mummy Bear and Daddy Bear kissed them goodbye and set off. "They'll be back home soon," said Granny Bear.

Suddenly Little Bear jumped off Granny Bear's knee. "Mummy Bear! Daddy Bear!", he cried as the snow whirled in. "When will you come back?" Mummy Bear kissed Little Bear again. "We'll be back the day after tomorrow," she said. "Now go and put on your blue suit. And then you build a wonderful snow den with Granny Bear."

Then she took off her scarf and put it around Little Bear's neck. "Will you look after this for me," she asked, "until I come back?" Little Bear nodded.

After they had gone the scarf helped him to brush his teeth and tidy his bed. Then he put on the blue bear suit. The scarf went everywhere with Little Bear that day. Together they jumped along in Mummy Bear and Daddy Bear's footprints, slid down snow hills and skidded on the frozen lake. Then they built a snow den and filled it with treasures and had tea in it. At bath time the scarf watched from a safe place while Little Bear raced his boats until Granny Bear came in. "Goodness, what a mess," she said, helping Little Bear into a towel. "You'd better run and get a cloth before I read you a bedtime story."

The next day Little Bear woke up and looked out of the window. It was still snowing and the world was white, even Mummy Bear and Daddy Bear's footprints had gone. "Granny Bear!" cried Little Bear. "I've had one sleep. When are Mummy Bear and Daddy Bear coming?" "You'll have to sleep one more time," replied Granny Bear. "Now go and brush your teeth and put on the yellow suit. Remember

the yellow suit means that Mummy Bear and Daddy Bear will be back after one more sleep."

The yellow suit and Mummy Bear's scarf helped Little Bear through the second day. They went on a nice long walk together and in the afternoon Little Bear helped Granny Bear to stir the cake mixture. "This is the welcome-back cake for Mummy Bear and Daddy Bear," said Granny Bear. "We'll bake it today and eat it tomorrow when they are back." Later Little Bear had a bath and went to bed. "When are Mommy Bear and Daddy Bear coming?" he asked. "After just one sleep," said Granny Bear.

The next day Little Bear woke early and looked out of the window. But there was no sign of Mummy Bear and Daddy Bear. "Granny Bear," cried Little Bear. "I've had one sleep. Where are they?" "Do you remember what Mummy Bear told you?" asked Granny Bear. "She said when you are wearing the red suit they'll be back home soon. So hop off, brush your teeth and put the red suit on."

Unit 13 Story time, rhyme time

6

That day Little Bear stayed inside and the scarf and the red suit helped him through the morning. "They'll be back in time for lunch," called Granny Bear, "come and help me make it." While Little Bear was putting the bowls out they suddenly heard the crunch of snow outside and there were Mummy Bear and Daddy Bear. "You came back," said Little Bear. "We always do, don't we?" smiled Mummy Bear. "Yes," said Little Bear.
And while they were hugging him he took the scarf off. "You can have this back," he said, "now I've got you."

Working with the text and pictures

A Connect the sentences parts.
1. When the letter arrived …
2. Mummy Bear and Daddy Bear had to go and help Uncle Bear …
3. Little Bear did not know how long three days were …
4. On leaving Mummy Bear gave Little Bear her scarf …
5. On the first day Little Bear put on his blue suit …
6. After Mummy Bear and Daddy Bear had left …
7. On the second day …
8. Mummy Bear and Daddy Bear returned …
9. When Mummy Bear was back home …

   a) … he helped Granny Bear make a cake.
   b) … so that he didn't feel alone.
   c) … Little Bear went into the snow and built a snow den.
   d) … she could have her scarf back.
   e) … when Little Bear was just laying the table for lunch.
   f) … it was early in the morning and everybody was still in bed.
   g) … because he had had an accident.
   h) … so Mummy Bear gave him three suits to wear, one for each day.
   i) … on the second day the yellow suit and on the third day the red suit.

B Describe pictures 1 – 6 using the story that you have read.
Write one or two complete sentences to each picture but do not copy the text.

C What kind of children's book is "When are you coming back?"
Go back and look at the text "Books and stories for children" for your answer.

Story time, rhyme time **Unit 13**

Working with the book

Imagine that after reading the story you think it might be a good idea to prepare a reading for a small group of children. You tell your nursery group teacher about your plan. She does not know the story and asks you to give her a short summary. She also wants to know why you have chosen this book.

A Summarizing the story *Production*
The following text is the beginning of a summary. Finish it by writing 8–10 sentences.
In the story "When are you coming back?" Mummy Bear and Daddy Bear have to leave for a few days while Little Bear is staying behind with Granny Bear. …

B Analysing the book *Production*
"A good children's book helps children develop their imagination, deals with their feelings and fears using a set of characters that have great appeal to children."
Is the book "When are you coming back?" a good children's book according to the definition above? Use extracts from the book to explain your opinion.

C Reading out aloud *Interaction*
Do a book reading in class. Some of you can act as children. They can comment or ask questions during the reading. Take turns reading out aloud. Be prepared to answer questions and to show the pictures while reading.

Grammar box: **Conjunctions** – Konjunktionen

- Konjunktionen verbinden Satzteile. Sie können Gegensätze, Gründe, die zeitliche Abfolge ausdrücken und haben daher eine wichtige Bedeutung für die Aussage eines Satzes.

and – und	so – daher, so	before – bevor
but – aber	because – weil	whether/if – ob
however – jedoch	since/as – da/weil	
although/even though – obwohl	when – als/wenn (zeitlich)	
while – während (zeitlich)	after – nachdem	
whereas – wohingegen		

Practising grammar

Put in a suitable conjunction from the list above. Sometimes more than one is possible.
1. … the children are sleeping, Mary and Janet have their lunch break.
2. The children never start eating … they have washed their hands.
3. I don't know … I'll be able to finish in time.
4. Some children find it difficult to do without a nap after lunch … others sleep for two hours every day.
5. One girl is playing with a cuddly toy dog … another one is painting a picture.
6. Tom is never ill … many of the children he works with have a cold.
7. … Janet come back home after her first day at the nursery school, she was tired.
8. Little Bear is wearing his mother's scarf … this helps him while his mother is away.
9. … Mummy Bear is back, Little Bear doesn't need the scarf any longer.
10. Nora has a temperature … Janet calls her mother.

Unit 13 Story time, rhyme time

Nursery rhyme time – traditionals

Nursery rhymes are one of the first ways that children discover the rhythm and rhyme of a certain language. They are educational and fun. The nursery rhymes on these pages have been favourites with British children for a long time and they know them by heart!

Humpty Dumpty

Humpty Dumpty sat on a wall
Humpty Dumpty had a great fall;
All the King's horses and all the King's men
Could not put Humpty Dumpty together again.

The Cat and the Fiddle

Hey, diddle, diddle!
The cat and the fiddle,
The cow jumped over the moon;
The little dog laughed
To see such fun
And the dish ran away with the spoon.

Tom, Tom, the Piper's Son

Tom, Tom
The piper's son
Stole a pig
And away he ran,
The pig was eat
And Tom was beat
And Tom went crying
Down the street.

Production

Working with the text

Learn one of the nursery rhymes by heart and then practice speaking it out loud so that you can hear the rhythm and the rhymes of the language.

Story time, rhyme time Unit 13

Activities with nursery rhymes

Many nursery rhymes are excellent to create finger games.
This way children not only learn about language and rhymes but also use movement.
This develops their motor skills and helps them to remember the words.

Two Little Blackbirds

Two little blackbirds sitting on the hill	(Start with your hands behind your back.)
One named Jack	(Bring one hand to the front.)
One named Jill	(?)
Fly away, Jack!	(Put the hand representing Jack behind your back.)
Fly away, Jill!	(?)
Come back, Jack!	(?)
Come back, Jill!	(?)

Five Little Ducks

5 little ducks went out one day
Over the hills and far away,
Mommy (daddy) duck called
Quack quack quack,
But only 4 little ducks came back.

4 little ducks went out one day
Over the hills and far away,
Mommy (daddy) duck called
Quack quack quack,
But only 3 little ducks came back.

3 little ducks went out one day
Over the hills and far away,
Mommy (daddy) duck called
Quack quack quack,
But only 2 little ducks came back.

2 little ducks went out one day
Over the hills and far away,
Mommy (daddy) duck called
Quack quack quack,
But only 1 little duck came back.

1 little duck went out one day
Over the hills and far away,
Mommy (daddy) duck called
Quack quack quack,
But no little ducks came wondering back.

No little ducks went out one day
Over the hills and far away,
Mommy (daddy) duck called
Quack quack quack,
And 5 little ducks came wandering back.

Hands-on tasks

Interaction

A **Complete the directions for the rhyme "Two Little Blackbirds", then present the rhyme with movements.**

B **Work in pairs. Develop movements for the rhyme "Five Little Ducks", then perform it in class. You may ask some of your classmates to act as "children" who follow along with your moves.**

Unit 13 Story time, rhyme time

Creative writing

Production

**Form groups of 3–4 students and write the story of "Jamaica's Find".
Then read out the stories to each other.**

Jamaica is the girl on the book cover. Her find is the little toy dog in her arms. She loves it and wants to keep it for herself but then she thinks again.

Think of these questions:
- Where does Jamaica find the toy dog?
- Does she take it home?
- If yes, what does her family say?
- What does she decide?
- Is Jamaica happy at the end?
- If yes, what has happened?

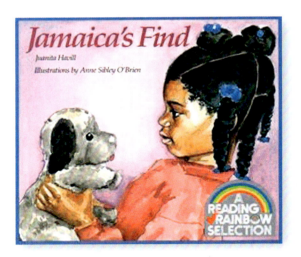

Let's sing a song

"Twinkle, Twinkle, Little Star" is the first stanza of the poem "The Star" by Jane Taylor. It is a popular English lullaby. Babies love it especially if you imitate the twinkling of a star with your hands while singing.

Twinkle, Twinkle, Little Star

Story time, rhyme time Unit 13

Old McDonald's Farm

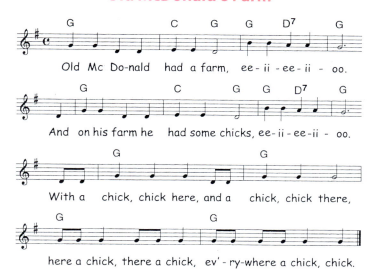

2. some ducks … quack, quack
3. some cows … moo, moo
4. some pigs … oink, oink
5. some dogs … bow, wow
6. some sheep … baah, baah
7. some cats … meow, meow
8. a car … rattle, rattle

Itsy Bitsy Spider
or "Eentsy Weentsy Spider"

The itsy-bitsy spider
Climbed up the water spout
Down came the rain
And washed the spider out.
Out came the sun
And dried up all the rain
And the itsy-bitsy spider
Climbed up the spout again.

Hands-on task

Interaction

Choose one of these songs and think of how to introduce the song to preschoolers. Present your song introduction to your classmates and perform the song in class according to your ideas.

Unit 13 Story time, rhyme time

Books and stories for children

cover ['kʌvə]	Bucheinband
source [sɔːs]	Quelle
pleasure ['pleʒə]	Vergnügen
(to) share [ʃeə]	hier: zusammen lesen
(to) curl up [kɜːl ʌp]	hier: es sich gemütlich machen
(to) escape [ɪ'skeɪp]	hier: sich entspannen, zerstreuen
imagination [ɪˌmædʒɪ'neɪʃn]	Fantasie, Vorstellungskraft
image ['ɪmɪdʒ]	Bild
powerful ['paʊəfʊl]	mächtig
non-discriminatory [nɒn-dɪskrɪmɪ'nətɔːrɪ]	nicht diskriminierend
rocking chair ['rɒkɪŋ tʃeə]	Schaukelstuhl
(to) knit [nɪt]	stricken
hidden [hɪdn]	versteckt
message ['mesɪdʒ]	Botschaft
(to) rescue ['reskjuː]	retten
(to) pop up [pɒp ʌp]	hochkommen, herauskommen
tri-dimensional ['traɪ-dɪ'menʃənl]	dreidimensional
feely book [fiːlɪ bʊk]	Tastbuch
sensory development ['sensərɪ dɪ'veləpmənt]	sensorische Entwicklung
factual books ['fæktʃʊəl bʊks]	Sachbuch
dual-language ['djuːəl-læŋgwɪdʒ]	zweisprachig
collection [kə'lekʃn]	Sammlung

Organizing a reading-aloud activity

(to) vary ['veri]	variieren
suspense [sə'spents]	Spannung
(to) predict [prɪ'dɪkt]	vorhersagen

When are you coming back?

(to) snuggle [snʌgl]	kuscheln
(to) hug [hʌg]	umarmen
suit [suːt]	hier: Strampelanzug
snow den [snəʊ den]	Schneehütte
(to) whirl [wɜːl]	wirbeln
(to) nod [nɒd]	nicken
(to) slid [slɪd]	rutschen
(to) skid [skɪd]	schlittern
treasure ['treʒə]	Schatz
(to) stir [stɜː]	rühren
bowl [bəʊl]	Schüssel
crunch [krʌntʃ]	Knirschen

Nursery rhyme time – traditionals

(nursery) rhyme [raɪm]	Reim
fiddle ['fɪdl]	Fiedel, Geige
motor skills [grəʊs 'məʊtə skɪls]	Motorik

Creative writing

exhibition [ˌeksɪ'bɪʃn]	Ausstellung

Let's sing a song

(to) twinkle ['twɪŋkl]	funkeln
stanza ['stænˌzə]	Strophe

Unit 14 — Children and TV

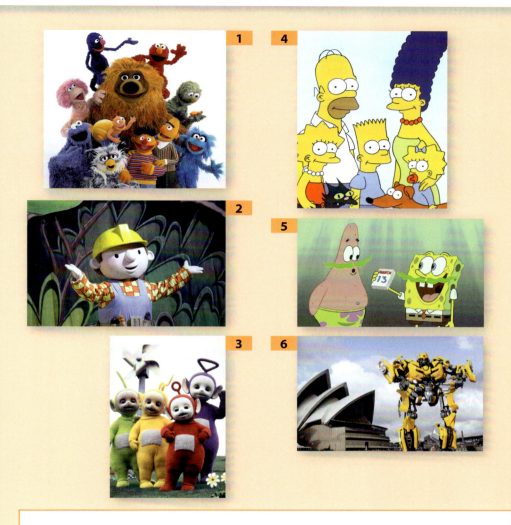

Look at these TV heroes

- Do you recognize these TV heroes? Tell your classmates about them (Who are they? What is typical about them?)
- Do you think these are good examples of children's programmes? Or do you think they are not meant for children? Give reasons.
- Which programme would you recommend for children aged 4 to 6? Give reasons.
- Should children under three watch TV? Discuss in class.
- Is there a programme which you think is appropriate for very young children? Say why.

Hands-on task

Production

What kind of children's programme did you like to watch in your childhood? Give a short summary of the programme and say why you liked to watch it.

Unit 14 Children and TV

Sesame Street – one of the most famous children's programmes

"You've never seen a street like *Sesame Street* before. You're gonna love it!" With this sentence Gordon – one of the main 'human actors' of the first episodes – welcomed thousands of children onto Sesame Street, a typical street in the heart of inner-city New York.

Today everyone knows that *Sesame Street* is one of the most famous and successful children's programmes ever.

But when the programme started in 1969 some parents and TV experts were sceptical at first about its chances of success. *Sesame Street* was very different from the typical children's programmes on TV until then and some parents were astonished and didn't want to believe that this programme could teach their children anything.

Compared to *Sesame Street* the old programmes were rather boring. Before *Sesame Street* started, children's programmes like *Mister Roger's Neighbourhood* were very popular on TV. In these programmes a rather old actor presented various subjects to children but the atmosphere was somewhat stiff. Most of the time *Mister Roger* spoke very slowly to the children in a lecturing tone, but this was regarded as the only way to make a show for children. People were worried that children wouldn't learn if there wasn't an elderly looking man talking to them like a strict and stiffly smiling teacher. That makes it clear why people called *Sesame Street* a revolution in children's programming.

First of all it was quite unusual to have human actors talking to and above all acting with cloth puppets as if they were human partners. These puppets known as *Muppets* were created by Jim Henson for a show in 1954. The Muppets gave the show its typical flavour but that wasn't the only new aspect about it. Its style was completely new and different. This new experiment was a fast-paced children's programme of sketches and entertaining sequences to teach children various preschool subjects like the letters of the alphabet, words,

numbers and social skills. The first programme presented a fast series of funny stories. Even today the show still works with quick and catchy sketches all dealing with basic subjects. Compared to the extremely languid *Mister Roger*, *Sesame Street* was all quickness. It was and still is great fun. The show often makes fun of pop culture and singers and popular songs are satirized. These funny sequences soon became very popular. They made the show interesting and also amusing for parents to watch along with, too. Over the years *Bert and Ernie*, *Oscar the Grouch*, *Big Bird*, *Kermit the Frog* and the *Cookie Monster* became familiar in every household.

In Marc Bernadin's book "Entertainment Weekly – 100 Greatest TV Shows of All Time" *Sesame Street* is recognized as number 20 of the best shows ever. Marc Bernadin thinks that *Sesame Street* has completely changed children's programming. He calls the show's concept an example of "edutainment" because it successfully combines education and entertainment.

Making a game out of learning is the show's recipe for success. Put a funny *Kermit* in front of the children instead of a boring *Mister Roger* and let this amusing frog go though a funny story or let him sing a song in front of a large letter and a child will listen attentively because the puppet and the story are funny and the tune of the song is catchy. This concept made children of many countries fall in love with it.

Children and TV Unit 14

Working with the text

A Say if these statements are true or false. If the statement is false, correct it.
1. Sesame Street takes place in the heart of inner-city New York. For this reason it is a programme only created for American children.
2. When the programme started in 1969 everyone was enthusiastic about it.
3. Sesame Street represented something completely new. It was just the opposite to what people were used to in children's programming.
4. Right from the beginning parents were convinced that Sesame Street would be very successful at teaching their children.
5. Grown-ups also like to watch Sesame Street because they can learn a lot as well.
6. The show's only aim is to entertain children.

B Explain what function the following names and numbers have in the text.
Example: inner-city New York – The original Sesame Street is a street in the heart of inner-city New York.

Form sentences with these:

1969	Mister Roger's Neighbourhood	The Muppets
1954	Cookie Monster	20

C Answer the following questions on the text.
1. Why were parents and experts sceptical at first ?
2. Before Sesame Street children's programmes were rather boring. Explain why.
3. What was unusual about Sesame Street?
4. Why was Sesame Street "completely new and different"? How does the show work?

Working with language

Try to explain in your own words what the following expressions from the text mean.

Look at page 175 ("Wörter und Ausdrücke auf Englisch erklären") for help.

line 27: in a lecturing tone	line 43: fast-paced children's programme
line 40: typical flavour	line 68: "edutainment"

Unit 14 Children and TV

Hands-on tasks

A **Imagine the following situation.** *Production*
Leo is one of your nursery school children. He is 5 years old. He knows that his friends are allowed to watch TV after nursery school and at weekends. He eagerly asks his mother for permission to watch TV, too, but she is very unsure about it and up till now she hasn't allowed him to watch TV or only very rarely. Now she asks you for help.
Can you give her some advice? What would you suggest and why?

Ab 3 bis 99 Jahren

In einer für Kinder nicht zu schnellen Folge bunter Bilder wird hier eine der schönsten Janosch-Geschichten präsentiert. Der Originaltext des Kinderbuchs wird von einem Schauspieler zu den Bildern vorgetragen und mit einer eingängigen Musik unterlegt.

Zum Inhalt:
Ein kleiner Bär und ein kleiner Tiger leben an einem Fluss. Eines Tages treibt eine Bananenkiste vorbei, auf der steht, woher sie kommt, aus "Pa-na-ma". Panama wird das Land der Träume für den Bären und den Tiger und beide machen sich auf, dieses Land zu suchen. Als sie nach vielen Abenteuern endlich glauben, ihr Traumland gefunden zu haben, sind sie da, wo sie immer gelebt haben.

Mediation

B **Sarah Berner comes from Great Britain and has been living in Germany with her German husband for two years now. On his fifth birthday her son Thomas got a German DVD with a story called "Trip to Panama" by Janosch. Mrs Berner asks Susanne Reuter – her son's nursery nurse – for help. Take over Susanne Reuter's role and try to answer in English.**

Hallo Frau Reuter! Thomas hat diese DVD zum Geburtstag bekommen, aber ich kann die Beschreibung auf der Rückseite nicht ganz verstehen. Können Sie mir helfen und mir das Wichtigste auf Englisch sagen?

Yes, I can try, let me see …

And do you think this DVD is good for Thomas?

Of course, …

Grammar box: **Adverbs** – Adverbien

Look at the following text passages again. What's the difference?

line 8 – 9: *Sesame Street is one of the most famous and **successful** children's programmes.*

but line 68 – 69: *(The show is called edutainment) because it **successfully** combines education and entertainment.*

Successful is an **adjective** but *successfully* is an **adverb**.

Bildung:	
Adverbien werden durch Anhängen von "ly" an das Adjektiv gebildet.	nice (**Adjektiv**) → nicely (**Adverb**) correct → correctly

Achtung:	
"y" am Ende des Adjektivs wird zu "i + ly":	easy – easily ; happy – happily
Nach Konsonant entfällt "le":	simple – simply
Stummes "e" enfällt:	whole – wholly , true – truly
Adjektiv auf "ly" → **kein** Adverb mit "ly", sondern:	friendly – in a friendly way
Adjektiv auf "ic" → Adverb mit "-ally":	fantastic – fantastically
Adjektiv auf "ll" → Adverb mit "y":	dull – dully , full – fully
Adjektiv difficult → **kein** Adverb auf "ly", sondern:	difficult – with difficulty
Adjektiv "good" → **kein** Adverb auf "ly", sondern:	well

- Adjektiv und Adverb haben manchmal die gleiche Form und gleiche Bedeutung. Dazu gehören Zeitangaben wie *daily, hourly, weekly, monthly etc.*
  Außerdem: *early, likely, fast, long, far, straight, low*

- Manche Adjektive haben zwei verschiedene Adverbformen:

Adjektiv	1. Adverb	2. Adverb
right (richtig)	right (richtig)	rightly (zurecht)
hard (hart)	hard (hart)	hardly (kaum)
fair (fair)	fair (fair)	fairly (ziemlich)
pretty (hübsch)	pretty (ziemlich)	prettily (hübsch)
late (spät)	late (spät)	lately (in letzter Zeit)
just (gerecht)	just (nur)	justly (gerecht)
ready (fertig)	ready (fertig)	readily (bereitwillig)
short (kurz)	short (kurz)	shortly (in Kürze)

Practising grammar

A Transform these adjectives into adverbs.
1. fast
2. long
3. sweet
4. angry
5. far
6. fantastic
7. basic
8. hard
9. daily
10. easy
11. probable
12. good

Unit 14 Children and TV

Walt Disney and Donald Duck

Two of Walt Disney's most famous cartoon figures are Mickey Mouse and Donald Duck.
Walter Elias Disney – an American film producer (1901 – 1966) – created them in the early 1930s but they are still very popular today and children all over the world know and love them.

B Work through the following text describing things which are typical of a Donald Duck story. Fill in the missing adverbs.

*Example: Donald Duck's mood often changes from being **happy** to being **angry**. He can (…) talk to Daisy but then suddenly he (…) stamps his feet.*
*Donald Duck's mood often changes from being happy to being angry. He can **happily** talk to Daisy but then suddenly he **angrily** stamps his feet.*

1. Donald Duck is a hothead and it's not unusual to see him being **angry** or even **furious**. Quite often he … clenches his fist and his face blushes …
2. Most often **surprising** things happen to him but he … manages to turn every problem into a happy ending.
3. Every story ends with a **happy** end and you can see Donald jumping up and raising his arms …
4. Donald loves Daisy. She is very **dear** to him and he is very **attentive** towards her. He … loves her and always listens to her …
5. When he is together with Daisy he seems to be very **contented** and he always smiles at her …

Grammar box: Use of Adjective and Adverb – Gebrauch von Adjektiv und Adverb

Adjective	Adverb
→ Bezieht sich immer auf ein Nomen oder eine Person *She is a nice girl.* *She is nice.*	→ Kann sich beziehen auf … ● **ein Verb** *She sings very nicely.* ● **auf ein Adjektiv** *Today the weather is extremely hot.* ● **auf ein anderes Adverb** *She sings extremely well.* ● **auf einen ganzen Satz** *Unfortunately, I missed my bus yesterday morning.*

Ausnahmen:

→ **kein** Adverb bei Verben, die einen Zustand beschreiben → *to be, to become, to get, to grow, to turn (werden), to remain, to stay, to keep (bleiben), to seem (scheinen)*

→ **kein** Adverb bei Verben der Sinneswahrnehmung → *to look, to feel, to smell, to sound, to taste*

Children and TV Unit 14

Practising grammar

Adjective or adverb? Fill in the correct form of the words in brackets.

Nowadays it is … (1 normal) for almost every household to have access to … (2 various) TV channels and the Internet. But some experts say that this … (3 enormous) progress in technology can be a … (4 serious) problem for parents. The … (5 vast) choice of programmes and Internet links confront parents with … (6 important) questions, for example: "What is … (7 good) or … (8 bad) for my child?" – "Are there programmes and TV heroes which are … (9 harmful) for my child?" – "What does my child see and have access to while surfing the Internet?" – "Are there any … (10 serious) risks?" – "What … (11 sensible) rules should I make for using the Internet?"
Nursery nurses are also … (12 regular) confronted with these …. (13 important) questions. Parents … (14 increasing) ask for help because they feel … (15 absolute) left to deal alone with this … (16 immense) problem. What …. (17 useful) advice is out there for parents? Today there are lots of … (18 violent) or …. (19 satirical) cartoon programmes which are not …. (20 real) designed for children but which they like to watch. Children who surf the web can … (21 hard) be controlled. All kinds of … (22 violent) programmes are already shown in the afternoon when children sit in front of TV. Sometimes parents do not know about the … (23 alarming) content some programmes and Internet pages have. Others …. (24 complete) ignore the … (25 extreme) …. (26 unpleasant) effect TV and Internet may have on their children and they do not control or check them. Those parents often use TV and Internet as a babysitter and leave their children alone in front of TV or computer for too many hours. They do not see the … (27 negative) impact TV and Internet may have on the child's …. (28 mental) health.

Children's TV heroes – what should they look like?

Sandra Brown works as a nursery nurse at the Tiny Mouse Nursery School. At circle time the children in her group regularly tell her about their TV viewing habits. Sandra knows that some of her children watch TV for too many hours each day, unsupervised by their parents. She
5 is also worried about the role models children are adopting from TV programmes as some of her children seem to be fond of mystery, science fiction or comic heroes which are not appropriate for their age group. One Wednesday afternoon, Sandra wants to discuss this problem with her colleagues Mary and Katherine at their staff meeting.

10
Mary	Okay, let's start our staff meeting. Today we need to talk about how we want to spend our yearly budget. I prepared a list of picture books which I'd like to buy. Maybe we'll have some money left over for new classroom equipment. But first, are there any other topics we should talk about?
15 Sandra	Yes, I'd like to mention our children's TV and computer habits. During the last few weeks I've become more and more worried about the TV programmes the preschoolers in my group seem to watch and the computer games they play at home. And …
Katherine	But what role do you see for us there? They watch TV or play their computer games at home – so parents have to take responsibility for their own kids. Why should that be our
20	problem?

→ continued

Sandra:	Oh, I think there is a problem for us with the kind of programmes the children watch. They copy behaviour which is anti-social and this has an impact on the atmosphere in my group.
Mary:	You're thinking of violent behaviour, aren't you?
25 Sandra:	Not only that. Of course, some children like to start fights which they imitate from violent scenes on TV. But I'm also thinking of anti-social behaviour like bullying or bad language which they pick up quickly from TV. And some children have become too competitive, always wanting to be the first and the best – just like their TV hero. Then they can't cope with disappointment.
30 Mary:	Yes, I know just what you mean. There are also more and more parents asking me for help. They want to get advice. Very often they don't know what kind of programme is appropriate for their child's age.
Katherine:	Maybe you're right. Our children are searching for role models and if parents leave them alone with the telly, you can bet they'll find the wrong ones to copy.
35 Mary:	I always tell parents to watch with their children and make sure their child's favourite TV hero doesn't behave violently in any way or do dangerous stunts. For me, it's also really important that the programme promotes social well-being and kindness. I believe that sharing and friendship is very important.
Sandra:	Yes, but I also think a real good children's programme should make sure that the children learn while they are watching it. The programme should be educational in some way. It should encourage children to use new words, for example.
Katherine:	You're right. I think it is also important that programmes should not be racist or exclude people – for example, anyone with special needs. It should also promote equality between people of all races. Some of our children may have reservations about people from different ethnic backgrounds – and it's important to help them to grow up without prejudices.
Sandra:	Yes, tolerance is important. Generally, I think that the children in my group watch TV for far too long, sometimes three or more hours a day. Maybe we should talk about the problem at our next parents' evening?
50 Mary:	We shouldn't only talk about our children's TV habits but also produce a handout so that parents have some guidelines.
Katherine:	That could be hard work! What programmes do you want to recommend? There are lots for children – and I don't know all of them! As a mother, I can give some advice from my own experience but I'm not an expert.
55 Sandra:	Yes, that's true – so we'll have to do some research and preparation for the next parent evening.
Mary:	Okay, that's a good idea. We should all search for expert advice to put in a handout before our next staff meeting. And now let's talk about our budget ….

Working with the text

A Answer the following questions on the text.
1. What does Sandra get to know about her children's TV habits and what is she worried about?
2. Why does Katherine think children's TV habits are not a problem they should talk about in their staff meeting?
3. What kind of bad habits do the children copy from TV programmes?
4. What topics should a "good" TV programme have, according to Mary? Explain.
5. Sandra wants TV programmes to be "educational". Explain what she means.
6. What topics are important according to Katherine?

Children and TV Unit 14

B **Think of further arguments relating to how a good children's TV programme should look. Refer to the points of view given in the text and add your own explanations.**
1. A good children's TV programme should teach children good behaviour because …
2. It should also be educational because …
3. One very important matter programmes should deal with is tolerance because …
4. There should not be any kind of violence because …
5. To my mind, a good children's programme should … (add your own point of view)

Hands-on task

Production

During the parents evening dealing with children's TV and computer habits, Sandra is confronted with the arguments below. Look at them carefully.

To be honest, I use the TV set and computer as a babysitter because when I come home from work I'm too exhausted to watch my son – and I have to do my housework. But I don't feel bad about it because in the early evening the crime stories he may see are just harmless compared to the series and films they show in the late evening when my son is in bed.

I'm really worried about what children can see on TV, and the idea of them surfing the Internet and finding totally unsuitable material really alarms me. For that reason, I have very strict rules. My daughters are not allowed to watch TV or sit in front of the computer without my supervision. I let them watch one children's series every second or third day but only if they didn't go on their computer first. They have to choose, TV or computer – but not both.

My mother didn't allow me to watch TV when I was a little child. Now I spend far too much time in front of the television. I believe that is a reaction to the no-telly-at-all-rule in my childhood. So, I don't restrict my daughter's watching times but I always make sure she is watching something meant for her age group.

TV and computers are part of modern technology and I believe that children have to make use of them to keep up-to-date. For that reason I don't restrict my children's TV and computer times.

Sit in small groups and work out a role play with these arguments. Think of how Sandra should react to those points of view. Make use of the word box below and present your role play in class.

Giving point of views

I can only underline the fact that …

I think / believe that …

I absolutely support the opinion that …

To my mind …

It's not correct to … because …

I'm convinced that …

I support your attitude that …

I agree / disagree with you.

I'm not of your opinion because …

In my opinion …

I would never consent to …

handwerk-technik.de

Unit 14 Children and TV

Sesame ['sesəmɪ] Street – one of the most famous children's programmes

children's programme ['tʃɪldrəns 'prəʊgræm]	Kinderprogramm
human ['hjuːmən]	menschlich
success [sək'ses]	Erfolg
successful [sək'sesfʊl]	erfolgreich
expert ['ekspɜːt]	Experte/Expertin, Sachverständige/r
boring ['bɔːrɪŋ]	langweilig
subject ['sʌbʒɪkt]	hier: Thema
stiff [stɪf]	steif
lecturing tone ['lektʃəɪŋ təʊn]	belehrender Ton
regard s.th. as [rɪ'gɑːd æz]	etwas ansehen als
elderly looking ['eldəlɪ ʊkɪŋ]	älter aussehend
strict [strɪkt]	streng
above all [ə'bʌv ɔːl]	vor allem
cloth puppet [klɔːθ 'pʌpɪt]	Stoffpuppe
flavour ['fleɪvə]	Geschmack, Stil
fast-paced [fɑːst-peɪsd]	in schneller Folge, schnell wechselnd
entertainment [ˌentə'teɪnmənt]	Unterhaltung
entertaining [ˌentə'teɪnɪŋ]	unterhaltend
catchy ['kætʃɪ]	eingängig
(to) represent [ˌreprɪ'zent]	repräsentieren, darstellen
(to) satirize ['sætəraɪz]	satirisch darstellen
amusing [ə'mjuːzɪŋ]	belustigend, lustig
grouch [graʊtʃ]	Muffel, Miesepeter
languid ['læŋgwɪd]	matt, träge
sequences ['siːkwənsez]	Folgen
familiar [fə'mɪljə]	gewohnt, vertraut
education [ˌedjuː'keɪʃn]	Erziehung
recipe ['resɪpɪ]	Rezept
attentively [ə'tentɪvlɪ]	aufmerksam
tune [tjuːn]	Melodie
eagerly ['iːgəlɪ]	hartnäckig
rarely ['reəlɪ]	selten
aim [eɪm]	Ziel

Walt Disney and Donald Duck

hothead [hɒt hed]	Hitzkopf
attentive [ə'tentɪv]	aufmerksam
contented [kən'tentɪd]	zufrieden

Children's TV heroes

vast [vɑːst]	enorm
role model [rəʊl 'mɒdəl]	Vorbild
habit ['hæbɪt]	Gewohnheit
appropriate [ə'prəʊprɪət]	geeignet, passend
(to) take responsibility [rɪˌspɒntsɪ'bɪlɪtɪ]	Verantwortung übernehmen
(to) copy ['kɒpɪ]	kopieren, hier: nachahmen
impact on ['ɪmpækt]	Einfluss auf
violent ['vaɪələnt]	gewaltsam, gewalttätig
(to) bully ['bʊlɪ]	„mobben"
(to) promote [prə'məʊt]	werben für, hier: vermitteln
social well-being ['səʊʃəl ˌwel'biːɪŋ]	hier: gutes Sozialverhalten
kindness ['kaɪndnəs]	Freundlichkeit
race [reɪs], racist ['reɪsɪst]	Rasse, rassistisch
prejudice ['predʒʊdɪs]	Vorurteil

Giving points of view

(to) underline ['ʌndəlaɪn]	unterstreichen
(to) support the opinion that [sə'pɔːt ðə ə'pɪnjən ðæt]	die Meinung unterstützen, dass
to my mind [tu: maɪ maɪnd]	meiner Meinung nach
it is not correct to [ɪt ɪz nɒt kə'rekt tuː]	es ist nicht korrekt zu …
(to) be convinced [bɪ: kən'vɪnsd]	überzeugt sein
(to) consent to [kən'sent tuː]	zustimmen zu
attitude ['ætɪtjuːd]	Haltung
(to) agree with [ə'griː]	zustimmen
(to) disagree with [dɪsə'griː]	nicht zustimmen

Unit 15 — Nursery school as a movie topic

Let's talk about the movies

There are not many films that deal with the topic kindergarten or nursery school. Why do you think that is?
Do you know any films with the actor Arnold Schwarzenegger?
What do you remember about them?
Is the movie "Kindergarten Cop" a typical Schwarzenegger film?

Look at this scene from the movie "Kindergarten Cop".
- Describe the situation. What does Schwarzenegger look like?
- How does he probably feel?
- Put yourself in the place of the children and imagine what they are thinking.

Compare this picture to the first one.
- What does Schwarzenegger look like here? Look at his clothes, his posture, …
- Does he enjoy the situation more?
- Imagine what he and the children are talking about.

handwerk-technik.de

Unit 15 Nursery school as a movie topic

The movie "Kindergarten Cop"

In the film "Kindergarten Cop" the actor Arnold Schwarzenegger plays police agent John Kimble who works undercover as a nursery nurse in a nursery school in order to find a dangerous criminal. The following scene clearly shows that he still has a few problems with his new job …

Who is my daddy and what does he do? Scene 6 (DVD timer 34:55–40:55)

All the children of the kindergarten class:
"I pledge allegiance to the flag of the United States of America and to the republic for which it stands, one nation, under God, indivisible, with liberty and justice for all."

5 Kimble: *(watching a fat child eating, then lifting him up to his eye level)* "Are these all your lunches?"
Child 1: *(shakes his head)*
Kimble: *(threatening)* "You mean you eat other people's lunches? Stop it!"

10 *The child spits out fries – Kimble puts him back on the ground.*

Kimble: "Now we're going to do something extremely fun. We're going to play a wonderful game called 'Who is my daddy and what does he do?'"
Child 2: *(putting up his hand)*
15 Kimble: "Yes?"
Child 2: "Is your daddy a fireman?"
Child 3: "He's probably big. Is he a wrestler?"
Child 4: "Is he a basketball coach?"
Kimble: *(touching his head)* "No, no, no, no."
20 Dominic: "What's the matter?"
Kimble: "I have a headache."
Lowell: "It might be a tumor."
Kimble: "It's not a tumor. It's not a tumor at all. What I meant was: you tell me
25 who is your daddy and what does he do!"
Children: "Oh!"
Kimble: "Get it? We start right here. You."
Child 5: "My dad repairs cars driven by
30 women who are pinheads."
Child 6: "My dad doesn't do anything since the crash."
Child 7: "My dad gives money to people that don't have money, then
35 people use that money, then they give other money back and they give the same amount of money back to my dad."

Nursery school as a movie topic Unit 15

Lowell: "My dad doesn't live with us anymore. He lives in New York and drives a taxi. My mom hopes he's going to die real soon."

Kimble takes notes.

Child 8: "My dad watches TV all day long."
Child 9: "My dad works on computers, and he's, umm, the boss of his company, and, umm, he has a moustache and a beard."
Kimble: "Mm-hmm."
Child 9: "Yeah. He doesn't have that much hair because – and he – his head is so big that he can't wear any hats."
Child 10: "My dad's divorced. My mum's divorced."
Child 11: "My dad, umm, is a psychologist and he helps people that are hurt or lost their feelings, and, umm, that's it."
Twin girls: *(together)* "Our mum says that our dad is a real sex machine."
Kimble: "Good."
Dominic: "I don't know what my dad does. I haven't seen him in a long time. He lives in France."
Child 3: "My dad is a gynaecologist and he looks at vaginas all day long."
Child 12: "Mi papá trabaja en la casa, y él juega conmigo mucho." (My father works at home and he plays a lot with me.)
Kimble: "Thank you. Very good. Okay, next. What's his name with his back to me?"
Dominic: "His name is Zach Sullivan. He doesn't like anyone to talk to him."
Child 11: "He's a poo-poo head."
Child 13: "Yeah, he's a poo-poo face."
Child 11: "He's a ca-ca poo-poo."
All children "Poo-poo ca-ca! Poo-poo ca-ca!"

Camera zooms in on Zach who plays car-crash in the back of the room by himself.

Kimble: "Quiet. That's enough. Hey Zach. Did your daddy teach you this game? Come on, Zach, let's all play together. It's so much more fun."
Zach: "Leave me alone!"

The bell rings.

Unit 15 Nursery school as a movie topic

Working with the text

A Questions on the text
1. How does the day start in this kindergarten?
2. What is the "wonderful game" that Mr Kimble proposes?
3. At first the children misunderstand Mr Kimble's idea. Explain what exactly they understand.
4. What are the dads' occupations? Give examples.
5. Do all the children really know what their dads do?
6. Why do some of the children call Zach a "poo-poo head"?
7. How does Mr Kimble react when all the children start shouting "poo-poo ca-ca"?

B Text analysis
"Who is my daddy and what does he do?"
Let's look at the answers that the children give. What do we learn about the children's families, about their way of life, their problems?
Copy the following table on a sheet of paper. Fill in the information from the text.

	Dad's occupation	Problems
child 6	His dad is unemployed, he doesn't do anything.	He had a crash, he is probably ill.
...		
...		

C Discuss the following questions with a partner or in a group.
1. If you saw a child stealing something from another child's bag or lunch box, how would you react? Would you react "Kimble-style"?
2. When there is a child in a nursery class who doesn't want to play with the other children, like Zach Sullivan in the movie scene, what would you do to integrate him or her into the group?

D Technical aspects of film-making
In this scene Kimble / Schwarzenegger is sometimes shown from a low-angle camera perspective.
What impression does this make on the viewer?

Nursery school as a movie topic Unit 15

In one scene of the movie the boy who steals other children's lunches is eating "fries". British people would call them "chips". Isn't it all very confusing? Look at the list below to learn about differences between British and American English.

Grammar box: British English (BrE) and American English (AmE)

- Diese Liste mit Unterschieden zwischen BrE und AmE soll nur einige Beispiele enthalten, um einen Eindruck zu vermitteln.

Unterschiede	British English	American English	Anmerkungen
1. Aussprache	tomato [aː]	[ei]	
	park [aː]	[ar]	Im AmE ist **r** nach einem Vokal hörbar.
	can't, dance [aː]	[æ]	
	body [ɒ] (offenes 'o')	[ʌ] ('a' wie in 'but')	Im AmE klingt '**body**' fast wie '**buddy**'.
	city [t]	[d]	**t** nach Vokal klingt im AmE wie **d**, z. B., **city**' wie '**siddy**'.
	Tuesday [tjuːzdei]	[tuː]	AmE verzichtet oft auf **[j]** vor **u**.
	suit [sjut]	[suːt]	
	z [zed]	[ziː]	Letzter Buchstabe des Alphabets
2. Rechtschreibung	theatre	theater	re – er
	colour	color	our – or
	to criticise	to criticize	s – z
	to travel (travelling, travelled)	to travel (traveling, traveled)	ll – l
			AmE bevorzugt vereinfachte oder an Aussprache angepasste Schreibung.
3. Wörter mit unterschiedlicher Bedeutung im AmE und BrE	nursery school	kindergarten	Kindergarten
	boot	trunk	Kofferraum
	cinema	the movies	Kino
	underground	subway	U-Bahn
	caretaker	janitor	Hausmeister
	chips	fries	Pommes frites
	traffic lights	stop lights	Verkehrsampel
	car park	parking lot	Parkplatz
	taxi	(yellow) cab	Taxi
4. Unterschiedliche Ausdrücke	I think, I believe	I guess	Ich denke, ich meine

Unit 15 Nursery school as a movie topic

Practising grammar

A A trip to London
Complete the text in American English. Choose the correct words.
Last week I went to London by car. As there was an accident on the … (1 motorway/highway) I had to take the … (2 detour/diversion). I stopped in front of a … (3 theater/theatre) to ask the way. A young man told me to turn right at the … (4 crossroads/intersection) and ask again at the … (5 gas station/petrol station). There a friendly … (6 sales clerk/shop assistant) told me to take the second exit of the … (7 traffic circle/roundabout). After I had passed a … (8 zebra crossing/crosswalk) I saw a … (9 bookstore/bookshop) and a large …(10 car park/parking lot). I parked my car there and walked to the … (11 subway/underground) to get to the … (12 center/centre) of London.

B Check the following sentences for elements of either British or American English. Write down the word in each sentence which you think is typically British or American and mark it "AmE" or "BrE".
Check the meaning and also the spelling.

1. English is my favourite subject at school.
2. Have you seen Dick's new truck?
3. The park is in the center of our town.
4. Mr Barnes, our caretaker, found my key.
5. I like French fries, they're very crispy.
6. Have you been to the movies lately?
7. The bus entered a parking lot so everybody could go to the washroom.
8. The accident happened because the blue car didn't stop at the traffic lights.
9. Tom told me to get off the underground at Tower Hill.
10. We met John when we travelled to Canada.

C Pronunciation exercise
Read the following sentences out loud. Read them
a) with a British accent,
b) with an American accent. Make it sound very British or very American!

1. In the dark corner of the garden center in the city the police officers found his body.
2. My name is Zach, Z-a-c-h, and I live next to Van Courtland Park in New York City.

Nursery school as a movie topic Unit 15

Working with the text

A Creative writing
Production

When Mr Kimble discovers that one of the boys is stealing other children's lunches he reacts rather violently. After all the children have gone home, Mrs Schlowsky, the head teacher, invites Mr Kimble to her office.
Write a dialogue between Mrs Schlowsky and Mr Kimble.
Mrs Schlowsky could try to show Mr Kimble an alternative way of dealing with that boy. Of course Mr Kimble defends his point of view …
Choose a partner for this exercise. You could also turn your dialogue into a small role play and act it out in class.

These words and phrases will help you:	Some verbs:
behaviour can be: violent, wild, decent,	to scold, to tell s.o. off, to discuss, to convince,
quiet children can be: impulsive, aggressive, shy	to give a (good / bad) example, to show an alternative, to show a way out,
adults can be: friendly, understanding, helpful, unfriendly, critical	to explain, to encourage, to stop s.o. from doing s.th.

For more information on role play look at page 190.

B Group work
Form groups of 3 – 4 students and discuss the following problem. Try to find a solution that is acceptable for all group members. Write the most important things of your strategy on a poster and hang it up in the classroom.
If you were in Mr Kimble's place, how would you handle the "poo-poo, ca-ca" situation (line 78) when the group picks on one of the children because he behaves in a funny way?

C Internet research
Use the Internet to find out some information about the "Pledge of Allegiance" in the United States: Who says it and where does this tradition come from? Summarise your findings and present your results to the class.

D Letter tiles
The words of this sentence have been completely scrambled. Put them back into the right order.

C H	G W	W O R	E A	I T H	B	C A	F U L	E M E
N B	L Y	K I N	N E	J O	E S S	S T R	I L D	R E N

Unit 15 Nursery school as a movie topic

movie (AmE) ['muːvɪ]	Film
cop (AmE) [kɒp]	Polizist (Umgangssprache)
The movie "Kindergarten Cop"	
(to) work undercover [wɜːk ˌʌndəˈkvə]	im Geheimen / verdeckt arbeiten
(to) pledge [pledʒ]	geloben, fest versprechen
allegiance [əˈliːdʒəns]	Treue
indivisible [ˌɪndɪˈvɪzəbl]	unteilbar
liberty [ˈlɪbəti]	Freiheit
justice [ˈdʒʌstɪs]	Gerechtigkeit
fries [ˈfraɪz]	Pommes Frites
coach [kəʊtʃ]	Trainer / in
pinhead [pɪnhed]	Dummkopf (Umgangssprache)
amount [əˈmaʊnt]	Summe
moustache [məˈstɑːʃ]	Schnauzbart
freckles [ˈfrekls]	Sommersprossen
gynaecologist [ˌgaɪnɪˈkɒlədʒɪst]	Gynäkologe / Gynäkologin, Frauenarzt / -ärztin
psychologist [saɪˈkɒlədʒɪst]	Psychologe / Psychologin
(to) zoom in on s.o. [zuːm ɪn ɒn]	an jemanden (mit der Kamera) dicht heranfahren, heranzoomen
leave me alone [liːv miː əˈləʊn]	Lass mich in Ruhe
Working with the text	
alternative way [ɔːlˈtɜːnətɪv weɪ]	andere, alternative Art und Weise
behaviour (BrE), behavior (AmE) [bɪˈheɪvjə]	Verhalten, Benehmen
decent [ˈdiːsnt]	anständig, ordentlich
(to) scold s.o. [skəʊld]	jmd. (aus)schimpfen
(to) convince [kənˈvɪns]	überreden, überzeugen
tiles [taɪls]	(Dach-)Ziegel
(to) scramble [ˈscræmbl]	vermischen, durcheinander bringen

Wörter mit unterschiedlicher Bedeutung im AmE und BrE (siehe auch Seite 159)

British English	American English	Deutsch
motorway	highway	Autobahn
detour	diversion	Umleitung
crossroads (nur pl.)	intersection	Kreuzung
petrol station	gas station	Tankstelle
shop assistant	sales clerk	Verkäufer / in
roundabout	traffic circle	Kreisverkehr
zebra crossing	crosswalk	Zebrastreifen
bookshop	bookstore	Buchhandlung
car park	parking lot	Parkplatz
underground	subway	U-Bahn
lorry	truck	Lastwagen

Unit 16 — Working abroad

European countries

Which of the European countries on this map can you name in English?
What are the names of their capitals?
Have you ever visited or do you come from any of these countries?
In which of them would you like to spend your holidays?

Which is which?

Find the right combinations of flags and maps.
Belgium   –   Croatia   –   Great Britain   –   Greece   –   Ireland

handwerk-technik.de

Unit 16 Working abroad

Changing places – Frederic's diary

How easy is it to settle in Germany? Frederic is writing a diary of his move to Germany, where he is working as a teacher in the town of Meißen near Dresden.

Nottingham, 17th July 20..

A true European background
I'm French and I've been married to Anne, who is British, for 13 years. We have two children, Kingsley, 8, and Imogène, 2, who are bilingual. Last year we sat down as a family to talk about our goals for the next two years. One of the most popular goals was to go and live abroad for a year. It had to be somewhere in Europe, preferably in a German- or French-speaking country. I've been teaching French and some German for the past ten years in secondary schools in Nottingham and Derbyshire. When the prospect of a teaching job in Germany turned up, our first reaction was a little prejudiced: wouldn't it be all grim and grey?
I went there for a whole weekend interview in January. And here I am: I will be teaching from August in a school in Meißen, Germany.

Breaking the ice
We found a school for Kingsley where we had a taster lesson and despite the language barrier he felt immediately welcome. He was proud to be able to introduce himself in German: "Mein Name ist Kingsley." It took many hours of discussion but it was worth it! The teacher asked if anyone in the class had heard about a famous character in Nottingham. A little girl put up her hand quickly and answered: "Ro… Robbie Williams!" The whole stay was a lovely experience and we can't wait to be back.

Meißen, 20th November 20..

Man muss jetzt Deutsch sprechen! One has to speak German now!
Kingsley starts school and Imogène starts her nursery school. I start teaching and Anne starts meeting the local community.
All up at 6 a.m.! Kingsley's primary school starts at 7:20 a.m. We all go as a delegation. The head-teacher and staff are waiting in front of the school to welcome the children. The sight of our car with its British number plates creates quite an excitement! Poor Kingsley is crawling under the weight of school books and one cushion that every child must bring for his or her chair. He gives me a sad look as I leave him with his teacher and classmates.

Wrong classroom? Wrong planet?
My first teaching day feels so strange: 25 well-behaved 14- to 15-year-olds, absolutely silent, with no posters on the walls (not allowed – would damage the paint). I am taken by surprise and at first I think I have entered the wrong classroom – or even the wrong planet!
I start with a few icebreakers, some of which involve moving around the classroom, but my students seem to be affected by a strange paralysis, and for the first time in ten years of teaching, I am rapidly losing my confidence. I have planned quizzes, games and text comprehension activities; I try using some humour but end with 25 blank expressions.
I finish the lesson exhausted, thank the students for their cooperation and I am about to go and throw myself into the river Elbe when suddenly they all stand up and rap the tables. They're now all smiling and some even come to shake hands and thank me. Now who's looking puzzled?

Working abroad Unit 16

Working with the text

A Right or Wrong?
Work on the following statements. If you think a statement is correct, say "Yes, that is correct", but check if you can add more information from the text. If you think the sentence is wrong, correct it.
Example: Frederic was a teacher in Nottingham.
Yes, that is correct, but he was also a teacher in Derbyshire. He taught German and French.
1. Frederic is British and he has been married to a French woman for eight years.
2. Kingsley spoke perfect German.
3. The headteacher welcomed the children.
4. The only thing that Kingsley had to bring to school was a cushion for his chair.
5. When Frederic entered the classroom there was a terrible noise.
6. The students were very pleased with the lesson.
7. They all slapped him on the shoulder after the lesson.

B Comment
Answer the following questions, giving your personal opinion.
1. Could you imagine working in another European country as Frederic and his family did? What would be the pros and cons of such a plan?
2. Why did the German students suffer from "a strange paralysis" (line 43) when Frederic asked them to move around in the classroom?
3. Why did Frederic want to "throw (himself) into the river Elbe" (line 47) after that first lesson?
4. Why did the students rap the tables and shake Frederic's hand afterwards?

Working with language

A Find the missing words. If you are not sure, look at the text again.
1. When you speak two languages you are …
2. Small children go to … , later they go to … school.
3. Many people are … against immigrants.
4. The future of students without a good school education is …
5. At school there are the … , the teachers and the …teacher.
6. In some schools students seem to suffer from …
7. Not even an ice… could take away the … expression on their faces.

B Which of the words in the text fit the following explanations?
1. all the teachers of a school
2. a school where children go after primary school
3. when you decide to live somewhere for a long time
4. large pictures which you put on walls to make them look nice
5. not in your own country

C Now try to explain the following words.
1. classmates
2. a diary
3. to introduce oneself
4. a game
5. a poster

Unit 16 Working abroad

D Translation of a text into English

Mediation

The headmaster of the school Frederic has applied to wants to contact Frederic by letter. As his English has become a little "rusty" over the years he asks a colleague to write the letter in English for him. He gives him a sheet with the notes you find below.
Write the headmaster's letter. Use his notes, but remember – you are not expected to write a word-by-word translation.

Sehr geehrter Herr T.,

vielen Dank für Ihr Schreiben vom April.
Ich möchte Ihnen sagen, dass an unserer Schule schon ein Lehrer aus Frankreich und eine Lehrerin aus Amerika arbeiten; wir sind jedoch trotzdem an ihrer Mitarbeit sehr interessiert. Bitte schreiben Sie uns, an welchen Schulen Sie bisher gearbeitet und welche Altersgruppen Sie unterrichtet haben. Wir würden Sie gern persönlich kennen lernen; teilen Sie uns bitte mit, wann Sie für ein Gespräch nach Meißen kommen könnten.

Viele Grüße

If you don't know what an English letter looks like, refer to page 183 ("Der Geschäftsbrief").

Grammar box: Conditional sentences (Type III) – Bedingungssätze (Typ III)

- Mit Bedingungssätzen des Typs III drückt man aus, was in der Vergangenheit hätte geschehen können, wenn die Situation anders gewesen wäre.
  If **I had known** that you were in London, **I would have come** to see you!
  (But I didn't know you were in London.)
  If **I had heard** the alarm, **I would have called** the police.
  (But I was fast asleep and couldn't hear it.)

- Der if-Satz (= Nebensatz) kann am Anfang oder am Ende eines Satzes stehen.
- Er wird gebildet mit *had + 3. Verbform (Past Perfect)*.
- Der Hauptsatz wird gebildet mit *would + have + 3. Verbform*.

→ Vorsicht: Im if-Satz niemals *would* verwenden! Kein *would* nach *if!*

Vgl. hierzu auch Grammar boxes Conditional type I und II in Unit 10.

Working abroad Unit 16

Practising grammar

A Make up conditional sentences type III.
Use the structure explained in the grammar box.
Example: I hurried to catch the underground to be on time for my interview. If I … (miss) the train, I … (be) late for the interview.
– If I had missed the train, I would have been late for the interview.
1. And if I … (miss) the interview, I … (not get) this job.
2. If I … (not get) this job, I … (be) in financial trouble.
3. If I … (be) in financial trouble, I …. (sell) my new car.
4. If I … (sell) the new car, I … (go) to work by bus.
5. And if I … (go) to work by bus, my buddies … (laugh) at me.

B Put the verb into the correct form.
Take care, this time the if-clause is at the end of the sentence.
1. We … (not hear) of Frederic and his family if he … (stay) in Nottingham.
2. And we … (not meet) his son Kingsley if he … (go) to school in Britain.
3. Frederic … (lose) his confidence if his students … (not rap) the tables.
4. We … (not read) his story if he … (jump) into the river Elbe.
5. You and I … (not learn) about Frederic's story if he …(not put) it on the Internet.

C Make up sentences using 'if' (type III) for each of the following situations.
1. We had a car crash because the driver in front stopped abruptly.
   If the driver in front hadn't …, we… not …
2. I have been so busy lately. That's why I haven't written to you before.
   If I … not …, I …
3. Mike walked home last night because he missed the last bus.
   If he …
4. She didn't try very hard. Maybe that's the reason she lost the game. …
5. Mr Smith didn't realise that it was wet and cold outside. So he slipped and fell. …

D Now that you have become an expert in the use of the English conditional, try this mixed exercise. Conditional clauses type I, II or III – you decide which one must be used.
1. Kingsley is a smart boy. If he … (to go) to a German school for one year, I'm sure he … (to speak) German perfectly.
2. During his first lesson in Meißen Frederic thinks: if I … (not – to have) my quizzes and icebreakers, I … (to be) completely lost now.
3. If they …. (to have) some posters on the wall, the classroom … (to look) much nicer.
4. Do you really think Frederic … (to throw) himself into the river Elbe if everything … (to go) wrong during his first lesson?
5. If Frederic's family … (stay) in Great Britain, they … (to miss) many interesting experiences.
6. If you … (to be) interested in a stay abroad, I am quite certain that you … (to find) a way to realise your plans.
7. If people … (to be) more courageous – but we know they are not – more people … (to look) for work in another country.

Unit 16 Working abroad

Applying for a job abroad

When Larissa, a 22-year-old German nursery nurse, reads Frederic's story she is really excited. She says to herself: "If he can go to another country although he has a family with two small children, what about me? My English is not all bad and I'm young, independent, quite courageous … am I not?"

And one day while surfing the web she comes across the website of Southdown Infant School and discovers the following:

Southdown Infant School

Nursery Assistant   (Ref: 20a/12)

Part-time (20 hrs)
£8,103.85 – £8,566.59 per annum

We are seeking a nursery assistant to help provide a safe and stimulating environment to all children under the care of the nursery. You will be required to encourage the social, physical, emotional and educational development of each child in a multi-cultural environment while maintaining standards of safety, health and hygiene.

You will hold an under-five qualification at NVQ Level 3 or equivalent and experience of working with that age group. You must have proven skills in providing a high standard of childcare. A first-aid qualification would be advantageous.

Application forms can be obtained from our website www.southdowninfantschool.co.uk or you can write to the Personnel Section at Southdown Infant School, Mill Road, London N4 N4P.
Please quote the reference number in all correspondence.

Working with the text

When Larissa sees this advertisement she forgets the rainy weather in Britain and decides to write a letter of application to Southdown Infant School in London.
Help Larissa to write her letter. Start by saying who you are and what gave you the idea of applying for a job in Britain.
Include your qualifications and say what you are currently doing. Say what you hope to learn and why especially you are the right person for this job.

Hands-on task

Search for job offers for nursery nurses or nursery assistants in English-speaking countries. Imagine applying for one of them: Write your own letter of application and CV for the position.

Use the information about writing a letter of application given on page 183.

Working abroad Unit 16

The job interview

Four weeks after sending her application Larissa is really surprised to receive a letter that invites her to come to London for a job interview. In order to prepare for it, Larissa simulates an interview with a friend.

Imagine you are Larissa's friend. Think of questions that the interviewer will ask her. Use the information from Larissa's CV. You can also ask other questions.
Work with a partner. After about ten questions switch roles.

This is Larissa's CV (Curriculum Vitae):

Personal details
Name	Larissa Schönhoff
Address	Rembrandtstr. 24, 50737 Köln
Telephone	+49/221/234 756
E-Mail	LarissaS@emails.de
Nationality	German
Date of birth	January 18th, 1990
Marital status	unmarried

Work experience
June 2009 – the present	Nursery nurse at Kindertagesstätte Paulusstraße in Cologne, responsible for a group of 25 children from 3 to 6 years

Apprenticeship
2006 – 2009	Practical traineeship to be a nursery nurse at Städtische Kindertagesstätte in Köln-Weidenpesch, combined with continued theoretical training at vocational college
May 2009	Final examination; overall grade: "Gut" (A-B)

Education
2000 – 2006	Comprehensive school Lise-Meitner-Gesamtschule in Köln-Porz, overall grade: "Befriedigend" (B-C)
1996 – 2000	Primary school Grundschule Idastraße in Köln-Porz

Other skills
Basic computer skills (Windows),
basic knowledge in Excel and PowerPoint;
driving licence;
In charge of the students' paper shop at
Lise-Meitner-Gesamtschule for 2 years

Personal interests
Football, tennis, reading science-fiction literature,
member of the "Society for the Protection of Animal Rights" since 2006

References

Ms Petra Meier
Head nurse
Kindertagesstätte Paulusstraße
Paulusstraße 46
51143 Köln

Ms Hannelore Schwarz
Sachbearbeiterin
Jugendamt Köln
Ottmar-Pohl-Platz 1
51103 Köln

Unit 16 Working abroad

Thoughts about my work experience in Britain

Finally Larissa gets the job and starts working at Southdown Infant School in London. She stays there for one year and when she comes back she writes the following report about her time there:

5 I believe that my stay abroad was a new and thrilling challenge, as I really had to take care of myself and had to get along on my own for a year in a foreign country whose culture was unknown to me. I didn't know anyone and I
10 was having problems with the language and life was simply completely different.
At the beginning of my stay I had some difficulties with the language but in the end I always found a way of making myself
15 understood. Facial expression and sign language always played an important role. After a little while I got used to communicating in another language and it became easier and easier to
20 understand others and to express myself. At first it was also difficult to get used to things in my new nursery as many situations and methods were unknown to me. In England children wear school
25 uniforms and there is generally more discipline in classes, so there is a lot to marvel at and you simply need time to get used to things.
I spent my year in London at Southdown
30 Infant School which accepts children from 3 to 7 years. The children who are 3 or 4 years old go to the "nursery" which can be compared to our "Kindergarten". This belongs to the school. As children in Great Britain start
35 school when they are 4 years and 6 months old and because a wide variety of methods is used to teach them reading, writing and maths, you also find various ways of working with the children there.
40 During lessons children work almost exclusively in small groups and there is always a teacher and at least one assistant. I spent most of the time in a class of 6- and 7-year-olds and I was not only able to watch but also
45 to take part in the teaching.
It was really very exciting to see the children count to 100, to watch them write small stories in no time at all or to see them read a book. Even the 5-year-olds knew the letters of the
50 alphabet, learnt to write short sentences and to read. Apart from that they could easily calculate with numbers up to 10.
Nevertheless, I think it's hard for small children to go to school until late in the afternoon.
55 At the beginning a lot of things in the daily routine were new and seemed strange to me. With them I discovered many new insights and gained a lot of exciting experience.

Working with the text

Mediation

A Give those of your colleagues whose English skills are a bit "rusty" a summary of the report above, in German.

Working abroad Unit 16

[For tasks B, C, D work with a partner.]

B Find a headline for each of the paragraphs.
Example: Paragraph 1 could be called: Going abroad; a thrilling experience; six weeks in a foreign country

C Questions on the text
1. How long did Larissa stay in London?
2. What did she do when she couldn't find the right words in English?
3. What did Larissa like about her work at Southdown Infant School and what was difficult for her?
4. What is different between Southdown Infant School and a nursery school as you know it?
5. Do you think that she enjoyed her year in London? Find reasons to support your answer.

D Creative writing
After the first two weeks Larissa writes a letter to Jenny, her best friend at home. She still has problems getting used to all those new people and strange things around her. Write Larissa's letter to Jenny.
Use the following words and ideas if you like, but you can also bring in your own thoughts.
You could talk about:
- the nursery – different from the nursery at home
- language problems – everybody talks so fast
- food – strange!
- school uniforms – old-fashioned!
- weather – surprisingly dry and sunny
- nursery nurses – very friendly

D Role play

See also page 190 for information about role playing.

Rules: One player is the moderator. He or she 'directs' the discussion a little, sums up at the end and makes sure that a solution is found.
You are given a few minutes to prepare your roles. Everybody should write down a few key words but do not just prepare lines of text to read out to the others!
A good start is to give everybody the chance to begin with a short statement. Try to finish with a solution that is acceptable to everyone.

Going to Calgary
For this game 5 people are needed: a 15-year-old girl, her mother, her father, her elder brother, her boyfriend.
Your mother's cousin David who moved to Canada 10 years ago has written an e-mail offering you a 6-month stay with his family in Calgary. He has even talked to the woman in charge of the local day-care center and you could work there for a few hours every day as a trainee.
Discuss the pros and cons of going to Canada with your mum, dad, your boyfriend and your elder brother. Think of the following things:

- Calgary is a lively, interesting city with over a million inhabitants.
- You could practise your job, which would be very good to mention in a job application.
- You will meet many people, make new friends and learn a lot of new things.
- Maybe you will feel a little lonely at first, miss your family, your boyfriend …?

Go on and find more points and reasons for and against.

Unit 16 Working abroad

Solutions European countries (capitals are in brackets)
Albania (Tirana), Austria (Vienna), Belarus (Minsk), Belgium (Brussels), Bosnia and Herzegovina (Sarajevo), Bulgaria (Sofia), Croatia (Zagreb), Denmark (Copenhagen), Estonia (Tallinn), Finland (Helsinki), France (Paris), Germany (Berlin), Great Britain (London), Greece (Athens), Hungary (Budapest), Ireland (Dublin), Italy (Rome), Latvia (Riga), Lithuania (Vilnius), Luxembourg (Luxembourg), Malta (Valletta), Moldavia (Chisinau), The Netherlands (Amsterdam), Norway (Oslo), Poland (Warsaw), Portugal (Lisbon), Rumania (Bucharest), Slovakia (Bratislava), Slovenia (Ljubljana), Spain (Madrid), Sweden (Stockholm), Switzerland (Bern), Turkey (Ankara), Ukraine (Kiev), Serbia and Montenegro (Belgrade)

Changing places – Frederic's diary

diary ['daɪərɪ]	Tagebuch
(to) settle ['setl]	sich niederlassen
former ['fɔːmə]	früher, ehemalig
bilingual [baɪ'lɪŋgwəl]	zweisprachig
goal [gəʊl]	Ziel
secondary school ['sekəndərɪ skuːl]	weiterführende Schule
prejudiced ['predʒʊdɪst]	auf Vorurteilen beruhend
grim [grɪm]	düster
taster lesson [teɪst ə 'lesn]	Probestunde, Unterricht zum Ausprobieren
primary school ['praɪmərɪ skuːl]	Grundschule
headteacher [hedtiːtʃə]	Schulleiter(in)
staff [stɑːf]	die Mitarbeiter, die Lehrkräfte
(to) crawl [krɔːl]	kriechen, hier: fast zusammenbrechen unter der Last
cushion ['kʊʃn]	(Sitz)kissen
(to) damage ['dæmɪdʒ]	beschädigen
icebreaker [aɪsbreɪkɜː]	"Eisbrecher", hier: Übung oder Aktivität, die die Stimmung lockert
confidence ['kɒnfɪdəns]	Selbstvertrauen
blank expressions [blæŋk ɪ'kspreʃənz]	ausdruckslose Gesichter
(to) rap the table [ræp ðə 'teɪbl]	auf den Tisch klopfen (als Zeichen für Beifall)
puzzled ['pʌzld]	verwirrt

Applying for a job abroad

job advertisement [dʒɒb əd'vɜːtɪsmənt]	Stellenanzeige
(to) seek [siːk]	suchen
(to) stimulate ['stɪmjʊleɪt]	anregen, Anreize schaffen
multi-cultural ['mlti-'kʌltʃərəl]	von vielen Kulturen geprägt
NVQ, National Vocational Qualification ['næʃənl vəʊkeɪʃn ˌkwɒlɪfɪ'keɪʃn]	staatlich anerkannte berufliche Qualifikation
equivalent [ɪ'kwɪvələnt]	gleichwertig
proven skills [pruːvən skɪls]	nachgewiesene Fertigkeiten
advantageous [ˌædvən'teɪdʒəs]	vorteilhaft
(to) quote [kwəʊt]	angeben, sich auf etw. beziehen

The job interview

CV, Curriculum Vitae [kə'rɪkjʊləm 'viːtaɪ]	Lebenslauf

Thoughts about my work experience in Britain

thrilling [θrɪlɪŋ]	spannend
facial expression ['feɪʃl ɪk'spreʃn]	Gesichtsausdruck
(to) marvel at s.th. ['mɑːvl æt]	sich über etwas wundern
(to) gain [geɪn]	gewinnen
insight ['ɪnsaɪt]	Einblick
(to) justify ['dʒʌstɪfaɪ]	rechtfertigen, beweisen

Methodenseiten

Wortschatz erweitern und Vokabeln lernen

Vokabeln zu lernen ist mühsam! Andererseits ist es noch viel mühsamer, über Dinge zu reden, die man nicht benennen kann … Mit ein paar einfachen Tipps und Tricks ist Vokabeln lernen gar nicht so schwer:

Tipp 1: Alles an seinem Platz
Vokabeln sollten einen festen Platz haben, z. B. ein Vokabelheft oder eine bestimmte Stelle im Ordner oder Ringbuch. Das Format ist dabei nicht wichtig.

Tipp 2: Nicht alles auf einmal
Vokabeln sollten in überschaubare Einheiten aufgeteilt werden. Man muss selbst herausfinden, wie viele man sich pro Sitzung merken kann. 10 – 15 neue Wörter pro Lerneinheit sind eine gute Zahl. Nicht so viel auf einmal, aber dafür regelmäßig lernen ist besser, d. h. jeden Tag oder jeden zweiten Tag eine Portion.

Tipp 3: Vokabeln abschreiben
Die meisten Leute können sich leichter merken, was sie nicht nur gelesen, sondern auch geschrieben haben. Außerdem gehört die richtige Schreibung einfach dazu – nicht nur dann, wenn der nächste Vokabeltest bevorsteht.

Tipp 4: Karteikärtchen anlegen
Man kann entweder alle zu lernenden Wörter auf Karteikärtchen schreiben oder man schreibt nur diejenigen Wörter auf, die man sich schlecht merkt.
Die Kärtchen kommen in eine Box mit Fächerunterteilung. Mehrere Kategorien sind ratsam: Ganz vorne die Gruppe der neuen Wörter, die noch nicht sicher „sitzen", ganz hinten sind die Vokabeln, die man schon sicher weiß. Dazwischen können mehrere Zwischenstufen sein. Beim Lernen wandern die Wörter in der Box langsam von vorne nach hinten, bis sie schließlich im Fach der fest eingeprägten Vokabeln landen. Diese werden nur gelegentlich wiederholt, die vorderen Kategorien entsprechend öfter.

Noch ein Trick:
Um Probleme mit der Rechtschreibung bei ähnlicher Schreibung im Deutschen und Englischen *(Theater – theatre)* zu vermeiden, ist es empfehlenswert, jeder Sprache eine Farbe zuzuordnen:
z. B. deutsch = blau, englisch = rot.
Das deutsche Wort kommt auf die eine, die englische Bedeutung auf die andere Seite.

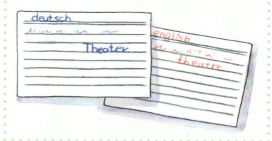

Tipp 5: Feste Verbindungen beachten
Im Englischen gehen Wörter oft feste Verbindungen mit anderen Wörtern ein. Diese feststehenden Ausdrücke sollte man sich notieren: Also nicht nur „*homework = Hausaufgaben*", sondern „*to do the homework = die Hausaufgaben machen*".

Tipp 6: Bezüge zu Bekanntem herstellen
Wenn man Wörter in Zusammenhänge stellt, also Neues mit Bekanntem verbindet, kann man sich das Lernen erheblich erleichtern (vgl. auch Seite 182 „Mindmap"). Nützlich ist es auch, mit den Vokabeln Sätze zu bilden und diese auf das Kärtchen zu schreiben.

Übrigens gibt es auch PC-Programme, mit denen man Karteikärtchen am Bildschirm ausfüllen und verwalten kann.

Methodenseiten

Textfragen schriftlich beantworten

Wenn Textfragen schriftlich beantwortet werden sollen, dann geht man Schritt für Schritt folgendermaßen vor:

Schritt 1: Lesen Sie den Text sorgfältig durch.

Schritt 2: Lesen Sie alle Fragen durch und stellen Sie sicher, dass Sie sie verstanden haben.

Schritt 3: Ordnen Sie zu, welche Zeilen Ihres Textes zu Ihrer Frage gehören. Sie können dies tun, indem Sie unterstreichen (mit verschiedenen Farben für die verschiedenen Fragen) oder indem Sie Stichworte herausschreiben.

Schritt 4: Schauen Sie alle Wörter nach, die Sie verstehen müssen, um die Frage zu beantworten. Dies kann mithilfe des Vokabelverzeichnisses im Anhang oder mit einem Wörterbuch geschehen.

Schritt 5: Aus den markierten Teilen des Textes bzw. den Stichworten verfassen Sie nun die Antwort auf Ihre Frage:

- Benutzen Sie einen Teil der Frage, um Ihre Antwort einzuleiten.

- Verwenden Sie Synonyme (= Wörter gleicher Bedeutung) und umschreiben Sie. (Vgl. auch Seite 175)

- Schreiben Sie vollständige Sätze.

Schritt 6: **Schreiben Sie niemals Sätze aus Ihrem Text ab!**

Schritt 7: **Beginnen Sie Ihren Antwortsatz nicht mit** *"Because ..."*!

Wörter und Ausdrücke auf Englisch erklären

Wörter können auf viele verschiedene Arten erklärt werden.

Zum Beispiel können Sie …

… ein Wort mit gleicher oder sehr ähnlicher Bedeutung nennen:
Disease *is the same as illness. Another word for disease is illness.*

… ein Wort mit entgegengesetzter Bedeutung nennen:
The opposite of **healthy** *is ill.*

… Größe, Form oder Farbe beschreiben:
A **pumpkin** *is a vegetable. It is orange and has the shape of a head but can be a lot bigger.*

… beschreiben, was man damit tut:
A **sink** *is the place where you wash dishes.*

… das Wort einem Oberbegriff zuordnen:
A **puppet** *is a kind of toy.*

… den Ausdruck in einen bekannten Zusammenhang einordnen:
The **block area** *is one part of the nursery school classroom.*

… ein Beispiel geben:
One example of **disease** *is chicken pox.*

… eine Definition geben:
The **nuclear family** *is a family type where father, mother and their children live together. There are more family members but they do not live in the same home.*

… mehrere der genannten Möglichkeiten kombinieren:
A **pumpkin** *is a vegetable. It is orange and has the shape of a head but can be a lot bigger. It is a popular Halloween decoration.*

Wenn Sie regelmäßig üben, Wörter zu umschreiben, werden Sie nach einiger Zeit feststellen, dass Sie Ihren persönlichen Wortschatz geläufiger anwenden können. Möglicherweise werden Sie sich immer weniger in der Situation (Klassenarbeit etc.) befinden, dass Sie ein ganz bestimmtes Wort verwenden wollen, es Ihnen aber nicht auf Englisch einfällt. Dann werden Sie es umschreiben können.

Konnektoren und Einleitungen

Introduction	Einleitung
Today,	Heute
Nowadays, …	Heutzutage
It is often claimed that …	Es wird oft behauptet, dass
It is a well-known fact that …	Es ist allgemein bekannt, dass
According to …	Laut / Gemäß
Structuring arguments	**Argumente strukturieren**
At first, I would like to / Firstly, …	Erstens
Secondly, …	Zweitens
Finally, …	Schließlich
First of all …	Zunächst einmal
To begin with I would like to mention that …	Zu Beginn möchte ich erwähnen, dass
In addition, …	Zusätzlich
Moreover, …	Darüberhinaus
Besides, …	Nebenbei (bemerkt)
Furthermore, …	Außerdem
Another advantage is …	Ein weiterer Vorteil ist
To add another point, …	Um (noch) einen Punkt hinzuzufügen,
Another reason is …	Ein weiterer Grund ist
Last but not least, …	Nicht zuletzt
Comparisons and contrasts	**Vergleiche und Gegensätze**
On the one hand … on the other hand …	Auf der einen Seite … auf der anderen Seite
I have to admit, however, that …	Ich muss jedoch zugeben, dass
Nevertheless, …	Nichtsdestotrotz
In spite of / Despite all those reasons …	Trotz all der Gründe
Although it is true …	Obwohl es stimmt….
In contrast to the text I think …	Im Gegensatz zum Text denke ich
Contrary to the popular idea,	Entgegen der allgemeinen Vorstellung
In comparison with …	Im Vergleich mit
Compared to …	Verglichen mit
Giving an example	**Beispiel geben**
…, for example,… … e.g. … …, for instance, …	zum Beispiel

Logical consequence	Logische Folge
So, Therefore That is why … Because of this, …	Deshalb
For these reasons …	Aus diesen Gründen
As a result, …	Als Ergebnis

Conclusion	Schluss
To conclude … In conclusion …	Zusammenfassend
All in all I think …	Alles in allem denke ich …
To sum up, …	Zusammengefasst
In brief, I cannot accept that …	Kurz gesagt, ich kann nicht akzeptieren, dass
Weighing the pros and cons, I come to the conclusion that …	Wenn man das Für und Wider abwägt, komme ich zu dem Schluss, dass

Personal opinion	Persönliche Meinung
I think that	Ich denke, dass
In my opinion To my mind …	Meiner Meinung nach
I am of the opinion that …	Ich bin der Meinung, dass
From my point of view … In my view … The way I see it, …	Meines Erachtens / Meiner Meinung nach / Meiner Ansicht nach
I must admit that …	Ich muss zugeben, dass
I am convinced that …	Ich bin überzeugt, dass
It's all right as far as I'm concerned.	Es ist okay, was mich betrifft.
I (entirely) agree / disagree with the author.	Ich stimme dem Autor (völlig) zu / Ich muss dem Autor (völlig) widersprechen.

Methodenseiten

Häufige Fehlerquellen im Englischen

Falsch	Richtig

Simple Present – Bei Verben im Simple Present gilt folgende Regel: *he/she/it* – „s" muss mit! **Vgl. Unit 1**

He **ask** his mother for help.	He asks his mother for help.
She **eat** a lot of biscuits.	She eats a lot of biscuits.
It **play** in the garden.	It plays in the garden.

Fragen im Simple Present – Bei Fragen im Simple Present erfolgt die Umschreibung mit *to do*.

What colour **has** snow?	What colour does snow have?
Goes he to school every morning?	Does he go to school every morning? **Vgl. Unit 1**

Verwechslung von there – they're – their
Die Worte klingen gleich, aber haben unterschiedliche Bedeutung:
there = dort; they are = sie sind, their = ihre

They always had good weather in **there** holidays.	They always had good weather in their holidays.
Their very excited about their trip to Paris.	They are very excited about their trip to Paris.
They will visit a lot of museums **their**.	They will visit a lot of museums there.

Verwechslung von it's – its
Die Worte klingen gleich, aber haben unterschiedliche Bedeutung:
it's (it is) bedeutet *es ist*. *Its* ist ein Pronomen und heißt *sein/ihr*. **Vgl. Unit 1**

The dog looked at **it's** puppies.	The dog looked at its puppies.
Its a wonderful day today.	It's a wonderful day today.
Is it your car? No, **its** Rita's.	Is it your car? No, it's Rita's.

Verwechslung von become – get
Das deutsche *„bekommen"* heißt im Englischen *„to get"*. *„To become"* heißt übersetzt *„werden"*!

I want to **get** a teacher.	I want to become a teacher.
If children watch too much TV, they will **become** nightmares.	If children watch too much TV, they will get nightmares.

Verwendung von this – these
„This" wird im Singular verwendet. *„These"* ist Plural und wird nur dort verwendet.

I don't understand **this** things.	I don't understand these things.
Oh, look at **this** wonderful flowers.	Oh, look at these wonderful flowers.
I like **these** coloured shirt very much.	I like this coloured shirt very much.

Falsch	Richtig

Satzbau – Adverbien der unbestimmten Häufigkeit stehen vor einer einteiligen Form des Verbs oder nach dem ersten Hilfsverb.

You drive **always** too fast.	You always drive too fast.
I go **never** to the supermarket.	I never go to the supermarket.
We don't arrive **usually** late.	We don't usually arrive late.

Genitiv-S – Der s-Genitiv wird für Personen verwendet. **Vgl. Unit 4**

This is the **car of Jim**.	This is Jim's car.
The **childrens** mother was in hospital.	The children's mother was in hospital.
Janet lives in a **students** hostel. She shares a kitchen with five other students.	Janet lives in a students' hostel. She shares a kitchen with five other students.
We liked the **film's** beginning.	We liked the beginning of the film.

Verwendung von will – want – Das deutsche „wollen" heißt im Englischen „to want". Das englische „will" heißt „werden" und wird für die Zukunft verwendet. **Vgl. Unit 6**

Mum, I **will** watch a video, please.	Mum, I want to watch a video, please.
I **will** become a teacher.	I want to become a teacher.

Verwendung von want + Infinitiv – Im Deutschen heißt es: „Ich möchte, dass…." Im Englischen muss man dafür *want + Infinitiv* benutzen.

I want **that** the children eat the cake.	I want the children to eat the cake.
My mother wants **that** I do the dishes.	My mother wants me to do the dishes.

Verwechslung von do – make – „Do" ist ein Vollverb mit den Bedeutungen *machen, tun, verrichten, erledigen*.

I will **make** my homework this afternoon.	I will do my homework this afternoon.
I know I must **make** more sports.	I know I must do more sports.
Katie **made** the shopping.	Katie did the shopping.

Verwendung von would im if-Satz – Im Bedingungssatz Typ II steht Simple Past im if-Satz und Conditional I im Hauptsatz. Der Typ II wird verwendet, wenn die Bedingung als unmöglich oder unwahrscheinlich angesehen werden kann. **Vgl. Unit 10 + 16**

If he **would understand**, it would be easier.	If he understood, it would be easier.
If he **wouldn't eat** so much, he wouldn't be so fat.	If he didn't eat so much, he wouldn't be so fat.

Wörtliche Übersetzung aus dem Deutschen
Vorsicht: Nicht alles lässt sich wörtlich vom Deutschen ins Englische übersetzen.

The **most people** live in the cities.	Most of the people live in the cities.
Do you **mean** the weather will be better soon?	Do you think the weather will be better soon?
It gives a lot of games in the nursery school.	There are a lot of games in the nursery school.

Methodenseiten

Einen zusammenhängenden Text schreiben

Breast-feeding is a good start for babies (Unit 10)
Today, a lot of women go back to work after having a baby because they need to earn money or want to look after their career. But who will look after the baby? Who will feed the baby? Is there an alternative to breast milk or is breast milk the best food for babies?
Mothers who want to feed their babies have to think about the right food. It takes some time to get used to breast-feeding and some mothers do not like it. **Firstly,** because they say that their breasts get bigger or sometimes sore. **Secondly,** because they find it makes them feel unsexy.
Sometimes it can also cause health problems e.g. mastitis. The breasts get swollen and infected. This is quite painful and the mother then needs to see a doctor immediately.
If a mother does not or cannot breast-feed her baby, formula milk is an alternative, **however,** you have to follow some rules when preparing a bottle and choose the correct formula milk. This can be difficult **because** there are so many different types, depending on the age of the child or the number of ingredients.
Family members can help by preparing the bottle or also by bottle-feeding the child, which is good. But formula milk costs money and the preparation of bottles can be time consuming.
Breast milk, **on the other hand,** is free and always **available.** To produce enough milk the mother needs to eat **a balanced diet** and some extra calories. She also needs to keep her fluid intake. Mothers should eat healthy food to get the extra nutrients **because** whatever a mother eats passes directly into the bloodstream, then into the breast milk and finally into the baby. Therefore, mothers must be careful what they eat and drink. Alcohol is not allowed, **for example.**
To add another point, breast-feeding can help mothers **to return to their pre-pregnancy weight. Another advantage** is that breast milk is easy for the baby to digest and it contains antibodies **which help** to protect the baby from infections.
Breast-feeding **also** gives a mother a special feeling of closeness to her baby **because** she holds it close and spends a lot of time with it.
Last but not least, breast milk contains all the **ingredients** a baby needs in the right proportions and **at the right temperature.**
Therefore I am of the opinion that breast milk is the best baby food. It has advantages for both mother and child. And if fathers want to help or the mother has no time because she has to work, the breast milk can be pumped into bottles and warmed up when it is time to give a feed. Furthermore, there are laws to protect mothers and give them time off or longer breaks at work in order to look after the baby.

Einige Tipps, wie man seinen Ausdruck verbessern kann:

Ein Text sollte mit einer Einleitung beginnen.

Benutzen Sie Konnektoren[1], um Ihre Sätze zu verbinden. Dies sorgt für einen abwechslungsreichen Satzbau.

Gliedern Sie Ihren Text! Sinnvolle Absätze erleichtern das Lesen und man kann Ihren Gedanken besser folgen.

Begründen Sie Ihre Argumente oder geben Sie Beispiele an, um Ihre Aussagen zu belegen.

Ein großer Wortschatz hilft, sich genau auszudrücken. Nutzen Sie – wenn möglich – Fachbegriffe. Dazu muss man immer wieder Vokabeln lernen!

Eine Erörterung wird mit einer kurzen Zusammenfassung und der eigenen Meinung abgeschlossen.

---

[1] *For more information on connectors see page 176.*

Eine Erörterung („Essay") schreiben

Ein „essay" zu schreiben heißt, einen zusammenhängenden Text mit einer ausgewogenen Argumentation zu verfassen. So gehen Sie vor:

Schritt 1: Lesen Sie sich die Aufgabenstellung gut durch.

Meist wird eine Einstiegsbehauptung („statement") abgegeben, zu der Sie sich eine Meinung bilden müssen.

Schritt 2: Sammeln Sie Argumente für und gegen die These, Behauptung oder Aussage.

- Erstellen Sie daraus eine Liste.
- Bringen Sie Ihre Argumente in eine Reihenfolge. Welches ist das Wichtigste? Welches ist weniger wichtig?

Schritt 3: Schreiben Sie eine Einleitung („introduction").

- Die Einleitung bezieht sich auf die Einstiegsbehauptung oder Aussage. Sie greift ein aktuelles Thema auf und führt zu einer Fragestellung. Sie soll den Leser ansprechen und zum Weiterlesen motivieren.
  Gut ist es, wenn man sich z. B. auf aktuelle Ereignisse, auf Zeitungsartikel oder Statistiken beziehen kann. Der Leser soll den Eindruck bekommen, dass das Thema heutzutage relevant ist.

Schritt 4: Schreiben Sie den Hauptteil („main part").

- Der Hauptteil enthält zunächst alle Argumente FÜR die These, gefolgt von den Argumenten GEGEN die Einstiegsbehauptung – oder umgekehrt, je nachdem, welcher Meinung Sie sind.
- Man beginnt mit den Argumenten der Seite, die NICHT der eigenen Meinung entspricht.
- Folgen Sie dem „Prinzip der Sanduhr": Beginnen Sie mit dem stärksten Argument der Gegenseite und enden Sie mit dem stärksten Argument der Seite, für die Sie sind.

- Um einen ausgewogenen Text zu bekommen, sind 3 – 5 Argumente pro Seite angemessen.
- Jedes Argument sollte begründet oder mit Beispielen belegt werden.
- Der Text sollte gut geliedert sein. Jedes Argument bildet einen eigenen Absatz.
- Achten Sie darauf, Ihre Gedanken und Sätze mit **Konnektoren**[2] zu verbinden.

Schritt 5: Schreiben Sie den Schluss („conclusion").

- Leiten Sie aus dem Gesagten Ihre eigene Meinung ab. Begründen Sie Ihre Meinung.
- Greifen Sie dabei die Einstiegsfrage wieder auf, geben Sie eine Antwort dazu oder machen Sie einen (Verbesserungs-)Vorschlag.

[2] *For more information on connectors see page 176.*

Methodenseiten

Die Mindmap

Wozu?	Wie?

Die Mindmap (auch Netzbild genannt) eignet sich überall da, wo Gedanken gesammelt und dargestellt werden sollen, z. B.
• zur Visualisierung eines Themas, eines geplanten Projektes;
• zum Einstieg in ein Thema oder ein Projekt. Hier können mit der Mindmap zunächst Gedanken gesammelt werden;
• zur Vertiefung eines Themas, da in der Mindmap Gedanken nicht nur gesammelt werden, sondern gleichzeitig Strukturen sichtbar gemacht und Beziehungen hervorgehoben werden.
 	
Nachteil
Bei vielen Gedanken kann die Mindmap unübersichtlich werden.
	Vorbereitung
	Man benötigt
	• eine größere Schreibfläche, z. B. Tapete, ein Plakat oder Papierbogen einer Flipchart
	• verschiedene Stifte in verschiedenen Farben und Stärken
	
	Durchführung
	• Der Ausgangspunkt ist immer ein in der Mitte des Plakats aufgemalter Kreis, in dem das Thema, zu dem gesammelt werden soll, in einem Schlagwort, in Stichworten oder in einem Fragesatz (= Problemstellung) angegeben wird.
	Beispiel: Eine Mindmap erstellen oder Wie erstellt man eine Mindmap?
	• Jetzt kann man Ideen zum Oberthema sammeln und anfügen. Dabei ist wichtig, dass man
	  ☞ Hauptpunkte sucht und anschreibt,
	  ☞ Unterpunkte an diese Hauptpunkte anhängt, sodass das Bild von innen nach außen wächst,
	  ☞ Beziehungen durch Pfeile und Verästelungen darstellt, sodass eine Art „Ideenbaum" entsteht,
	  ☞ mit unterschiedlichen Farben und Symbolen arbeitet, die Beziehungen hervorheben, „Knotenpunkte" oder wichtige Fragen / Oberpunkte verdeutlichen.

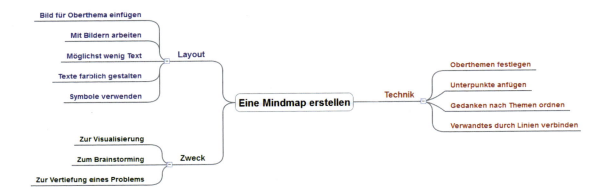

Der Geschäftsbrief

Die Form des Geschäftsbriefs ist bei vielen formalen Anlässen einzuhalten, auch bei einer Bewerbung.

Vorsicht:
Der Aufbau im Englischen unterscheidet sich von dem eines deutschen Geschäftsbriefs!

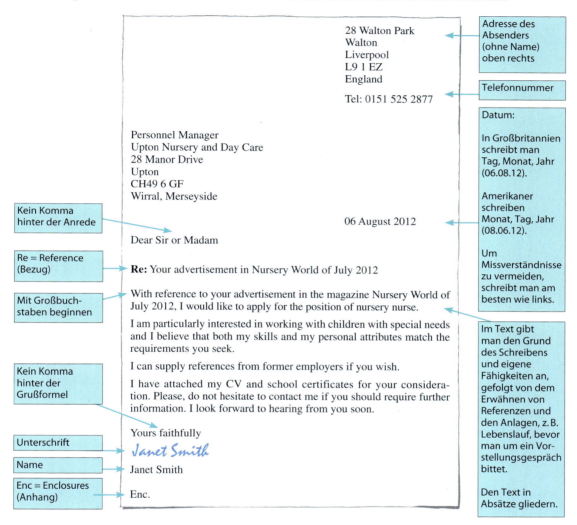

Anreden und Grußformeln

Anrede und Grußformel am Schluss des Briefes richten sich danach, ob man die Person kennt, an die man schreibt:

Dear Sir or Madam	Yours faithfully
Dear Madam	Yours faithfully
Dear Sir	Yours faithfully
Dear Mr Black	Yours sincerely
Dear Mrs Gray	Yours sincerely
Dear Sarah	Yours / Love / Best wishes

Amerikaner schreiben als Grußformel:
Sincerely yours …

Methodenseiten

Mediation

Mediation heißt, einen Inhalt von einer Sprache in eine andere zu übertragen. Dieser Inhalt kann in verschiedenen Formen vorliegen: schriftlich (z. B. Sachtext, Gebrauchsanweisung, Zeitungsartikel), als Hörtext (z. B. Dialog, Interview), sogar als Bild- und Textkombination (z. B. Cartoon, Werbung).
Bei einer Mediationsaufgabe im Englischunterricht kann es um eine Übertragung vom Deutschen ins Englische gehen, meist wird jedoch ein englischsprachiger Ausgangstext in Deutsche übertragen.
Eine Mediation ist **keine Übersetzung,** bei der es darum geht, möglichst wörtlich zu übertragen!

Umsetzung
Jede Mediationsaufgabe beinhaltet eine berufliche Handlungssituation, aus der hervorgeht, für wen die Mediation ist (z. B. Eltern, Erzieherkollegen) und welcher Aspekt des Textes bearbeitet werden soll. Daraus geht auch hervor, in welcher Form Sie ihre Mediation schreiben sollten (z. B. als Brief, Ratschlag, Zusammenfassung). So gehen Sie vor:

1. Lesen Sie die Aufgabenstellung genau, damit Sie alle Aspekte der Aufgabenstellung erfassen.

2. Beim ersten Lesen des Textes sollten Sie unbekannte Wörter nachschauen.

3. Beim zweiten Lesen sollten Sie jene Teile des Textes unterstreichen, die für die Aufgabe wichtig sind. Achtung: Unterstreichen Sie niemals ganze Sätze, sondern markieren Sie nur wichtige Aspekte. Klammern Sie Beispiele ein – diese sollten nicht übertragen werden.

4. Beim dritten Lesen schreiben Sie an den Rand des Textes Stichwörter auf Deutsch, die Ihnen helfen sollen, den Hauptinhalt zusammenzufassen.

5. Fassen Sie nun den Inhalt auf Deutsch in vollständigen Sätzen zusammen.

6. Es ist wichtig, den gesamten Zusammenhang verständlich zu machen. Dazu ist es manchmal sinnvoll, Informationen zu ergänzen, die im Ausgangstext nicht vorhanden sind. So könnte z. B. ein Preis in englischen Pfund (£) für einen deutschen Leser viel aussagekräftiger sein, wenn man einen ungefähren Wert in Euro (€) als Zusatzinformation hinzufügt. Auch der umgekehrte Fall, das Weglassen von Informationen, kann sinnvoll sein, wenn sonst nur Selbstverständliches wiederholt würde.

Beispiel

English	Translation	Mediation
Sharing a book that is about other children in similar circumstances can help children. They may enjoy the story and then feel ready to talk about how they are feeling. For example, there are books about children who have lost a parent.	Es kann Kindern helfen, mit ihnen gemeinsam ein Buch über Kinder in ähnlichen Lebensverhältnissen zu lesen. Sie mögen die Geschichte und fühlen sich dann bereit, darüber zu sprechen, wie sie sich selbst fühlen. Es gibt z. B. Bücher über Kinder, die einen Elternteil verloren haben.	Es kann Kindern helfen, über ihre eigenen Erfahrungen zu sprechen, wenn man mit ihnen Bücher über Kinder liest, denen es ähnlich geht.

Feedback geben

Feedback geben bedeutet, jemandem zu sagen, welchen Eindruck seine Präsentation auf einen persönlich gemacht hat.

Warum Feedback?
- Feedback kann helfen, die eigene Präsentation zu verbessern.
- Feedback ist nicht dazu da, jemanden persönlich anzugreifen.

Diese Regeln helfen Ihnen,

wenn Sie Feedback geben:
- Seien Sie professionell.
- Seien Sie ehrlich, genau und fair.

wenn Sie Feedback bekommen:
- Keine Rechtfertigungen.
- Es ist eine Chance – nutzen Sie sie.

Feedbackbogen
Er ist nützlich, um Beobachtungen festzuhalten. Diese Beobachtungen sind die Grundlage für ein Feedback, auch auf Englisch. Folgender Beobachtungsbogen bezieht sich auf die „Reading-aloud activity" in Unit 13. Mit anderen Beobachtungskriterien kann er für vielfältige Aktivitäten und Präsentationen genutzt werden.

Giving feedback
For: reading-aloud activity (Unit 13)

Useful expressions

I think that …	In my opinion …	To my mind …
I saw / heard …	I couldn't see / hear …	
I would suggest that …	My suggestion would be that …	
I didn't understand …	Could you explain …	

Ratings: ++ = Excellent   + = Good   0 = OK   – = Not good at all

	Student / Group 1	Student / Group 2	Student / Group 3	Student / Group 4
The reading • is fluent • loud enough • uses voice for meaning	++ too quiet …			
The readers work with pictures	+			
The readers use props	–			
The children can be active	++			

Beispiel
I think that your reading was very fluent, but a bit too quiet, I couldn't hear everything clearly. You worked a lot with a pictures and I saw that the children liked that. In my opinion you prepared your activity in a way that the children could be very active. I suggest that you use some props to make your reading even livelier.

Informationen im Internet suchen

Suchmaschinen

Die am meisten genutzte Suchmaschine ist Google. Auf den meisten Computern ist sie als Standardsuchmaschine oder sogar als Startseite eingerichtet. Einen Begriff „googlen", das kann inzwischen jeder. Man kann die Suche mit Google aber auch nach eigenen Vorstellungen anpassen.
So gehen Sie vor:
Wenn man die Suche nach einem bestimmten Begriff gestartet hat, erscheint unten auf der Seite eine Zeile mit Optionen. Ganz links in dieser Zeile findet sich der Link „Erweiterte Suche". Wenn man dieses Stichwort anklickt, erscheint ein recht umfangreiches Untermenü, mit dessen Hilfe man seine Suche sehr viel präziser gestalten kann. Man kann sich z. B. nur Ergebnisse in einer bestimmten Sprache anzeigen lassen, man kann die Suche auf ein bestimmtes Land beschränken oder auf Seiten, die erst vor kurzem aktualisiert worden sind. Dies sind nur einige der Möglichkeiten, zudem gibt es von der Seite „Erweiterte Suche" aus unter dem Link „Sie können auch ..." noch weitere Untermenüs mit noch weitergehenden Voreinstellungen.
Zwar laufen über 80 Prozent aller Suchen über Google, was aber hauptsächlich damit zu tun hat, dass Google in den wichtigsten Browsern fest eingebaut ist. Probieren Sie ruhig einmal andere Suchmaschinen, die ebenfalls gute Ergebnisse liefern, z. B. bing.com, yahoo.com oder ask.com.

Online-Wörterbücher

Eine wichtige Informationsquelle für den Fremdsprachenunterricht sind natürlich Online-Wörterbücher, von denen es mittlerweile eine große Anzahl gibt, die hier nicht alle vorgestellt werden können. Nachfolgend wird auf 3 Wörterbücher besonders hingewiesen.

Leo.org

Eines der bekanntesten und von Schülern häufig benutzten ist www.leo.org. Hier bekommt man meist eine größere Zahl von Übersetzungsmöglichkeiten für einen gesuchten Begriff. Das Problem dabei ist es, zu entscheiden, welches Wort am besten in den eigenen Text passt.

Wenn man z. B. für das deutsche Wort „Schloss" die Übersetzungen „belt buckle, castle, feeder-selecting device, lock" angeboten bekommt und keines der englischen Wörter kennt, geht man so vor:

- In einem anderen Wörterbuch nachschauen,

- das Wort „googlen" oder

- den wahrscheinlichsten Begriff noch einmal rückübersetzen lassen.

Oft findet man auch Hilfe in den **Diskussionsforen** am Ende der LEO-Ergebnisliste, wo Nutzer Fragen an die „Nutzergemeinde" zu konkreten Übersetzungsproblemen stellen und mitunter lebhafte Diskussionen über die richtige Übersetzung entstehen.
Anmerkung zum „Lautsprecher": Wer sich in der Aussprache unsicher ist, kann sich das Wort durch Anklicken des Symbols vorsprechen lassen.

Methodenseiten

BEOLINGUS

Gut geeignet für Schüler ist auch das Online-Wörterbuch „BEOLINGUS" der TU Chemnitz unter **http://dict.tu-chemnitz.de/**. Es bietet nicht nur Übersetzungen an, sondern liefert gleich Anwendungsbeispiele mit, die zeigen, in welchen Kontexten und wie genau ein Wort „funktioniert". Außerdem verlinkt BEOLINGUS Begriffe mit dem Lexikon „Wikipedia".

Linguee

Ein etwas anderes, aber gerade für die Schule sehr gut geeignetes Wörterbuch ist **www.linguee.com**. Diese Website bietet eine sehr praktische Möglichkeit zu überprüfen, ob die eigenen Formulierungen richtig sind. Diese Seite ist einerseits ein Wörterbuch, d.h., man kann sich Wörter Deutsch-Englisch, Englisch-Deutsch übersetzen lassen. Man kann aber auch mehrgliedrige Ausdrücke kontrollieren lassen, man bekommt also eine Antwort auf die Frage „Kann man das so auf Englisch sagen?"

Wenn man sich also nicht ist, ob man mit seiner Übersetzung des Satzes „die Sonne geht unter" = „the sun goes down" richtig liegt, bzw. wenn einem Zweifel kommen, weil das doch recht Deutsch und irgendwie komisch klingt, dann gibt man es bei linguee.com ein – und tatsächlich, es werden Beispiele angezeigt, man kann das also so sagen.

Urheberrecht

Einen Punkt sollten Sie noch beachten. Die meisten Informationen sind im Netz frei zugänglich. Das heißt aber nicht, dass Sie Texte, Bilder und Videos einfach benutzen dürfen – auch nicht für ein Referat oder eine Präsentation in der Klasse. Hier gelten die Regeln des Urheberrechts, nach denen man sich vorher die Genehmigung vom Rechteinhaber einholen muss.
Grundsätzlich gilt:

- Texte dürfen in geringem (!) Rahmen zitiert werden. Dabei ist es gleich, ob sie aus dem Internet, aus Büchern oder anderen Printmedien stammen.
Wichtig ist, dass Sie die genaue Quelle nennen, z. B.:
Schmidt, Peter: „Fachkräfte für Kitas gesucht".
URL: www.spiegel.de
(gefunden am: 20.06.2012)

- Für die Nutzung von Bildern und Videos brauchen Sie immer die Einwilligung desjenigen, der die Rechte daran hat (Anfrage beim Urheber, Fotograf o. Ä.).
Ausnahme: Webseiten, die ihre Bilder ausdrücklich zur freien Nutzung anbieten (Clipart-Galerien o. Ä.).

Wer diese Bestimmungen nicht respektiert, riskiert unter Umständen, dass er eine kostenpflichtige Abmahnung bekommt.

handwerk-technik.de

Die Präsentation

Die vier Kriterien der Präsentation

- **Einfachheit:** einfache Sprache nutzen, möglichst wenig Fremdwörter einsetzen, kurze Sätze, Fachbegriffe erklären
- **Gliederung:** gegliederter Vortrag, Übersichtlichkeit herstellen, evtl. dem Publikum Gliederung des Vortrags vorstellen
- **Kürze:** nur wichtige Dinge darlegen, für das Thema wesentliche Informationen weitergeben, keine Nebensächlichkeiten ausführen
- **Stimulans / Anregung:** motivierende Impulse setzen durch Beispiele oder Bilder

Vorbereitung eines Vortrags

Legen Sie Stichwortkarten an:
- auf A6-Karteikarten
- Schreiben Sie in gut lesbarer Schrift je ein Teilthema auf die Karteikarte und unterstreichen Sie diese farbig.
- Notieren Sie sich wichtige Stichworte zu dem jeweiligen Teilthema, keine ganzen Sätze.
- Ausnahme: Wer sehr nervös ist, kann sich zur Sicherheit den Einstiegs- und Schlusssatz notieren oder diese auswendig lernen.
- Verwenden Sie unterschiedliche Schriftgrößen, damit Ihnen Wesentliches sofort ins Auge fällt.
- Kennzeichnen Sie durch Symbole (!,?,☺), was Sie besonders betonen wollen.

Beim Zuhörer „ankommen"

- Schauen Sie den Zuhörer an.
- Machen Sie die Zuhörer gespannt durch einen interessanten Einstieg.
- Stellen Sie einen Bezug zum Zuhörer her, indem Sie z. B. einen aktuellen, lebensnahen Aufhänger anwenden.
- Sprechen Sie die Zuhörer auch während des Vortrags immer wieder direkt an bzw. geben Sie dem Zuschauer das Gefühl, von Ihnen direkt angesprochen zu werden.
- Sprechen Sie frei und deutlich.
- Machen Sie Pausen.
- Variieren Sie die Stimm- und Tonlage, um den Inhalt zu unterstreichen.
- Setzen Sie Mimik und Gestik ein.
- Visualisieren Sie Ihren Vortrag, sodass Sie den Zuhörer nicht nur über das „Ohr", sondern auch über das „Auge" erreichen.

Visualisierung

Flipchart
Zum Festhalten der Themenschwerpunkte / Überschriften / Gliederung

Overhead-Projektor
Folienpräsentation zur schrittweisen Gedankenvermittlung, dem Vortrag folgend können wichtige Informationen visualisiert werden

Pinnwand
Visualisierung von Postern / Plakaten und Beispielen, zur Aufnahme von Ideen aus dem Zuhörerkreis

Dias, Kurzfilm, Pläne, Modelle
Visualisierung von Beispielen, die den Vortrag unterstützen oder vertiefen

Powerpoint-Präsentation
Auch hier schrittweise Gedankenvermittlung durch Visualisierung wichtiger Informationen (vgl. auch Seite 189 „Folie oder Plakat gestalten")

Handouts
nach der Präsentation als eine Zusammenfassung der wichtigsten Informationen („Was man sich merken sollte")

Folie oder Plakat gestalten

Folie und Plakat sollen Informationen visualisieren und damit einen Themenvortrag unterstützen oder ein Thema in seinen wesentlichen Punkten verdeutlichen. Mit dieser Art der Visualisierung können folgende Ziele verfolgt werden:
- den Zuhörer zu motivieren oder einen visuellen Anreiz zu bieten
- das Behalten von vorgetragene/wichtigen Informationen zu erleichtern
- ein besseres Verständnis für ein bestimmten Thema herzustellen
- wichtige Informationen zu betonen

Bei Folien, die durch Fernmedien (Overheadprojektor, Beamer) präsentiert werden, gelten die gleichen Gestaltungsregeln wie für das Plakat:

Eine Folie bzw. ein Plakat muss
→ deutlich erkennbar,
→ kontrastreich und
→ auf ein Thema begrenzt sein.

Farben
- Farbig ist ansprechender als nur Schwarz-Weiß
- Aber: **keine** grellen Farben
- Wichtige Informationen farblich hervorheben
- Nicht zu „bunt", höchstens drei Farben, sonst entsteht zu viel Unruhe
- Grundsätzliche Informationen in einer neutralen Farbe festhalten (z. B. Schwarz)
- Texte können durch Farbunterlegung hervorgehoben werden.

Vorsicht: Keine zu grellen Farben oder dunkle Farben wählen, die den Kontrast zur Schrift verschwinden und den Text undeutlich werden lassen.

Schrift
- Weitgehend einheitliche Schriftart und Schriftgröße wählen, keine Unruhe erzeugen
- Buchstabengröße so wählen, dass diese auch in einigem Abstand erkannt werden können (Folie: Hand Schriftgrad 18 – 24 Pt, Computer 14/16/18 Pt – 1 Pt entspricht 0,375 mm)
- Titel und wichtige Informationen können durchaus größere Schriftgrade als 24 Pt haben
- Wichtige Informationen können durch Fettdruck und Unterstreichung hervorgehoben werden
- Sperrung und durchgehende Großbuchstabenverwendung eignen sich eher für die Hervorhebung einzelner Worte

Bilder und Skizzen
- Nicht zu viele Bilder, damit der Überblick nicht verloren geht
- Bilder mit ausreichender Erklärung versehen
- Bilder müssen zum Text passen
- Bildunterschriften/Erklärungen zum Bild in kleinerer Schrift gestalten
- Nur aussagekräftige Bilder verwenden, Bilder nicht als bloße Ausschmückung nutzen
- Bilder müssen in angemessener Größe zum Text erscheinen
- Besser farbige Bilder einsetzen

Aufbau und Gestaltung
- Klare Gliederung der Aussagen, die direkt mit dem Auge erfasst werden kann
- Folie/Plakat nicht überladen. Faustregel: Niemals mehr als 6 – 8 Zeilen mit 6 Wörtern
- Stichwörter, **keine** ganzen Sätze
- Wenn Sätze, dann kurze Merksätze
- Mit Titel und Untertitel arbeiten, d. h. Unterpunkte zu Überschriften einrichten, insbesondere komplizierte Sachverhalte in Teilaspekte und Unterpunkte auflösen
- Kernaussagen markieren (Farbe, Schrift oder Rahmen setzen)
- Gestaltungselemente (Symbole, Grafiken) zur Hervorhebung und Verdeutlichung von Informationen und als Gliederungshilfen (z. B. Pfeilsymbole) nutzen

Das Rollenspiel

Rollenspiele eignen sich gut, um gemeinsam Inhalte und Wortschatz zu diskutieren oder um eine Lerneinheit zu wiederholen und anzuwenden. Sie sind meist mit Arbeit verbunden, vermitteln aber in der Regel allen ein Erfolgserlebnis, ein Gefühl von „das habe ich selbst erarbeitet, das kann ich jetzt".

Ablauf eines Rollenspiels – vier Phasen
- Vorstellung des Themas
- Individuelle Vorbereitung auf die eigene Rolle
- Eigentliches Rollenspiel in der Gruppe
- Auswertung und Diskussion über den Verlauf des Rollenspiels

Phase 1: Vor Beginn sollte die Lehrperson eine kurze Einführung in das Thema geben und erklären, wie das Rollenspiel ablaufen soll.

Phase 2: Zur Vorbereitung des Rollenspiels bekommen alle Teilnehmer/innen eine kurzgefasste schriftliche Einweisung. Daraus können sie entnehmen, welche Rolle sie übernehmen und was sie inhaltlich zu vertreten haben.
Alle Teilnehmer/innen lesen die Informationen durch und machen sich Gedanken darüber, was sie bei der Diskussion vortragen wollen. Notizen können gemacht werden, es soll aber kein Text geschrieben werden, der lediglich vorgelesen wird – es soll eine spontane Diskussion entstehen.

Zur Rollenverteilung
Die Rollen können entweder von der Lehrkraft verteilt oder von den Teilnehmer/innen eigenständig festgelegt werden. Es sollte niemand gezwungen werden, eine Rolle zu übernehmen, die ihm absolut nicht liegt. Eine Person sollte eine Moderatoren- oder Leitungsfunktion innehaben und z. B. Teilnehmer/innen, denen es schwer fällt sich zu äußern, durch Fragen oder gezieltes Ansprechen in die Diskussion einbeziehen.

Phase 3: Als Einstieg bietet sich an, dass jeder Schüler in einem kurzen Statement den Standpunkt der eigenen Rolle vorstellt. Dies dient auch dazu, den anderen Teilnehmer/innen zu verdeutlichen, wer welche Meinung vertritt.

Phase 4: Die Dauer der Diskussion kann von vornherein auf eine bestimmte Zeit begrenzt werden, man kann das Rollenspiel aber auch – ohne Berücksichtigung des Zeitaspekts – dann für beendet erklären, wenn eine Einigung oder Lösung des vorgegebenen Problems erreicht wurde.

Abschluss
Am Ende jedes Rollenspiels sollte eine Reflexionsphase stehen, in der alle Teilnehmer/innen Rückmeldung geben können:
- zum Verlauf,
- wie sie sich fühlten,
- ob sie mit dem eigenen Beitrag zufrieden waren,
- was beim nächsten Rollenspiel geändert werden kann.

Vgl. auch: Feedback geben, Seite 185.

Unregelmäßige Verben

Infinitive (1. Verbform)	Past Tense (2. Verbform)	Past Participle (3. Verbform)	
(to) be	was (sg.), were (pl.)	been	sein
(to) beat	beat	beaten	schlagen
(to) become	became	become	werden
(to) begin	began	begun	beginnen, anfangen
(to) bite	bit	bitten	beißen
(to) bleed	bled	bled	bluten
(to) blow	blew	blown	blasen
(to) break	broke	broken	brechen, zerbrechen
(to) bring	brought	brought	bringen, mitbringen
(to) build	built	built	bauen
(to) burn	burnt	burnt	brennen
(to) buy	bought	bought	kaufen
(to) can	could		können
(to) catch	caught	caught	fangen, ergreifen
(to) choose	chose	chosen	wählen
(to) come	came	come	kommen
(to) cost	cost	cost	kosten
(to) cut	cut	cut	schneiden
(to) deal (with)	dealt	dealt	sich kümmern, sich beschäftigen mit
(to) do	did	done	machen, tun
(to) draw	drew	drawn	zeichnen, malen
(to) dream	dreamt	dreamt	träumen
(to) drink	drank	drunk	trinken
(to) drive	drove	driven	(Auto) fahren
(to) eat	ate	eaten	essen
(to) fall	fell	fallen	fallen
(to) feel	felt	felt	fühlen
(to) fight	fought	fought	bekämpfen, kämpfen
(to) find	found	found	finden
(to) fly	flew	flown	fliegen
(to) forget	forgot	forgotten	vergessen
(to) forgive	forgave	forgiven	vergeben, verzeihen
(to) freeze	froze	frozen	frieren, gefrieren
(to) get	got	got	bekommen, kommen
(to) give	gave	given	geben
(to) go	went	gone	gehen, fahren
(to) grow	grew	grown	wachsen
(to) have	had	had	haben
(to) hear	heard	heard	hören
(to) hide	hid	hidden	(sich) verstecken
(to) hit	hit	hit	schlagen, stoßen
(to) hold	held	held	halten, abhalten
(to) hurt	hurt	hurt	(sich) verletzen
(to) keep	kept	kept	behalten, halten
(to) know	knew	known	wissen, kennen

Anhang

Unregelmäßige Verben (Fortsetzung)

Infinitive (1. Verbform)	Past Tense (2. Verbform)	Past Participle (3. Verbform)	
(to) lead	led	led	führen
(to) learn	learnt	learnt	lernen
(to) leave	left	left	verlassen, abfahren
(to) lend	lent	lent	leihen, verleihen
(to) let	let	let	lassen
(to) lie	lay	lain	liegen
(to) lose	lost	lost	verlieren
(to) make	made	made	machen, anfertigen
(to) mean	meant	meant	bedeuten
(to) meet	met	met	treffen, begegnen
(to) pay	paid	paid	bezahlen
(to) put	put	put	setzen, legen, stellen
(to) read	read	read	lesen
(to) ride	rode	ridden	reiten, Radfahren
(to) ring	rang	rung	klingeln, läuten
(to) rise	rose	risen	aufstehen
(to) run	ran	run	rennen, laufen
(to) say	said	said	sagen
(to) see	saw	seen	sehen
(to) seek	sought	sought	suchen
(to) sell	sold	sold	verkaufen
(to) send	sent	sent	senden, schicken
(to) shake	shook	shaken	schütteln
(to) show	showed	shown	zeigen
(to) shut	shut	shut	schließen
(to) sing	sang	sung	singen
(to) sit	sat	sat	sitzen
(to) sleep	slept	slept	schlafen
(to) smell	smelt	smelt	riechen
(to) speak	spoke	spoken	sprechen
(to) spend	spent	spent	verbringen, ausgeben
(to) stand	stood	stood	stehen
(to) steal	stole	stolen	stehlen
(to) swim	swam	swum	schwimmen
(to) take	took	taken	nehmen, mitnehmen
(to) teach	taught	taught	lehren, unterrichten
(to) tear	tore	torn	zerreißen
(to) tell	told	told	erzählen
(to) think	thought	thought	denken
(to) throw	threw	thrown	werfen
(to) wake (up)	woke	woken	aufwachen
(to) wear	wore	worn	(Kleidung) tragen
(to) win	won	won	gewinnen
(to) write	wrote	written	schreiben

Alphabetische Vokabelliste   s. th. = something   s. o. = someone

A

ability	Fähigkeit
(to) be able to	fähig sein zu
able-bodied	nicht behindert
abnormal needs	abnormale Bedürfnisse
above all	vor allem
(to) abuse	missbrauchen
(to) abuse verbally	beschimpfen, beleidigen
(to) be abused	missbraucht werden
abusive	beleidigend
(to) accept	akzeptieren
access to	Zugriff auf
accessible for wheelchairs	rollstuhlgerecht
according to	gemäß, entsprechend, laut
(to) achieve	erreichen
(to) act out	darstellen, vorspielen
(to) activate	aktivieren, auslösen
activity quilt	Spieldecke
actor	Schauspieler
actress	Schauspielerin
actually	tatsächlich, eigentlich
(to) adapt	anpassen
adaptation	Anpassung
adapted to the needs of the disabled	behindertengerecht
adhesive tape	Klebeband
administrative	Verwaltung-…
(to) admit	zugeben
(to) adore	anbeten, über alles lieben, für etwas schwärmen
adult	Erwachsener
advantageous	vorteilhaft
advice	Ratschlag
(to) advise	raten
advisory team	Beratungsteam
agony aunt	Kummerkastentante
aim	Ziel
all in tears	unter Tränen
allegiance	Treue
(to) be allergic to s.th.	allergisch gegen etwas sein
(to) alter	verändern
(to) alter / design s.th. to fit the needs of the disabled	behindertengerecht umbauen / umgestalten
alternative way	andere, alternative Art und Weise
amount	Summe
amusing	belustigend, lustig
application	Bewerbung
appointment	Termin, Treffen, Verabredung
(to) approach	sich nähern
(to) be appropriate for	geeignet sein für
apron	Schürze
argument	verbaler Streit, Streitgespräch
arts	Kunst, die Künste
ashamed	beschämt
asterisk	Sternchen
astonished	erstaunt
attack	Angriff
(to) attend	besuchen (Kindergarten etc.)
attentive	aufmerksam
attitude towards	Einstellung zu
audio book	Hörbuch
aunt	Tante
autism	Autismus
automatic opening / close	automatisches Öffnen / Schließen
autumn (BrE), fall (AE)	Herbst
average	durchschnittlich, Durchschnitts-…
(to) avoid	vermeiden

B

backyard	Hof
bacteria (pl.)	Bakterien
balanced diet	ausgewogene Kost, ausgewogene Ernährung
barley	Gerste
bathtub	Badewanne
beaker	Becher
(to) bear s.th.	etwas ertragen
(to) become independent	unabhängig werden
(to) behave	sich verhalten
behaviour (BrE)	Verhalten, Benehmen
behavioural	verhaltensbezogen
(to) believe	glauben
bell	Klingel, Klingelton
belly button	Bauchnabel
bench	Bank
(to) benefit from	Nutzen ziehen von, profitieren von
besides	außer, außerdem
bilingual	zweisprachig
bin (BrE)	Mülleimer
birth defect	Geburtsfehler
black pudding	Blutwurst
blank expressions	ausdruckslose Gesichter
(to) blindfold s. o.	jmd. die Augen verbinden
block area	Bauecke
blocks	Bauklötze
bob up and down	auf und ab wippen, sich auf- und ab bewegen
bookcase	Bücherregal
boring	langweilig
(to) bounce up and down	auf und ab springen
bouncing cradle	Babywippe
bowl	Schüssel
box	Schachtel
brain damage	Gehirnschaden
breadcrumbs	Brotkrümel

Alphabetische Vokabelliste

breadwinner	Ernährer/in
break	Pause
breast	Brust
bricks	Bausteine
bright	hell
(to) bring to mind	ins Gedächtnis zurückbringen
brochure	Broschüre, Prospekt
broom	Besen
brother	Bruder
brother-in-law	Schwager
bruise	Bluterguss, blauer Fleck
(to) brush teeth	Zähne putzen
building blocks	Bauklötze
(to) bully	„mobben"
(to) bully s.o.	jmd. terrorisieren, tyrannisieren
bump	Beule
button	Knopf
by hearsay	vom Hörensagen
by touch	durch Anfassen

C

calm	ruhig
candy (AmE)	Süßigkeit
car tyre swing	Autoreifenschaukel
carbohydrates	Kohlenhydrate
cardboard	Pappe
cardboard boxes	Pappkartons
care	Betreuung
carpeted	mit Teppich ausgelegt
(to) carry out	etwas ausführen
carved pumpkin	ausgehöhlter Kürbis
case	Fall
castle	Schloss
(to) catch	fangen, hier: eine Krankheit bekommen
catchy	eingängig
cave	Höhle
(to) celebrate	feiern
cereals	Zerealien, Getreideflocken
cerebral palsy	spastische Lähmung
certificate	Zeugnis
chain	Kette
chairman	Vorsitzende, Vorsitzender
(to) chalk	mit Kreide bemalen
chart	Abbildung, Schaubild
(to) chase	verjagen, jagen
(to) check	überprüfen
cheek	Wange
chest	Brust
chicken pox	Windpocken
child abuse	Kindesmissbrauch
childminder (auch: day nanny)	Kinderbetreuer/-in, Tagesmutter
child with special needs	Kind mit einem besonderen Bedürfnis, mit Behinderung
childhood	Kindheit
children's programme	Kinderprogramm (TV)
child-size	in Kindergröße
chocolate-coated	mit Schokolade überzogen
(to) choke	würgen, ersticken
chopping board	Schneidbrett
circle	(Stuhl-)Kreis
circumstance	Umstand, Situation, Lebensumstände
city/town administration	Stadtverwaltung
(to) clear away	wegräumen
cleft palate	Gaumenspalte
(to) clench fists	Fäuste ballen
(to) climb up and down	herauf- und herabklettern
climbing apparatus	Kletterapparat
climbing frame	Klettergerüst
climbing pole	Kletterstange
(to) cling to s.o.	sich an jmd. hängen
cloth	Tuch, Lappen
cloth puppet	Stoffpuppe
clothes	Kleidung
clumsy	ungeschickt
coach	Trainer/in
coeliac disease	(med.) Zöliakie, Sprue
cold	Erkältung
cold pad	Kühlpad
colleague	Kollege, Kollegin
collection	Sammlung
college of further education	berufsbildende Schule, Berufskolleg
(to) compare	vergleichen
compared to	verglichen mit
(to) complain	sich beschweren
concept	Konzept
concussion	Gehirnerschütterung
confidence	Selbstvertrauen
conflict	Konflikt
confused	verwirrt
(to) consent to	zustimmen zu
consideration	Überlegung
(to) consist of	bestehen aus
contented	zufrieden
(to) convince	überreden, überzeugen
(to) be convinced	überzeugt sein
cop (AmE)	Polizist (Umgangssprache)
(to) cope, (to) cope with	bewältigen, meistern
(to) copy	nachahmen, kopieren
cot	Liege
(to) cough	husten
cousin	Cousine, Cousin
cover	Bucheinband
cozy	gemütlich, kuschelig
cracker	Keks, Cracker
cradle	Wiege
crafts	Handwerkskunst, Basteln
(to) crawl	kriechen
crayon	Buntstift
crèche	Krippe, Einrichtung für Unter-Dreijährige

Alphabetische Vokabelliste

Creepy Crawlies	ungefähr: 'Unheimliche Krabbler'	(to) dress up	sich verkleiden
crepe bandage	Mullbinde	dressing	Wundauflage
crossing	Kreuzung	(to) drift apart	sich auseinander bewegen, voneinander entfernen
crunch	knirschen		
crunchy	knusprig	(to) drop	fallen lassen
cuddly	anschmiegsam, knuddelig	dual-language	zweisprachig
		(to) dunk	(kurz) eintauchen
cuddly toy animal	Kuscheltier	dyspraxia	Motorikstörung
cupboard	Schrank		
(to) curl up	es sich gemütlich machen	**E**	
curtain	Vorhang	eagerly	hartnäckig
cushion	(Sitz-)Kissen	ear infection	Ohrenentzündung
customs	Sitten, Gebräuche	education	Erziehung
cut	Schnitt	educational standards	Erziehungsstandards
CV, Curriculum Vitae	Lebenslauf	effect	Wirkung
		elderly looking	älter / "ältlich" aussehend
D		elementary school	Grundschule
daily routine	Tagesablauf	elsewhere	woanders
(to) damage	beschädigen	embarrassed	verlegen
data sheet	Datenblatt, Karteikarte	employment	Berufstätigkeit
daughter	Tochter	emotional abuse	emotionaler Missbrauch
day-care business	Firma, die sich (gegen Bezahlung) um Kinder kümmert	(to) enable	befähigen, aktivieren
		(to) encourage s. o.	ermutigen, fördern
		(to) endure	ertragen, erleiden
(to) be deaf	taub sein	energetic	voller Energie
decent	anständig, ordentlich	enriching	bereichernd
(to) decide	(sich) entscheiden	entertaining	unterhaltend
decision	Entscheidung	entry	Eintrag
deficiency	Defizit, Mangel	environment	Umgebung
delivered	angeliefert	(to) equip with	austatten mit
(to) deny s. o. affection	jmd. Zuneigung verweigern	equivalent	gleichwertig
(to) depend on	abhängig sein von	(to) escape	flüchten, auch: sich entspannen, zerstreuen
depending on	abhängig von		
(to) describe	beschreiben	(to) exclude from	jmd. ausschließen von
description	Beschreibung	exclusion from	Ausschluss von
(to) be desperate	verzweifelt sein	exhibition	Ausstellung
(to) destroy	zerstören	(to) expect s. o.	jemanden erwarten
(to) develop	entwickeln	expert	Experte / Expertin, Sachverständige / r
development	Entwicklung		
diary	Tagebuch	(to) explore	erforschen
dictator	Diktator, Tyrann	(to) extend	erweitern
(to) digest	verdauen	extended family	Großfamilie
(to) dilute	verdünnen	eye pad	Augenauflage
disability	Behinderung, auch: Unfähigkeit		
		F	
(to) be disabled	behindert sein	(to) face	ins Auge sehen, konfrontiert werden mit
discontent	Unzufriedenheit		
disgust	Entsetzen, Ekel	facial expression	Gesichtsausdruck
dishes	Geschirr	factual books	Sachbuch
(to) distribute	verteilen, verbreiten	(to) fail	nicht schaffen
disturbed relationship	gestörte Beziehung	fall (AmE), autumn (BrE)	Herbst
diversity	Vielfalt		
(to) divide	unterteilen	(to) fall apart	auseinander fallen
divorce	Scheidung	familiar	gewohnt, vertraut
(to) be divorced	geschieden sein	family life	Familienleben
dodgers	Drückeberger	family member	Familienmitglied
doll	Puppe	family parties	Familienfeiern
Down Syndrome	Down-Syndrom	family placement	Familienpraktikum
(to) dress	(sich) anziehen	family portrait	Familienporträt, Familienbild
		family tree	Familienstammbaum

handwerk-technik.de

Alphabetische Vokabelliste

(to) fancy	gern mögen
fast-paced	in schneller Folge, schnell wechselnd
father	Vater
fault	Fehler
favourite	Lieblings-…
(to) feel poorly, feel unwell	sich elend / unwohl fühlen
feely book	Tastbuch
fiddle	Fiedel, Geige
fine motor skills	Feinmotorik
first-aid box	Erste-Hilfe-Koffer
(to) fix	fixieren, befestigen
flat	Wohnung
flavour	Geschmack, Stil, Aroma
floor	Fußboden
flu	Grippe
flushed	gerötet
(to) focus on	sich konzentrieren auf
fond	liebevoll
for the sake of	zum Wohl von, um jemandes Willen
forehead	Stirn
former	früher, ehemalig
foul	unflätig
fracture	Bruch
fractured	gebrochen
freckles	Sommersprossen
free play	Freispiel
(to) freeze	einfrieren
freezer	Gefrierschrank / -fach
frequently	häufig
fridge, refrigerator	Kühlschrank
fries	Pommes frites
(to) frighten away	verscheuchen
(to) be frightened	ängstlich sein
fruit	Obst
furious	(sehr) wütend
furnished with	möbliert mit

G

(to) gain (experience)	(Erfahrung) gewinnen
game	Spiel
GCSE, General Certificate of Secondary Education	Mittlerer Bildungsabschluss an britischen Schulen, vergleichbar mit dt. Realschulabschluss (Sekundarstufe I)
gently	vorsichtig, sanft
(to) get used to	sich gewöhnen an
ghoul	Geist, Erscheinung
(to) give delight	Freude machen
(to) give s.o. a helping hand	jmd. behilflich sein
glue, glue stick	Klebstoff, Klebestift
(to) go on an outing	einen Ausflug machen
goal	Ziel
goblin	Kobold
good mood	gute Stimmung
(to) grab around	umgreifen
grade	Klassenstufe
grandchildren	Enkelkinder
granddaughter	Enkelin, Enkeltochter
grandfather	Großvater
grandmother	Großmutter
grandparents	Großeltern
grandson	Enkel, Enkelsohn
grass pitch	Rasenfeld, Rasenfläche
grazed	abgeschürft
greasy	verfettet, fettig
great-grandchild	Urenkel
great-grandfather	Urgroßvater
great-grandmother	Urgroßmutter
great-grandparents	Urgroßeltern
grim	düster
(to) grip	greifen
(to) groan	stöhnen
gross motor skills	Grobmotorik
grouch	Muffel, Miesepeter
(to) grow corn	Mais anbauen
grown-up	Erwachsene / r
(to) be grown-up	erwachsen sein
(to) grunt	brummen
(to) guess	raten
(to) guide	führen
guided tour of the premises	eine Führung durch die Räumlichkeiten
guinea pig	Meerschweinchen
(to) gulp	hinunterschlingen, herunterschlucken
gynaecologist	Gynäkologe / Gynäkologin, Frauenarzt / -ärztin

H

habit	Gewohnheit
handbasin	Handwaschbecken
handbook	Handbuch
handle	Griff
handout	Flugblatt, Broschüre, Arbeitsblatt
hands-on	praktisch, im Praktikum
harmony	Harmonie
harvest	Ernte
(to) haunt the streets	sich auf den Straßen herumtreiben
(to) have an impact on	einen Einfluss haben auf
head	Kopf
headache	Kopfschmerzen
headteacher	Schulleiter / in
(to) heal	heilen
health care	Gesundheitspflege
health professionals	Fachkräfte im Pflegebereich
healthy	gesund
hearing impairment	Gehörstörung
hearing loss	Gehörverlust
helpful	hilfreich
hidden	versteckt
(to) hide	verstecken
(to) hit (hit, hit)	schlagen

Alphabetische Vokabelliste

holiday	Urlaub; auch: Feiertag	involved	beteiligt, einbezogen
hollow	hohl	iron	Bügeleisen
home corner	Puppenecke	ironing board	Bügelbrett
(to) hook	einhängen	irritable	reizbar
(to) hop	hüpfen	it is not correct to	es ist nicht korrekt zu …
hothead	Hitzkopf	it's obvious	es ist offensichtlich
(to) hug	umarmen	item	Gegenstand, Objekt
human	menschlich		
(to) hurt (hurt, hurt)	verletzen (seelisch / körperlich)	**J**	
husband	Ehemann	jealous	neidisch
hygiene	Hygiene	jigsaw puzzle	Puzzle
hygienic	hygienisch	job advertisement	Stellenanzeige
		job advisor	Arbeitsberater / in, Mitarbeiter / in des Arbeitsamts
I			
icebreaker	"Eisbrecher", Übung oder Aktivität, die die Stimmung lockert	job centre	Arbeitsamt
		(to) join hands	an die Hand nehmen, sich die Hände geben
illness	Krankheit	joy	Freude
image	Bild	(to) jump over	springen über
imagination	Fantasie, Vorstellungskraft	justice	Gerechtigkeit
immediate family circle	engster Familienkreis	(to) justify	rechtfertigen, beweisen
		K	
impact on	einen Einfluss auf	(to) keep a diary	ein Tagebuch führen
(to) improve	verbessern	(to) keep an eye on	ein Auge halten auf, nach jmd. schauen
(to) be in charge of	verantwortlich sein für		
inclusion	Aufnahme, hier: Inklusion	(to) keep eye contact	Augenkontakt halten
increasing	zunehmend	(to) keep out of each other's way	sich voneinander fernhalten
Independence Day	US-amerikanischer Unabhängigkeitstag		
		kindness	Freundlichkeit
independent(ly)	selbstständig, unabhängig	knee	Knie
		knife	Messer
Indian (auch: Native American)	Indianer, Ureinwohner USA	knight	Ritter
		(to) knit	stricken
indivisible	unteilbar		
infant, toddler	Kleinkind	**L**	
(to) inflict	zufügen, beibringen	language difficulties	Sprachschwierigkeiten
influence on	Einfluss auf	languid	matt, träge
(to) inform s.o.	jmd. informieren	lantern	Laterne
(to) be informed	informiert sein	lap	Schoß
ingredients	Zutaten, Inhaltsstoffe	lap tray	hier: kl. Tisch / Tablett, das sich am Rollstuhl befestigen lässt
(to) injure	körperlich verletzen		
insight	Einblick		
(to) inspect	inspizieren, überprüfen	(to) lay the table	den Tisch decken
intact	intakt, nicht beschädigt	learning problem	Lernproblem
integrated nursery school class	integrative Kindergartengruppe (Gruppe mit behinderten und nicht behinderten Kindern)	learning tool	Lernwerkzeug
		leave me alone	Lass mich in Ruhe
		lecturing tone	belehrender Ton
		leftover	Rest
		leg	Bein
intellectual deficit	intellektuelles (geistiges) Defizit	liberty	Freiheit
		librarian	Bibliothekar / in
intellectual difficulties	intellektuelle Schwierigkeiten	library	Bücherei
		lifestyle	Lebensstil, Lebensweise
(to) intimidate	einschüchtern	lift	Aufzug
intimidated	eingeschüchtert	light-skinned	hellhäutig
invalid chair	Krankenstuhl	limb	Glied
invalid toilet seat	Krankentoilettensitz	(to) be limited	eingeschränkt, beschränkt sein
invitation	Einladung		

Alphabetische Vokabelliste

linguistic competence	Sprachkompetenz	**N**	
(to) be linked with	verbunden mit	nap	kurzer Schlaf
literacy activities	Leselern-Aktivitäten	napkin	Serviette
lollipop sticks	Lolli-Stiele	nappy (BrE)	Windel
long-sleeved	langärmelig	nap room	Schlafraum
(to) look after	sich kümmern um	nasty	böse, gemein
(to) look forward to s.th.	sich auf etwas freuen	navel	Bauchnabel
		needs	Bedürfnisse
(to) look out for	Ausschau halten nach	neglect	Vernachlässigung
lumpy	klumpig	nephew	Neffe
		nevertheless	trotzdem, dennoch
M		niece	Nichte
majority	Mehrheit	(to) nod	nicken
(to) make mud pies	Kuchen aus Sand bauen	noise	Geräusch
malformation	Missbildung	non-discriminatory	nicht diskriminierend
malfunction	Fehlfunktion	norm	Normalität, Regel
marbles	Murmeln	nose bleed	Nasenbluten
marriage	Ehe	nuclear family	Kleinfamilie
(to) be married to	verheiratet sein mit	nursery (auch: nursery school)	Kindertagesstätte, Kindergarten
married life	Eheleben	nursery nurse (BrE)	Kinderpfleger/in, Mitarbeiter/in im Kindergarten
(to) marvel at s.th.	sich über etwas wundern		
mattress	Matraze		
mean	gemein, schäbig, knickerig		
measuring cup	Messbecher	nursery rhyme	Kinderreim
(to) meet	treffen	nursery school (BrE)	Kindertagesstätte, Kindergarten
mental disability	geistige Behinderung		
message	Botschaft	nutrients	Nährstoffe
messy area	unordentlicher Bereich, wo Kinder Dinge liegen lassen dürfen	nutrition	Ernährung
		nutritional weaning	Fläschchen-Entwöhnung
		NVQ, National Vocational Qualification	britische staatlich anerkannte berufliche Qualifikation
milestone	Meilenstein, Ziel		
mime game	Pantomime-Spiel		
minding hours	Betreuungsstunden	**O**	
mirror	Spiegel	oat	Hafer
(to) miss	vermissen	(to) obey	gehorchen
mistreatment	Missbrauch, Misshandlung	occupational therapist	Beschäftigungstherapeut/in
(to) be mistreated	missbraucht/misshandelt werden	old-fashioned	altmodisch
		only child	Einzelkind
(to) moan	stöhnen	on request	auf Nachfrage
mobile	Mobilé, Windspiel	Open Day	Tag der offenen Tür
(to) modernise	modernisieren	openness	Offenheit
moron	Schwachkopf, Depp (Umgangssprache)	opportunity	Gelegenheit, Möglichkeit
		organic	biologisch
morsels	Häppchen, Bissen	outburst	Ausbruch
mother	Mutter	outdoor, outside	außen, außerhalb, im Freien
motor skills	Motorik	outing	Ausflug
mouse (sg.); mice (pl.)	Maus; Mäuse	outskirts	Stadtrand
moustache	Schnauzbart	oven	Backofen
movie (AmE)	Film	overall grading	Gesamtbewertung
multi-cultural	von vielen Kulturen geprägt	own	eigen
mummy	Mumie		
mushy peas	Erbsenpüree/-brei		

Alphabetische Vokabelliste

P

package	Paket
packaging	Verpackung
paediatrician's practice	Kinderarztpraxis
(to) pad over	hinüber trotten
paper tissue	Papiertaschentuch
(to) be paralysed	gelähmt sein
paralysis	Lähmung
participation	Teilnahme, Beteiligung
patchwork family	Patchwork-Familie (eine Familie, die sich aus zwei Familien neu zusammensetzt)
pattern	Muster
pavement	Bürgersteig
(to) pay attention to s.o.	jmd. beachten, jmd. Aufmerksamkeit schenken
peaceful	friedlich
pedestrian bridge	Fußgängerbrücke
pedestrian crossing	Fußgängerüberweg
pedestrian subway	Fußgängerunterführung
pedestrian, walker	Fußgänger
peekaboo	Kuckuckspiel
peel	Schale
(to) perform	aufführen, vortragen; auch: leisten, arbeiten
(to) be permitted	erlaubt sein
personality	Persönlichkeit
pet zoo	Streichelzoo
physical abuse	körperliche Misshandlung
physical disability	körperliche Behinderung
physical violence	körperliche Gewalt
physiotherapist	Physiotherapeut/in
(to) pick on s.o.	herumhacken auf jmd.
(to) pick s.o. up	jemanden abholen
picture lotto	Memory (Spiel)
(to) pile up	auftürmen, aufhäufen
pillow	Kissen
(to) pinch	zusammendrücken, zwicken
pinhead	Dummkopf (Umgangssprache)
placement	hier: Praktikumsstelle
plaster	Pflaster
plastic mould	Spielförmchen, Sandförmchen
plate	Teller
(to) play a message	eine Melodie/Nachricht abspielen
play and learning environment	Spiel- und Lernumgebung
(to) play a trick on s.o.	jmd. einen Streich spielen
(to) play area	Spielbereich
(to) play ball games	Ballspiele spielen
(to) play chasing games	Nachlaufspiele spielen
play dough	Knete
play hide and seek	Verstecken spielen
play with the sand	mit Sand spielen
playground, play area	Spielplatz, Außengelände
playing field	Spielfeld
pleasant	angenehm
pleasure	Vergnügen
(to) pledge	geloben, fest versprechen
(to) point	zeigen
(to) poke	hineinstecken
poorly	kränklich
(to) pop back	plötzlich zurückkommen
(to) pop up	hochkommen, herauskommen
(to) possess	besitzen, in Besitz nehmen
potty-training	Sauberkeitserziehung
poultry	Geflügel
(to) pour	gießen
powerful	mächtig
(to) predict	vorhersagen
prejudice	Vorurteil
prejudiced	auf Vorurteilen beruhend
preparation	Vorbereitung
preparatory	vorbereitend
preparatory grade	Vorbereitungsklasse, Vorschulklasse
(to) prepare	zubereiten, vorbereiten
prepared	vorbereitet
pre-pregnancy weight	Gewicht vor der Schwangerschaft
preschool children	Kinder im Vorschulalter
preschooler	Vorschulkind
(to) pretend	so tun, als ob
(to) be pretty sure	sich sicher sein
(to) prevent	verhindern
primary school	Grundschule
(to) proclaim	proklamieren, verkünden
profession	Beruf
(to) promote	fördern, unterstützen
properly, thoroughly	sorgfältig, gewissenhaft
props	Requisiten
(to) prosper	gedeihen, zu Wohlstand kommen
proven skills	nachgewiesene Fertigkeiten
(to) provide with	bereitstellen, versorgen mit
psychologist	Psychologe/Psychologin
public	öffentlich
(to) pull	ziehen
pulses	Hülsenfrüchte
puppet	Handpuppe
pure	rein, unverfälscht
puzzled	verdutzt, verwirrt

Q

qualifications	Qualifikationen
quality childcare	Kinderbetreuung auf hohem Niveau
quarrel	Streit
(to) quench the thirst	den Durst löschen
quiet area	Kuschelecke
quite	ziemlich
(to) quote	zitieren, sich auf etw. beziehen

Alphabetische Vokabelliste

R

race	Rasse
racist	rassistisch
rage	Zorn
(to) raise a family	eine Familie gründen, ernähren
(to) raise money	Geld aufbringen
ramp, wheelchair ramp	Rollstuhlrampe
(to) rap the table	auf den Tisch klopfen (als Zeichen für Beifall)
rarely	selten
rash	Ausschlag
rattle	Rassel
reading-aloud	vorlesen
ready-cooked	vorgekocht
(to) reassure	beruhigen
reception class	Eingangsklasse, erstes Jahr
recipe	Rezept
recitation	Vortrag (eines Liedes)
(to) recognise objects	Objekte wahrnehmen
(to) recommend	empfehlen
(to) be made redundant	gekündigt werden (Arbeitsleben)
reference	Referenz, Bestellnummer
refrigerator (kurz: fridge)	Kühlschrank
regard s.th. as	etwas ansehen als
regularly	regelmäßig
(to) reject	ablehnen
relative	Verwandter
(to) release	loslassen
(to) remove obstacles	Hindernisse aus dem Weg schaffen
(to) represent	repräsentieren, darstellen
reputation	Ruf
(to) rescue	retten
residential area	Wohngebiet
(to) rest	sich ausruhen
rhyme	Reim
(to) ride a tricycle	Dreirad fahren
(to) rinse	ausspülen
risk assessment	Risikoeinschätzung
rocking chair	Schaukelstuhl
role model	Vorbild
rope ladder	Seilleiter, Strickleiter
rough	rau
rubber boots	Gummistiefel, "Wellies"
rude	unhöflich, unverschämt, grob
(to) run around	herumlaufen
(to) run s.th.	etwas betreiben (ein Unternehmen)
runny nose	laufende Nase
rye	Roggen

S

sachet	Tütchen
(to) be safe	sicher sein
safety	Sicherheit
sandpit	Sandkasten
sanitary facilities	Sanitäranlagen
(to) satirise	satirisch (komisch) darstellen
saucer	Untertasse
(to) be scared	Angst haben
sceptical	skeptisch
scissors (nur pl.)	Schere
(to) scold s.o.	jmd. (aus)schimpfen
(to) scramble	vermischen, durcheinander bringen
secondary school	weiterführende Schule
secret	Geheimnis
(to) seek	suchen
(to) seek medical help	ärztliche Hilfe holen
seesaw	Wippe
(to) seesaw	wippen
self (sg.), selves (pl.)	das eigene Selbst
semi-detached house	Doppelhaushälfte
semi-open	halb offen
sense	Sinn
sense of humour	Sinn für Humor
sensory	sensorisch, mit den Sinnen
sensory development	sensorische Entwicklung
sequences	Folgen
serious	ernst, ernsthaft
(to) settle	sich hinsetzen, sich niederlassen
(to) settle an argument	einen Streit beilegen
(to) settle in	sich einleben
severe	ernsthaft
sexual abuse	sexueller Missbrauch
shapes	Formen
(to) share (with)	teilen, auch: sich mitteilen
shelf (sg.), shelves (pl.)	Regal(e)
shoulder	Schulter
(to) show off	angeben
shy	schüchtern
sick-bed	Krankenbett
sight	Anblick
sign	Zeichen
single-parent family	Familie mit einem Elternteil
sink	Spüle
sister	Schwester
sister-in-law	Schwägerin
(to) be situated	sich befinden, liegen
skeleton	Skelett
(to) skid	schlittern
skill	Fähigkeit, Geschick
skin	Haut
skin tone	Hautfarbe
(to) skip	Seil springen
skipping rope	Hüpfseil
sleepy	schläfrig
(to) slid	rutschen
slide	Rutsche
(to) slide down	herunterrutschen

Alphabetische Vokabelliste

smeared	verschmiert	suggestion	Vorschlag
smell	Geruch	suit	hier: Strampelanzug
smooth	glatt	suitable	passend, geeignet
snow den	Schneehütte	summary	Zusammenfassung, Inhaltsangabe
(to) snuggle	kuscheln		
soaked with sweat	triefend vor Schweiß	(to) supervise	beaufsichtigen
soap opera	"Seifenoper", Fernsehserie	(to) support	unterstützen
social services	Sozialdienste	suspense	Spannung
social skills	soziale Fertigkeiten, Sozialkompetenz	(to) swear	fluchen
		swelling	Schwellung
social well-being	hier: gutes Sozialverhalten	swing	Schaukel
solution	Lösung, Problemlösung	(to) swing to and fro	vor und zurück schaukeln
(to) solve a problem	ein Problem lösen	(to) swirl	rühren
son	Sohn		
sore	wund	**T**	
sorting	Auswahl-, auswählen	table manners	Tischmanieren
sound (adj.)	ausgewogen, umfassend	(to) take a nap	ein Schläfchen machen
sound (n)	Klang	(to) take a rest, (to) rest	eine Pause einlegen
(to) sound	klingen		
source	Quelle	(to) take a risk	ein Risiko eingehen
special care	besondere Pflege, Fürsorge	(to) take care of, (to) care for	sich kümmern um
special needs	besondere Bedürfnisse (Behinderung)		
		(to) take responsibility	Verantwortung übernehmen
speech therapist	Sprachtherapeut/in	(to) take turns	sich abwechseln
speech/language impairment	Sprachfehler	task	Aufgabe
		taste	Geschmack
spirits	Geister	taster lesson	Probestunde, Unterricht zum Ausprobieren
(to) split	sich aufteilen		
sponge	Schwamm	telly (ugs.)	TV, Fernsehen
spoon	Löffel	temper	Wesen, Naturell, auch: Wut
(to) squeeze	zusammendrücken	temperature	(erhöhte) Temperatur, Fieber
stable	stabil	tense atmosphere	angespannte Atmosphäre
(to) stack	stapeln	texture	Oberflächenstruktur, auch: Oberfläche aus Stoff
staff	die Mitarbeiter, die Lehrkräfte		
		Thanksgiving	Erntedankfest
(to) be staffed with	mit Personal besetzt	theme time	Arbeit an einem Thema
stage	Phase	thrilling	spannend
(to) stammer	stottern, stammeln	throat	Kehle, Rachen
(to) stand s.th.	etwas ertragen	thumb	Daumen
stanza	Strophe	(to) tie back	zurückbinden, zusammenbinden
(to) stare at s.o.	jmd. anstarren		
(to) stay in one place	an einer Stelle stehen bleiben	tiles	(Dach-)Ziegel
		timetable	Stundenplan, Zeitplan
stew	Eintopf	timid	ängstlich, verängstigt
(to) stick	anheften	tiny	sehr klein, winzig
stiff	steif	teeny-weeny	klitzeklein (Umgangssprache)
(to) stimulate	anregen, Anreize schaffen	to my mind	meiner Meinung nach
sting	Stich	toddler	Kleinkind, "Krabbelkind"
(to) stir	rühren	toileting progress	Fortschritte bei der Sauberkeitserziehung
(to) stitch	nähen (Wunde)		
(to) storm at s.o.	auf jmd. einstürmen	tomb	Grab
strict	streng	topic	Thema, Themenstellung
styrofoam	Styropor	tortoise	Schildkröte
subject	Thema	tot	Kurzform von toddler: Kleinkind
(to) succeed	Erfolg haben		
success	Erfolg	totally	völlig, ganz und gar
successful	erfolgreich	towel	Handtuch
(to) suck thumb	Daumen lutschen	toy	Spielzeug
(to) suffer	leiden	toy spade	(Kinder-/Spiel-)Spaten
(to) suggest	vorschlagen	track	Schiene

Alphabetische Vokabelliste

training course	Lehre, Ausbildung	**W**	
trampoline	Trampolin	wagon	Waggon
trapped fingers	eingeklemmte Finger	(to) walk around	herumgehen
(to) treat s. o.	jmd. behandeln	(to) watch s. o.	jmd. beobachten, beaufsichtigen
treasure	Schatz		
treat	Süßigkeit, "Leckerchen"	weaning	Entwöhnung
triangles	Dreiecke	wedding photo	Hochzeitsfoto
tricycle	Dreirad	weekly	wöchentlich
tri-dimensional	dreidimensional	welcoming	einladend
trolley	Teewagen, Servierwagen	well-equipped	gut ausgestattet
(to) trust in	vertrauen in	well-trained	gut ausgebildet
tummy	Bauch	What a burden!	Was für ein schweres Schicksal!
tune	Melodie		
tweezers (nur pl.)	Pinzette	wheat	Weizen
twice	zweimal	wheelchair	Rollstuhl
(to) twinkle	funkeln	(to) whirl	wirbeln
twinkly	glitzernd	wide range	weites Angebot
twins	Zwillinge	widower, widow	Witwer, Witwe
(to) twist	verdrehen	wife	Ehefrau
typical (of)	typisch (für)	(to) wipe	(ab-)wischen
		(to) wish	wünschen
U		witch	Hexe
uncle	Onkel	withdrawn	zurückgezogen
(to) underline	unterstreichen	(to) withstand	standhalten, durchhalten
unpleasant	unangenehm	wooden	aus Holz
unsure	unsicher	wooden blocks	Bauklötze
upstairs	im oberen Stock	work diary	Arbeitstagebuch
usually	gewöhnlich, üblicherweise	work experience	Praktikum
		work report	Arbeitsbericht
V		(to) work undercover	im Geheimen / verdeckt arbeiten
vacancy	hier: freier Betreuungsplatz		
vacuum cleaner	Staubsauger	worktop	Arbeitsplatte
valuable	wertvoll	(to) worry	sich Sorgen machen
(to) vary	variieren	worry	die Sorge
vast	enorm	wound	Wunde
vegetable	Gemüse	wrists	Handgelenke
violent	gewaltsam, gewalttätig		
visual impairment	Sehstörung	**Y**	
visual loss	Sehverlust	(to) yawn	gähnen
vocational training	Berufsausbildung		
(to) vomit	sich erbrechen	**Z**	
		zebra crossing	Zebrastreifen
		(to) zoom in on s. o.	an jemanden (mit der Kamera) dicht heranfahren, heranzoomen

Bildquellenverzeichnis

©PLAYMOBIL/geobra Brandstätter GmbH & Co. KG, Zirndorf: S. 49/1, 3
action press gmbh & co. kg, Hamburg: S. 158 (Anita Weber/SIPAPress)
Arif, Shermin, Berlin: S. 62/5
Atheneum Books for Young Readers, New York, USA: S. 133/4
Cartoonstock, Bath, Großbritannien (www.cartoonstock.com): S. 177 (Piero Tonin)
Dienstbier, Akkela, Lilienthal: S. 11/3
Disney Press New York, USA: S. 133/5
dpa-Picture-Alliance GmbH, Frankfurt am Main: S. 8 (Bildagentur-online); 11/5; 140/1 (The Advertising Archives), 2 (Mary Evans Picture Library), 3 (The Advertising Archives); 145/1 (NDR/Sesame Workshop), 2 (EPA/EVERT), 3 (Mary Evans Picture Library), 4 (The Advertising Archives), 5 (Mary Evans Picture Library); 146; 150
DRK Kreisverband Wolfenbüttel e. V. – Integrations- und Therapiezentrum, Wolfenbüttel (www.itz-drk.de): S. 131
Fabian Helmich Photographie, München: S. 73/1
face to face Agentur GmbH, Hamburg: S. 155/1 (Moviestore Collection), 2 (Hollywood Picture Press); 156/1, 2 (Moviestore Collection)
Fiand, Ruth, Aachen: S. 23/1 – 5; 31; 37
Fotolia Deutschland, Berlin, © www.fotolia.de: S. 11/1 (Alena Ozerova); 16/2 (sdenness); 35 (pressmaster); 49/2,8 (es0lex); 56/2 (lisalucia); 59/1 (Laufer), 2 (Abdul Quaiyoom), 3 (WaD), 4 (tang90246), 5 (alexmillos); 60/1 (red2000),2 (aalto); 61/1 (kristina rütten), 2, 4, 7 (aalto); 62/1, 3 (aalto); 63/2 – 8 (notkoo2008); 69/4 (Ksenia kuznetsova), 11 (Chamillew); 71 (Jose Manuel Gelpi); 72/4 (Elwynn); 75 Pavel Losevsky); 76/4 (Elwynn); 79/1 (Monkey Business), 3 (Sergey Khamidulin); 81 (Wojciech Gajda); 82 (Paulista); 90/1 (Dan Race), 2, 3 (Vera Kuttelraserova), 4 (Mast); 97/2a (tigatelu),

2b (Africa Studio), 2c (valeriy555), 6 Somenski), 7 (Africa Studio), 8 (Joe Gough), 9 (eyetronic), 10 (Liv Friis-Larsen); 100/2 (olynia), 3a (bluedarkat), 3b (yvdavid), 4a (valeriy555), 4b (tigatelu), 4c (Africa Studio), 5 (Franziska Krause), 6a (M.studio), 6b (Pavel Timofeev), 7a (thecorner), 7b (yvdavid); 108/1 (st-fotograf); 114/1 (Tatyana Gladskih); 119 (fotofreaks); 124/1, 2 (Jaren Wicklund); 126 (Jaren Wicklund); 142/2 (style-o-mat); 170/2 (Petro Feketa)
Getty Images Deutschland, München: S. 79/4 (Aurora Creative); 145/6 (Matthew Vasilescu for Paramount Pictures Australia)
HABA – Erfinder für Kinder, Bad Rodach: S. 16/3; 49/6
Harper Collins Publishers, Glasgow, Großbritannien: S. 133/2
Houghton Mifflin Harcourt Company, New York, USA (Jamaica´s Find by Juanita Havill and Illustrated by Anne Shibley O´Brien): S. 133/1; 142/1
Independent Life Technologies, Cambridgeshire, Großbritannien: S. 130/1, 2
INTERTOPICS Pressebildagentur GmbH, Hamburg: S. 157 (SnapPhoto)
iStockphoto, Berlin: S. 12 (Chan Pak Ki); 13 (Chan Pak Ki); 43/1 (Chan Pak Ki); 49/10 (tweetyclaw); 61/6 (knape); 67 (Pamela Moore); 69/8 (Onur Döngel); 73/2 (Joseph Gareri); 85 (Chan Pak Ki); 97/3 (Chris_Elwell); 118/1; 123 (tiler84); 134 (Jani Bryson); 141 (Cheryl Graham); 143 (Bonnie Jacobs); 151/1 (David Stuard), 2 (Fred Froese)
KERSA GmbH & Co. KG, Mindelheim: S. 49/7, 9; 118/2
Kreber, Heidi, Aachen: S. 11/6; 17/1 – 5
LEO GmbH, Sauerlach (www.leo.org): S. 186
Linguee GmbH, Köln (www.linguee.de): S. 187/2
LITTLE TIGER Verlag GmbH, Gifkendorf: S. 148
Margarete Steiff GmbH, Giengen/Brenz: S. 49/4, 5
Marienschule Gemeinschaftsschule, Marienfeld: S. 28 Mars Holding GmbH, Verden: S. 97/4
Mattel GmbH, Frankfurt am Main: S. 69/7

Meyer, Rebecca Wachtberg: S. 1; 3/1 – 8; 4; 6/2, 3; 9; 14; 18/1 – 3; 20; 21; 26/1, 2; 30; 36; 39/1 – 4; 46; 47; 50/1 – 8; 51; 57; 66/1 – 3; 87; 94; 95; 98; 100/1; 104/1, 2; 136/1 – 3; 137/1, 2; 138; 153; 169; 170/1; 173; 174; 190
Philips Deutschland GmbH, Hamburg: S. 69/1
Produce for Better Health Foundation, Wilmington, USA: S. 105
Ravensburger AG, Ravensburg: S. 49/11
Schmidt, Hartmut W., Fotografie, Freiburg: S. 11/2, 4; 16/1; 43/3; 56/1, 3, 4; 80; 89; 93
Schmidt, Sabine, Hamburg: S. 107/1 – 3
Schweer, Anke, Wolfenbüttel: S. 2; 6/1; 7; 61/3, 5; 62/2, 4; 97/5; 99; 101
Shutterstock Images LLC, New York, USA: S. 43/2; 59/6 (Nicobatista); 69/2 (Onurz Kocamez), 3 (Daniel Trautmann), 5 (Ennpictures), 6 (Cheryl E. Davis),9 (Onur Döngel),10 (Zvonimir Orec); 70/1 (Goldmund Lukic), 2 (Criminalatt), 3 (Ilike); 72/1 (Monkey Business Images), 2 (Gelpi), 3 (Olga Bogatyrenko), 5 (Leviche v. Dmitry), 6 (Kotorniti), 7 (Zulufoto), 8 (Patricia Marks), 9 (Kokhan-Chikow), 10 (Lev Dolgachov); 74 (Mark Stay); 76/1 (Monkey Business Images), 2 (Gelpi), 3 (Olga Bogatyrenko), 5 (Leviche v. Dmitry), 103 (Marlon Lopez); 114/2 (Cresta Johnson); 160/1, 2 (opicobello); 163/1 (Enrique Ramos), 2 – 6 (opicobello), 7 – 11 (Bardocz Peter); 171 (opicobello)
Signal Iduna, Hamburg: S. 111
Techniker Krankenkasse, Hamburg: S. 97/1
Technische Universität Chemnitz (www.beolingus.de): S. 187/1
The Very Hungry Caterpillar von Eric Carle (Copyright © 1969 & 1987 von Eric Carle) – Mit freundlicher Genehmigung von dem Eric Carle Studio: S. 133/3
Toys"R"Us GmbH, Köln: S. 52/1 – 8
Unilever Deutschland Holding GmbH, Hamburg: S. 106/1 (Knorr),2; 108/2
Verlag Handwerk und Technik GmbH, Hamburg: S. 79/2; 112; 120; 128/1 – 4
www.w3.gwis.com: S. 63/1

Impressum

Zu diesem Buch sind eine Audio-CD
(Bestellnummer 16412)
und ein Lehrerhandbuch (16411) erhältlich.

ISBN 978-3-582-01641-6

Das Werk und seine Teile sind urheberrechtlich geschützt. Jede Nutzung in anderen als den gesetzlich oder durch bundesweite Vereinbarungen zugelassenen Fällen bedarf der vorherigen schriftlichen Einwilligung des Verlages. Die Verweise auf Internetadressen und -dateien beziehen sich auf deren Zustand und Inhalt zum Zeitpunkt der Drucklegung des Werks. Der Verlag übernimmt keinerlei Gewähr und Haftung für deren Aktualität oder Inhalt noch für den Inhalt von mit ihnen verlinkten weiteren Internetseiten.
Verlag Handwerk und Technik GmbH
Lademannbogen 135, 22339 Hamburg; Postfach 63 05 00, 22331 Hamburg – 2016
Internet-Adresse: www.handwerk-technik.de
E-Mail: info@handwerk-technik.de

Satz und Layout: Foto Grafik Design Harro Wolter, 20253 Hamburg

Druck und Bindung: Grafisches Centrum Cuno GmbH & Co. KG, 39240 Calbe